LUKE
The Gospel of Mercy

STUDY GUIDE

Fr. Jeffrey Kirby, STD   **Paul Thigpen, PhD**

In loving memory of

Dr. Thomas "Tom" Neil Buckley, KHS

husband, father, and friend

Nihil Obstat: Reverend Matthew Kauth, STD
                   Censor Deputatus

Imprimatur: Most Reverend Peter J. Jugis, JCD
                   Bishop of Charlotte
                   November 1, 2016
                   Feast of All Saints

The *nihil obstat* and *imprimatur* are official declarations that a book is free from doctrinal or moral error. No implication is contained therein that those who grant the nihil obstat and imprimatur agree with the contents, opinions, or statements expressed.

ISBN: 978-1-5051-0798-2

Catholic Scripture Study Programs published exclusively by
Saint Benedict Press, LLC
PO Box 410487
Charlotte, NC 28241
www.SaintBenedictPress.com

Printed and bound in the United States of America

WELCOME TO LUKE

The parable of the prodigal son. It's one of the most memorable stories Jesus ever told, remarkable for the image of divine mercy that it offers us. Like the father of a wayward child, Our Lord assures us, God rushes out to meet us as we make our way home.

Now the parable of the prodigal is remarkable for another reason as well: It's found only in the Gospel of Luke. In fact, commentators have long noted that throughout his Gospel, Luke focuses on God's mercy, presenting us with stunning insights into the gracious heart of God.

During this eighteen-week study, you'll be joining Fr. Jeffrey Kirby and Dr. Paul Thigpen to find out just why Luke has so often been called "the Gospel of mercy."

In the coming weeks, you'll …

* Meet the author of this beautiful, powerful Gospel, learning why he emphasized the reality of God's mercy for all people.

* Understand more deeply how the events surrounding Jesus' birth and in his youth revealed God's merciful plan for the world.

* Discover how Jesus' mission of mercy was launched at his baptism and strengthened by his testing in the wilderness.

* Delve into Jesus' teaching about both divine mercy and divine justice, examining his parables about the Good Samaritan, the prodigal son, the rich fool, the lost coin, the lost sheep, the Pharisee and the tax collector, and the rich man and the beggar.

* Hear how Our Lord mercifully transformed so many lives by healing the sick, raising the dead, casting out demons, and forgiving hardened sinners.

* Ponder the events at the conclusion of Jesus' earthly life that mercifully opened the gates of heaven: how he gave us the Eucharist and the priesthood, died and rose again in triumph, and promised the Holy Spirit to those who receive his forgiveness.

Finally, you'll gain a new appreciation for the Church—established through Christ's Apostles—as God's plan to extend his mission, through us, to the end of time. As the Apostle Paul, Luke's friend and mentor, once put it, Our Lord has chosen us to be "vessels of mercy" (Rom 9:23). God bless you as you encounter the life-changing Word of God and seek to live it out!

Conor Gallagher, Publisher

Š: LVC   Š· EV

St. Luke, Simone Martini, 1284–1344, Tempera and gold leaf on panel

TABLE OF CONTENTS

UNDERSTANDING YOUR GUIDE

What's inside your Study Guide for Luke: The Gospel of Mercy? Here's an overview.

Study Sessions

The *Study Guide* is divided into eighteen study sessions. Each session is further divided into a "Self-Study" section and a "Group Study" section. These sections are designated (along with the session number) by the caption in the colored bar along the outside edge of each page.

The following elements appear in each of the eighteen sessions of the Study Guide:

SELF-STUDY

The first section of each session, designated as "Self-Study," helps you prepare individually for the group study. Before coming together with the other participants, you can spend some time on your own reading the scriptural text, reflecting on the study notes in this section, and looking ahead to the questions for group discussion. Your group may have you write the responses to the questions you can answer before the session in order to prepare for a more rewarding group discussion.

Optional use of the self-study section: We highly recommend that you prepare for the group experience by using the "Self-Study" section. But we recognize that busy schedules don't always allow for that possibility. So even if you're sometimes unable to prepare ahead of time, the group session recaps, videos, and discussions will still offer you valuable insights into the scriptural text. As you view and listen, you can still take part in the conversation and take notes on the videos and discussions. In addition, as time allows, you can always go back to review the material in the book.

Session Reading

The scriptural citation at the bottom of the opening page of each session identifies the specific portion of the Gospel of Luke to be studied in that particular session. The scriptural texts quoted in the Study Guide and Leader Guide come from the Revised Standard Version, Catholic Edition (RSV-CE) translation of the Bible. Other Catholic versions are available, but you should be aware that the wording of the biblical text will vary in other translations.

Non-Catholic Bibles typically lack seven books that are found in the Catholic Bible. So make sure the version you choose is an approved Catholic Bible such as the RSV-CE or one of the editions of the *New American Bible* (NAB). The Douay-Rheims (DR) version is also an approved translation and an old favorite of many Catholics, but keep in mind that some of its older language may seem unfamiliar, and many of its books have names that differ from more contemporary translations.

Introduction

A short description of the scriptural passage being studied introduces the session.

Prayer to Prepare for Study

Prayer should be an integral part of every aspect of our lives, especially when we embark on a study of Scripture. We must ask God for the knowledge, wisdom, diligence, and humility necessary to understand his Word, and for the grace to change our lives by responding in faith and obedience to what he says.

This prayer, included at the beginning of every "Self-Study" section, is attributed to St. Thomas Aquinas (c. 1225–1274), a Doctor of the Church and one of the greatest students of Scripture who has ever lived. It's a beautiful, powerful petition to Our Lord for his grace as we study.

Study Notes

These extensive notes are in many ways the "meat" of this Bible study. They provide insights into the historical, cultural, moral, and wider biblical context of the entire passage under study. They will help you understand and reflect upon what you read in the Gospel; offer occasional comments on the text by the Church Fathers and other saints; and provide answers to common questions about difficult or puzzling passages.

GROUP STUDY

The second section of each session, designated as "Group Study," takes you and the other participants in your group through your study together. It includes prayers, videos, questions for reflection or discussion, and other aids to study: definitions of key words that may be unfamiliar; quotes from the saints and Church documents; and relevant citations from the *Catechism of the Catholic Church* (CCC).

Opening Prayer

The opening prayer is for the group to pray together. It's adapted from Scripture—Psalm 19:14—and is prayed at the beginning of each session.

Teaching Video

The Teaching Video, the first of two videos for each session, is hosted by Dr. Paul Thigpen. The Teaching Video for the first session, "An Introduction to Luke," offers an overview of the Gospel and its author. In the sessions following, while the study notes cover the entire text designated for each session, this video offers a more focused approach. It provides a close-up view of a specific portion of the Gospel passage under study, such as a particular scene, event, theme, character, or parable.

While you and the other participants are watching, you can take notes on the lines provided under various topical headings drawn from the video presentation. We recommend this activity to help you remember what you have heard.

Small Group Discussion

If your study has ten or more participants, you may hold discussions in small groups of five to seven. Each small group will have its own discussion leader prepared to guide the group. The small group discussion for each session will respond to two sets of questions, "Digging Deeper" and "Life Application."

Digging Deeper

The "Digging Deeper" questions prompt you in two ways: First, the questions help you recall some of the insights you have learned in reading the scriptural passage and the study notes. Second, the questions help you reflect more deeply by considering some wider issues raised by what you have learned.

Life Application

The "Life Application" questions are posed to help you consider how you might apply to your own life the key points from each session. After this discussion, you will be able to consider your answers in light of the insights provided by the "Life Application Video." Answers to these questions will vary according to the life circumstances of each participant.

Before turning to the second video, the group will take a five-minute break to socialize, stretch your legs, use the restroom, and enjoy refreshments.

Life Application Video

After returning from your break, you'll gather to watch the second video, a pastoral reflection from Fr. Jeffrey Kirby, STD. His insights focus on how to apply to your everyday life the scriptural passage being studied. We recommend that you simply listen instead of taking notes on this video.

How Then Shall We Live?

This section serves as a summary of the insights in the "Life Application Video." Since you haven't taken notes on the video, we recommend that you silently review this section to prepare for responding to the challenges in "Living It Out."

Living It Out

This section prompts you to pray, then discern and write down the changes that God is asking you to make in your life, especially over the course of the next week, based on what you have learned. You'll be given three to five minutes to sit quietly and reflect on the challenges you face in this regard. Then you'll have an opportunity to share what you're thinking and feeling if you're comfortable doing so.

Closing Prayer

Each session will close with the group praying aloud together the prayer provided. Each prayer has been chosen for its relevance to some aspect of that particular session. The closing prayers are drawn from Scripture and other traditional sources.

ADDITIONAL STUDY AIDS

Arranged throughout both the "Self-Study" and the "Group Study" portions of the guides are special sections with additional relevant information and insights. These are intended to supplement your knowledge and enhance your understanding of the scriptural passage being studied:

Words to Know

A list of key words or phrases that defines terms that might be unfamiliar or expounds upon their basic meaning.

Catechism Connections

Citations for relevant passages from the *Catechism of the Catholic Church*.

Rome to Home

Relevant excerpts from Church documents such as papal pronouncements and statements of ecumenical councils.

Voices of the Saints

Relevant quotes from saints throughout history.

My Personal Checklist

At the beginning of the first group session of *Luke: The Gospel of Mercy*, you'll have the opportunity to review "My Personal Checklist: Before the Study" (p. XIII), which is a list of some personal benefits that we hope you will receive through this experience. You'll have a minute or two to follow the instructions on the page.

At the end of the last session of the study, you'll have the opportunity to review "My Personal Checklist: After the Study" (p. 319), so you can reflect on the areas in which you have grown personally through the study. You'll have a minute or two to follow the instructions on the page. *Both of these checklists are for your use only; they should not be shared with anyone else unless you choose to do so.*

GROUP STUDY SESSION PLAN

What does a typical study session look like? Here's an overview.

Before the Group Study Session

* Read the "Session Reading" and "Introduction" in the "Self-Study" section of the *Study Guide.*

* Read the "Study Notes" in the "Self-Study" section of your *Study Guide* (as time allows).

* Write your answers to the "Digging Deeper" and "Life Application" questions in the "Group Study" section of your *Study Guide* (as time allows).

* For sessions 2 through 18, review the "Living It Out" challenges from the prior session in the "Group Study" section of your *Study Guide*. Then consider in what ways you have responded to these challenges.

The Group Study Session

* Opening Prayer

* Prior Session Recap

* Teaching Video with host Dr. Paul Thigpen

* Small Group Discussion

    * Digging Deeper

    * Life Application

* Break

* Life Application Video with host Fr. Jeffrey Kirby, STD

* How Then Shall We Live?

* Living It Out

* Closing Prayer

After The Group Study Session

* On your own before the next gathering (as time allows), review this session's material in the Study Guide, including the additional study aids: "Words to Know," "Catechism Connections," "Rome to Home," and "Voices of the Saints."

St. Luke, Guido Reni, Restored Traditions

MY PERSONAL CHECKLIST
Before the Study

Your word is a lamp for my feet, a light for my path (Ps 119:105 NAB).
You will know the truth, and the truth will make you free (Jn 8:32).

Here are some personal benefits you can receive through this study of *Luke: The Gospel of Mercy*. Check all those you hope to receive. At the end of the study, you'll have a chance to review the list again to reflect on the areas in which you've grown. *This checklist is for you only; it will not be shared with anyone else unless you choose to do so.*

- ❑ I want to know God more personally and intimately through studying his Word.
- ❑ I want to become more familiar with the Bible and learn how to study it.
- ❑ I want to find in the Bible the truth about God, myself, and others.
- ❑ I want to understand better the people who encounter Jesus in the Gospel so that I can learn from their experience.
- ❑ I want to understand more about God's mercy so that I can experience it more fully and extend it to others.
- ❑ I want to receive more hope and healing for the personal wounds I carry.
- ❑ I want to forgive myself for something in my past, even though it's difficult.
- ❑ I want to forgive someone else for something in my past, even though it's difficult.
- ❑ I want to be less attached to material possessions.
- ❑ I want to be more attentive and generous to those who are around me and to those who are most in need.
- ❑ I want to be more grateful for the mercy and other graces I've received from God.
- ❑ I want to be more willing to ask forgiveness from the people whom I've wronged.
- ❑ I want to become a more active member of my parish to help build the kingdom of God.
- ❑ I want to avoid rashly judging others.
- ❑ I want to honor the Lord's Day (Sunday) more fully and consistently.
- ❑ I want to prepare better for making good sacramental confessions.
- ❑ I want to reflect God's loving kindness to those around me.
- ❑ I want to appreciate more fully the meaning, the reality, and the power of the Eucharist.
- ❑ I want to accept more faithfully and joyfully the "crosses" I must bear in my life.

If you've checked some of the boxes above, *Luke: The Gospel of Mercy* can provide you with a life-changing experience. Join together with your community of faith to encounter God in his Word.

AN
INTRODUCTION
TO LUKE

It seemed good to me also, having followed all things closely for some time past, to write an orderly account for you, most excellent Theophilus.

LUKE 1:3

SESSION READING
LUKE 1:1–4

Introduction

The third Gospel is a beautiful and powerful portrait of Our Lord Jesus Christ. But it's much more than just a portrait. As a part of Sacred Scripture, the Gospel of Luke is heaven's own invitation to us to draw close to the Son of God. You could call it a divine summons: to know Jesus Christ; to love, serve, and become like him; and to awaken everyone we know to the good news of his salvation.

Salvation is possible because of the abundant mercy of God, flowing out from his heart to a blind and broken world. For this reason, St. Luke, the author of the third Gospel, returns again and again to the theme of divine mercy—God's offer of forgiveness, reconciliation, and transformation.

This session provides an overview of the author and the text by addressing these important questions: What do we know about Luke himself? How did he write this book, and why? What sets this Gospel apart from the other three biblical Gospels? And most importantly: Are we willing to let this book change our lives?

Prayer to Prepare for Study

Lord, my God, bestow upon me an understanding that knows You, diligence in seeking You, wisdom in finding You, a way of life that is pleasing to You, perseverance that waits trustfully for You, and confidence that I shall embrace You at the last. Amen.

—Prayer of St. Thomas Aquinas before study

Study Notes

These notes provide insights to help you understand and reflect upon the biblical text.

* According to ancient tradition, Luke was from Antioch in Syria, the only known Gentile (non-Jewish) author of the New Testament (Col 4:10–14).

* Luke was a disciple of St. Paul and learned the gospel from him (Phlm 1:24; 2 Tm 4:11). His writing reflects several themes from St. Paul, including a focus on God's mercy, salvation history, the redemption of the Gentiles, the work of the Holy Spirit, and the call of the disciple to continue the work of Jesus Christ.

* Luke wrote his Gospel and Acts of the Apostles as a single work (Lk 1:1–4; Acts 1:1–2). Some scholars believe that the Church later divided Luke's Gospel from Acts in order to have the four Gospel books and Acts parallel the five books of the Pentateuch in the Old Testament (Genesis, Exodus, Leviticus, Numbers, Deuteronomy). Given that division, it would seem to make sense that the books would be ordered Matthew, Mark, Luke, Acts, and John, so that the two parts of Luke's work would remain together. But from ancient times,

the Church has considered the Gospels the most important books in the New Testament, first in honor. So they were placed together and before all the other books.

✦ Why, then, wouldn't Luke have been listed as the fourth Gospel, with Acts placed immediately after it? The ordering of the Gospels in ancient lists varies, and some of those lists actually do place Luke fourth, perhaps for that very reason. Even so, the order that seems to be the most ancient is the present one. This order probably became standard because it reflects the chronological order of the Gospels' composition according to ancient tradition, with John last. So John had to be placed between Luke and Acts.

✦ Luke was a well-educated and well-traveled man. His writing displays a wide knowledge of the Mediterranean world, its geography and culture (see Acts, especially chapters 16–28). He also had an extensive knowledge of Jewish culture and history, including the Septuagint—the Greek translation of the Old Testament widely used at that time. He writes some of the most elegantly-styled Greek to appear in the New Testament.

✦ Luke was a physician by profession, so he emphasizes scenes of medical interest (such as healing miracles) in his Gospel and Acts (Col 4:14). It is possible that he studied medicine at the famous school in Tarsus and met the Apostle Paul while there.

✦ Luke was the only one among the "apostolic men" (those associated with the Apostles) and the Gospel writers who did not meet the Lord during his public ministry. Some traditions suggest that he was one of the seventy disciples sent out to preach (10:1–24) or the second disciple (along with Cleopas) who met Jesus on the way to Emmaus (24:13). But these suggestions are difficult to reconcile with Luke's own statement implying that he was not among the eyewitnesses to the events he recorded in his Gospel (1:1–4).

Winged cow with a book, symbol of Saint Luke the Evangelist. Detail of the frescoes with the Stories of Genesis, by Giusto de' Menabuoi, in the Baptistry of Padua / Alinari / Bridgeman Images

✦ The principal relics of Luke are contained in the Abbey of St. Giustinia in Padua, Italy. The saint's feast day is October 18, and his Gospel is used for the "C" cycle of Sunday Mass readings.

✦ One tradition holds that Luke wrote his Gospel (twenty-four chapters) and Acts of the Apostles (twenty-eight chapters) during St. Paul's two-year imprisonment, sometime between A.D. 62 and 68. But scholars debate the matter, and others consider a later date of A.D. 80 to 90 more probable for the full composition.

✤ Luke's writings are addressed to "Theophilus" (1:3) which means "loved by God" or "lover of God." There may have been an individual with this name or title, but it may well be a general designation for all people of good will (especially the Gentiles) who are seeking to be "lovers of God." Luke stresses the universal offer of salvation for all people in an attempt to receive a large Gentile hearing for the message of Jesus Christ.

✤ In his writings, Luke follows the classical historiographical tradition—the standard protocols for writing history in his culture. His opening prologue imitates the style of Greek and Roman historians of his day. He provides a geographical and chronological framework for his story by noting where events took place and who was occupying secular positions of power at various times. (There was no universally accepted method of dating at the time, so identifying publicly known rulers established a timeframe.)

✤ Luke's historical approach is reflected as well in that he attempted a chronological biography of Jesus, the only Gospel writer to do so (Lk 1:1–4). The other three Gospel writers had other concerns that governed the structure of their works: Matthew, writing primarily for a Jewish audience, makes frequent reference to the Law of Moses and the Prophets, emphasizing Jesus as both the new Moses and the new David. Mark provides a compact handbook for living the Christian way of life. And John's Gospel follows the Jewish liturgical year, showing Jesus as the new Temple.

| *St. Luke painting a portrait of Our Lady holding her infant son Jesus Christ by Giovanni Francesco Barbieri, best known as Guercino, Italy (16th century) / Restored Traditions*

✤ Writing from a Greek perspective, Luke is unique in his stress on the role of women and of Gentiles in the Lord's ministry, both in his Gospel and in Acts. He also echoes the Old Testament emphasis on God's care for the poor and lowly.

✤ Luke's style of narration could be described as a "foot and food" approach. His Gospel reflects a Mediterranean culture in that much of the narrative revolves around Jesus' walking or being at a meal. This narrative pattern culminates in the Emmaus scene at the end of his Gospel (24:13–35).

✤ As a physician, Luke is deeply aware of the human condition, so he provides some warm pastoral stories from the Lord Jesus that are not given in the other Gospels. These include the prodigal son, the Good Samaritan, and the good thief (15:11–32; 10:25–37; 23:39–43). He also uses precise medical terms typically found only in the technical medical literature of his day.

✤ Tradition teaches that Mary was one of the eyewitnesses interviewed by Luke in the writing of his Gospel (1:1–4). He includes details that could have been known only to Mary or to someone close to her, such as the events of the Annunciation and her pondering of events in her heart (1:26–38; 2:19, 51). One uncertain tradition that can be traced back to the eighth century claims Luke was an artist who drew several images of Mary that are now venerated in several churches throughout the world.

✤ Luke visited St. Paul frequently during his two-year house imprisonment (Acts 28:30), and may have had extensive access during this time to other early Church leaders—the "eyewitnesses" (Lk 1:2), such as St. Peter.

✤ Luke is frequently mentioned alongside St. Mark (Phlm 1:24; 2 Tm 4:11). He seems to have used Mark's Gospel (according to tradition, written at the feet of St. Peter) in the composition of his own Gospel.

✤ As a disciple of St. Paul, Luke was involved in his apostolic journeys. Beginning in Acts 16:10, Luke often speaks in the first person ("we") because of his involvement in the work.

✤ Eusebius, a fourth-century Bishop of Caesaria (d. before A.D. 341), is known as the "Father of Church History." He reported in his Ecclesiastical History (3.4): "They say that Paul was actually accustomed to quote the Gospel according to St. Luke."

To prepare for small group discussion, turn ahead now to this session's "Digging Deeper" and "Life Application" sections.

Rome to Home

Now more than ever, in a world that is often without light and without the courage of noble ideals, people need the fresh, vital spirituality of the Gospel. Do not be afraid to go out on the streets and into public places, like the first Apostles who preached Christ and the Good News of salvation in the squares of cities, towns and villages. This is no time to be ashamed of the Gospel! It is the time to preach it from the rooftops. Do not be afraid to break out of comfortable and routine modes of living, in order to take up the challenge of making Christ known in the modern metropolis. . . . The Gospel must not be hidden because of fear or indifference. It was never meant to be hidden away in private.

—St. John Paul II, *World Youth Day Homily, Denver, Colorado, August 15, 1993*

Opening Prayer

Let the words of my mouth and the meditation of my heart be acceptable in your sight, O Lord, my rock and my redeemer!

—Psalm 19:14

Teaching Video

This first video, hosted by Dr. Paul Thigpen, focuses on certain themes and passages from the Gospel of Luke. Here are some key highlights of his presentation, with room to take notes as you view the video to assist you in the group discussion.

Why Luke wrote the Gospel and the Book of Acts

_____

_____

_____

_____

What we know about Luke

_____

_____

_____

_____

Evidence that Luke was writing as both an historian and an evangelist

_____

_____

_____

_____

Major themes of the book

_____

_____

_____

_____

Literary genres in the book

_____

_____

_____

_____

Material unique to Luke's Gospel

_____

_____

_____

_____

Catechism Connections

These readings from the Catechism of the Catholic Church (CCC) will deepen your understanding of this session's presentations and discussions. The numbers identify the relevant paragraphs in the Catechism.

✤ The inspiration and truth of Sacred Scripture: CCC 101–108.

✤ The Holy Spirit interprets Sacred Scripture: CCC 109–114.

✤ The gospel is for the entire human race: CCC 831.

✤ The missionary mandate of the Church follows from her catholic nature: CCC 849–856.

Small Group Discussion

DIGGING DEEPER

1. Why would the early Christians need a reliable historical record of Jesus' life and ministry, and of the early days of the Church? Why would they need a written record in addition to the preaching of the Apostles?

_____

_____

_____

_____

Pentecost, 16th century, Portuguese painting / De Agostini Picture Library / G. Dagli Orti / Bridgeman Images

2. What aspects of Luke's training, skills, gifts, and personal experience made him especially well suited to write these particular books (his Gospel and the Book of Acts)?

_____

_____

_____

_____

3. Why would Luke consider it essential for the earliest Christians to recognize that God's offer of salvation was universal—for both Jews and Gentiles; men and women; the rich, prominent, and powerful; and the poor, lowly, and weak?

_____

_____

_____

_____

4. Why was it so important for Luke to emphasize the role of the Holy Spirit in the life of Jesus and the life of the early Church?

_____

_____

_____

_____

5. Why was it so important for Luke to place his account of Jesus' life and ministry, and of the early days of the Church, in the context of earlier events in salvation history?

_____

_____

_____

_____

LIFE APPLICATION

1. What do we hope to learn from Luke's Gospel that could strengthen our faith and hope in God, and deepen our love for him and for others?

_____

_____

_____

_____

2. What implications for our personal relationships do we find in the Gospel's declaration that God invites every single person to repentance and redemption in Jesus Christ?

_____

_____

_____

_____

3. In what practical ways might we get to know the Holy Spirit better and rely on him more to bear spiritual fruit in our lives?

_____

_____

_____

_____

| *The Four Evangelists (oil on panel), French School, (16th century) / Musee National de la Renaissance, Ecouen, France / Bridgeman Images*

Life Application Video

After breaking from your small group discussion, gather to watch the second video, a pastoral reflection from Fr. Jeffrey Kirby, STD.

Voices of the Saints

Luke writes his Gospel to Theophilus, that is, to the one whom God loves. But if you love God, it was also written to you. And if it was written to you, you too must fulfill the duty of an evangelist. Diligently keep this token of Luke's friendship close to your heart.

—*St. Ambrose of Milan*

How Then Shall We Live?

Silently review the following summary of Fr. Kirby's reflection to prepare for answering the questions in "Living It Out."

Look at what the Lord was able to accomplish in and through Luke, who was actually a Gentile, not one of the original Chosen People. And yet all that God has accomplished through this beloved physician, he seeks to do in and through each of us according to our own vocation and state in life.

Will we take the great leap of faith and allow God to do a great work in us and in the midst of our world today? Are we willing to leave our comfort zone—to be like Luke, the Gentile, leaving what he knew best and entering on a whole new journey? Will we dare to live in Jesus Christ and allow his grace to transform us and others through us?

God calls every one of us, as he called Luke, to share his good news, to live out the gospel, each of us in our own way. What work does God want to do in your life? Is he calling you to forgive or befriend someone? What good news is he asking you to carry to others, or to receive from others?

| *Light at the end of the tunnel, © GlebStock, Shutterstock*

Out of what kind of darkness is God calling you? What marvelous light does he desire to give you? What work does God want to accomplish in your marriage and family? And what about your neighbors? Is God calling you to go the extra mile for a neighbor? Is he calling you to a greater charity and service to others? Perhaps God wants to send you as a missionary into your work place.

And what about the poor? Do you recognize them in your life—those who need food, love, or the talents that only you possess?

Let's say to Jesus, "Yes, Lord, I will follow. I will let you work. Come, give me your grace, and let me be your instrument in my world today."

Living It Out

On your own, spend three to five minutes praying, discerning, and writing down the specific ways that God might be calling you to make changes in your life. Share and discuss afterwards only if you feel comfortable doing so.

Consider this week how God is calling you to …

✠ Move out of your comfort zone to share some aspect of the Gospel with someone you know.

✠ Demonstrate God's mercy to someone who needs it.

✠ Cooperate with the Holy Spirit to cultivate a particular virtue in your life.

| *The chair of St. Peter, detail of the stained glass window behind, 1665 (detail of 158488), Bernini, Gian Lorenzo (1598-1680) / St. Peter's, Vatican City / Photographer Craig Mace.*

Words to Know

Evangelists, the Four: Matthew, Mark, Luke, and John; according to ancient tradition, the writers of the four biblical Gospels.

Gentiles: People who are not Jews.

Gospel: Literally, "good news." In general, the term is used to refer to the "good news" of God's salvation in Jesus Christ. It is also used to refer to any one of the first four books in the New Testament that record the events of Christ's life, death, and resurrection: Matthew, Mark, Luke, and John.

Martyrology, Roman: A martyrology is a list for every day of the year of martyrs and other saints whose feasts or commemorations occur on each day, usually with a brief note about each one. The Roman Martyrology is the official martyrology of the Catholic Church, extensive though not exhaustive, and subject to historical revision.

Pentateuch: The first five books of the Old Testament: Genesis, Exodus, Leviticus, Numbers, and Deuteronomy. Also known as "the Law" or "the Book of the Law of Moses."

Prologue: A separate, introductory section of a literary work. Both the Gospel of Luke and the Gospel of John feature a prologue.

Septuagint: A Greek translation of the Hebrew Old Testament, begun in Alexandria, Egypt, in the third century B.C. and completed around 100 B.C. It also includes several books not found in the Hebrew Scriptures. Early Christians writing in Greek often quoted the Septuagint when citing the Old Testament.

Theophilus: Greek name meaning "lover of God" or "loved by God." Luke addresses his Gospel and the Book of Acts to Theophilus.

Closing Prayer

Lord, your word is a lamp to my feet, and a light to my path.

I am your servant; give me discernment so that I may know your decrees.

The unfolding of your words gives light; it imparts understanding to the simple.

I long for your salvation, Lord; your teaching is my delight.

—Adapted from Ps 119:105, 125, 130, 174

The Annunciation, before 1652 (oil on canvas), Le Sueur, Eustache (1617-55) / Louvre, Paris, France / Bridgeman Images

ANNUNCIATION
AND
VISITATION

*And the angel said … "Behold, you will conceive in your womb and bear
a son, and you shall call his name Jesus."*

LUKE 1:30–31

SESSION READING
LUKE 1:5–80

Introduction

After the elegant epilogue stating his method and intentions as an historian, Luke launches into his story. The remainder of the first chapter reports the remarkable events leading up to the birth of Jesus Christ.

The central figures of these events are, in order of appearance, Zechariah and Elizabeth, an elderly couple who have never been able to conceive a child; the Archangel Gabriel, a heavenly messenger with good news; Mary, a young virgin who is Elizabeth's cousin; Joseph, to whom Mary is engaged; and John, the child miraculously born to Zechariah and Elizabeth.

Gabriel announces God's startling plan to redeem his people, as he has promised long ago. John will be the messenger to prepare the way for the long-awaited Messiah, who will save his people from their sins. And Mary, though a virgin, will miraculously conceive and bear a Son named Jesus, who will be that Messiah and Savior, the Son of God.

Now let's take a closer look at the significance of these central figures; their biblical, geographical, historical, and cultural contexts; and their varying responses to the angel's good news. As Luke demonstrates, God's plan reveals to them, and to us, the marvel and the mystery of his mercy.

Prayer to Prepare for Study

Lord, my God, bestow upon me an understanding that knows You, diligence in seeking You, wisdom in finding You, a way of life that is pleasing to You, perseverance that waits trustfully for You, and confidence that I shall embrace You at the last. Amen.

—Prayer of St. Thomas Aquinas before study

Study Notes

These notes provide insights to help you understand and reflect upon the biblical text.

✤ The Old Testament Book of Ezekiel contains a vision of an angelic creature with four faces (Ez 1:1–14; the faces appear again in Rv 4:7). These four figures are known as the *Tetramorphs* (literally, "four forms"), and they include a man, a lion, an ox (or calf), and an eagle. As early as the second century, Christians found in these faces a symbolic representation of the Four Evangelists: Matthew, Mark, Luke, and John. Various arrangements were proposed to match each figure with a particular Evangelist. But the arrangement that finally prevailed in the Western Church symbolized Matthew by a man, Mark by a lion, Luke by an ox (or calf), and John by an eagle. For centuries now, sacred art has employed these images to represent the Gospels and their authors.

✤ Several explanations have been offered for the associations. One has to do with the way each Gospel begins. Matthew starts with Christ's human genealogy. Mark begins with John the Baptist crying out in the wilderness as a lion roars in the desert. Luke starts his account in the Temple, where oxen were sacrificed by the priests. And John's Gospel begins by soaring in the heavens like an eagle. The four figures can also remind us of four aspects of Our Lord's nature and ministry: his humanity (man); his divinity (eagle); his kingship (lion); and his priesthood (ox).

❖ Luke opens his narrative by noting that Caesar Augustus is the Roman emperor, for the Holy Land is occupied by Rome. Herod the Great is king of Judea (1:5). He is a client king, a puppet, of Rome and is known for his brutality and bloodlust. Later, his son, also named Herod, will be a client of Rome and will rule as the tetrarch of Galilee, figuring in the account of Jesus' passion (23:7–15). By noting both the Jewish king (even if only a puppet-king) and the Roman emperor, Luke situates his story both in Jewish salvation history and in universal salvation history.

❖ The events in the Gospel occur largely within the first-century A.D. Roman province that includes most of the area once ruled by Kings David and Solomon. This province has three divisions.

❖ Judea is the southernmost district, the area that became the Kingdom of Judah (or the Southern Kingdom) after the United Kingdom of Solomon was divided by civil war in the tenth century B.C. It includes the city of Jerusalem (with the Temple) and the town of Bethlehem, where Jesus is born. Judea is populated primarily by descendants of the ancient Israelite tribes of Judah and Benjamin.

The Ancient City of Jerusalem with Solomon's Temple, 1871 (colour litho), Unknown Artist, (19th century) / Photo © Zev Radovan / Bridgeman Images

✤ Galilee is the northernmost district. It has a mixed population of Jews and Gentiles who settled there in the centuries after the earlier Jewish inhabitants were deported by their Assyrian conquerors in the eighth century B.C. The city of Nazareth, where Mary and Joseph reside and where Jesus grows up, is located in Galilee, as is Capernaum, the town that becomes a center of his ministry.

✤ Samaria is the central district. Its habitants are largely descendants of Gentiles and the Israelites who separated from Judah after Solomon's death. We will learn more about this district when we study the parable of the Good Samaritan.

✤ At this time, the Levitical priesthood of the Old Covenant is still being exercised in the Temple of Jerusalem. This priesthood offers sacrifices and guards the fulfillment of the ceremonial law given by God and contained especially in the Book of Leviticus. Zechariah is a Levitical priest (1:5, 8–10). Mary and Joseph will later obey the ceremonial law when they have Jesus circumcised; when they go to the Temple for Mary's ritual purification, which ends the formal period of a mother's isolation after childbirth; and when they present him in the Temple (2:21–24). Ultimately, through his passion, death, and resurrection, Christ will completely fulfill the ceremonial law, and it will no longer be in effect for those who embrace the New Covenant in Christ.

✤ In this chapter, Luke records the fulfillment of several Old Testament prophecies: Isaiah's prophecy that the promised Messiah (or Christ) would be born of a virgin (Is 7:14; Lk 1:34); the prophecy that the Messiah would be of the house of David (2 Sm 7; Jer 23:5–6; Lk 1:27, 32–33); and Micah's prophecy, to be fulfilled by John, that a messenger would go before the Messiah to prepare his way (Mi 4:5–6; Lk 1:76).

| *The Holy Family, J. Palinka / Restored Traditions*

✤ In the account of Zechariah in the Temple, Luke's reference to an angel is just the first of many. In fact, in his Gospel he speaks more about the ministry of angels than any of the other Evangelists (1:11–19, 26–38; 2:9–15; 4:10; 9:26; 12:8–9; 15:10; 16:22; 20:36; 22:43; 24:4, 23) and in Acts as well (5:19; 6:15; 7:30, 35, 38, 53; 8:26; 10:3, 7, 22; 11:13; 12:7–11, 15, 23; 23:8–9; 27:23).

✤ Gabriel, whose name in Hebrew means "might of God" or "man of God," is recognized in Christian tradition as one of the archangels—that is, one of the principal angels. The term *archangel* occurs in Scripture twice: In Jude 9 ("the archangel Michael") and 1 Thessalonians 4:16 ("the archangel's call"). Ancient Christian tradition, drawing in part from even earlier

Jewish tradition, holds that the angels form a hierarchy—that is, they are organized in higher and lower ranks, with each rank having distinctive functions. (See also Eph 1:21, where the Apostle Paul seems to speak of ranks among the fallen angels, or demons, as well.) We have biblical references to seven angels whose special function it is to "stand before God's throne" (Tob 12:15; Rv chapters 8 through 11). In Gabriel's declaration to Zechariah, he seems to be saying that he is one of these seven angels (Lk 1:19).

✤ Gabriel is best known to Christians through his appearances to Zechariah and Mary as described in Luke's first chapter. Though he is never identified by name in the Gospel of Matthew, his role in these events surrounding Jesus' birth has led many to assume that he is also the angel who appears to Joseph in two dreams (Mt 1:20–24; 2:13).

✤ Gabriel appears as well in the Book of Daniel. In chapters 8 and 9, he explains the meaning of the prophet's visions. In Daniel 10, he is presumably the angel who tells Daniel how the Archangel Michael (Jude 9) came to his aid in answering the prophet's prayer. In both Old and New Testaments, then, Gabriel seems to have a role as God's special herald or messenger—which is, in fact, what the Greek word *angelos* literally means.

✤ In Luke's description of the angel's appearance to Zechariah, note the detail he provides that the angel is standing "on the right side of the altar of incense" (1:11). Such small details are typical of eyewitness reports. This particular detail is also suggestive: Given the layout of the Temple, the angel is apparently standing between the altar and the table holding the "bread of [God's] Presence" (Ex 25:30; see also Mt 12:4). The angel's appearance is setting into motion the events that lead up to the coming of the "bread of life" (Jn 6:35), the One who is "God [present] with us" (Is 7:14; Mt 1:22–23). Some see this bread as a foreshadowing of the Eucharist.

✤ The angel says to Zechariah that John "will be filled with the Holy Spirit, even from his mother's womb" (1:15). A common belief (explicitly taught by St. Thomas Aquinas and Pope Leo XIII, among others) holds that John was in a special category in this regard: He was sanctified (made holy) in the womb at the moment when Elizabeth, his mother, encountered Mary and "was filled with the Holy Spirit," and he himself leapt for joy inside her. If that is the case, both Mary and John were sanctified before their birth. The Church's liturgy suggests this special status: John and Mary are the only two saints whose nativities we celebrate as universal liturgical feasts.

✤ Nevertheless, there is of course an important difference here between Mary and John. Conception and birth are not at all the same thing. Our Lady was preserved from original sin from the first moment of her conception—from the very beginning of her existence. John, however, was not *conceived* without sin as she was. According to the ancient teaching, John was *born* without sin. Though he was conceived in original sin, he was sanctified months later by the Holy Spirit before he was born, while still in Elizabeth's womb (as if he were baptized in the womb). Of course, the other great difference between the two in this regard is that Our Lady was preserved as well from all actual sin throughout her life, while John was not.

✤ Gabriel greets Mary with the salutation "Hail" (or "Rejoice"), and then names her "full of grace" (1:28). The expression is from the Greek word *kecharitomene*, which is a past participle—an action completed in the past with an application in the present. The expression could also be translated as "Hail, you who have been perfected in grace." This is an important biblical declaration that helps the Church to understand the Immaculate Conception: namely, that by a singular and prevenient (anticipatory) grace, she was conceived without sin.

✦ The second-century text known as the *Protoevangelium of James* (also, the *Infancy Gospel of James*) witnesses to an ancient tradition that at this time, Mary was already consecrated to God as a virgin (with Joseph as her guardian), so she was not expecting to have marital relations with him. If this is true, it explains why she would not assume immediately that Joseph was to be the father of the promised Child. However, the Church did not judge the *Protoevangelium* to be divinely inspired as the four biblical Gospels are, and its historical reliability has been strongly challenged.

✦ The archangel announces to Mary that the birth of the Christ will happen by the power of the Holy Spirit as the Most High (God himself) overshadows her (1:35). This is a direct reference to the *Shekinah* of the Old Testament, a Hebrew term for God's presence among his people. It was described as a cloud over the Ark of the Covenant (see Ex 25:22; Lev 16:2). This action showed Mary to be the new Ark, the new carrier of God's presence among his people.

✦ In the kingdom of Solomon, who was King David's successor on the throne, his wife could not be his queen, for he had hundreds of wives! But he had only one mother, and she was recognized as the queen—what we would now call the "queen mother." She was known as "the Great Lady" (Hebrew, *Gebirah*), and the king showed her exceptional reverence: He bowed when she entered his throne room, and she was seated at his right hand, the first place of honor, as a pre-eminent member of the royal court. She wore a crown (Jer 13:18) and headed up the list of palace officials (2 Kgs 24:12–15). She also helped to shepherd the people (Jer 13:18–20) and was the advocate who presented their petitions to the king (1 Kgs 2:17–19). Later queens on David's throne were accorded this title and position as well.

✦ In this light, when Gabriel tells Mary that her Son will be the everlasting King who reigns on David's throne, the implication is that she herself will be the everlasting Queen Mother, the *Gebirah*, at the King's right hand. Because Jesus is King of the Universe (1 Tm 1:17; 6:13–16; Rv 17:14), his mother is Queen of the Universe. In recognition of this exalted honor, Catholics speak of Mary as Queen.

✦ Mary spoke with Gabriel "in the sixth month" of Elizabeth's pregnancy (1:26), then hurried off to see Elizabeth, remaining there for three months (1:56). Since pregnancies typically last nine months, this timeframe suggests that Mary stayed with Elizabeth until John was born. Spiritual writers have often noted that this action demonstrates Mary's prompt charity toward her elderly cousin: As soon as she heard of Elizabeth's situation, she hurried to help her.

✦ When Mary goes to visit her relative Elizabeth, the unborn John the Baptist leaps in Elizabeth's womb, and the older woman asks: "And why is this granted me, that the mother of my Lord should come to me?" (1:39–40, 43). Mary stays with her for three months (1:56). This is a direct parallel to the Old Testament account of King David's greeting the Ark of the Covenant: He asks, "How can the ark of the Lord come to me?"; he leaps, dancing, before the Ark; and the Ark remains in its place for three months (2 Sm 6:9, 11, 14). This parallel emphasizes that Mary is the new Ark of the Covenant.

⚜ "All generations will call me blessed" (1:48). This prophecy spoken by Mary in her canticle is fulfilled every time we pray the Hail Mary.

⚜ The literary form known as the "canticle" was a beautiful feature of ancient Jewish devotional life. Canticles were songs filled with petitions of praise and thanksgiving, along with important affirmations of faith. Three canticles found in this Gospel, filled with rich symbolism from the Old Testament, now appear in the Liturgy of the Hours, which is prayed every day in the Church. The name for each canticle comes from the first word (or words) in its Latin translation. The Canticle of Zechariah (1:67–79), called the *Benedictus*, is always prayed at *Lauds* (Morning Prayer). The Canticle of Mary (1:46–55), called the *Magnificat*, is always prayed at *Vespers* (Evening Prayer). The Canticle of Simeon (2:29–32), called the *Nunc dimittis*, is always prayed at *Compline* (Night Prayer).

| *The Magnificat (oil on canvas), Tissot, James Jacques Joseph (1836-1902) / Jewish Museum, New York, USA / Bridgeman Images*

To prepare for small group discussion, turn ahead now to this session's "Digging Deeper" and "Life Application" sections.

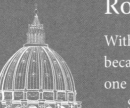

Rome to Home

With her "yes," [Mary] opened the door of our world to God himself; she became the living Ark of the Covenant, in whom God took flesh, became one of us, and pitched his tent among us (Jn 1:14).

So we cry to her: Holy Mary, you belonged to the humble and great souls of Israel who, like Simeon, were "looking for the consolation of Israel" (Lk 2:25) and hoping, like Anna, "for the redemption of Jerusalem" (Lk 2:38). Your life was thoroughly imbued with the sacred scriptures of Israel which spoke of hope, of the promise made to Abraham and his descendants (Lk 1:55). In this way we can appreciate the holy fear that overcame you when the angel of the Lord appeared to you and told you that you would give birth to the One who was the hope of Israel, the One awaited by the world. Through you, through your "yes," the hope of the ages became reality, entering this world and its history.

—*Pope Benedict XVI, Spe Salvi, 49–50*

Opening Prayer

Let the words of my mouth and the meditation of my heart be acceptable in your sight, O Lord, my rock and my redeemer!

Psalm 19:14

Teaching Video

This first video, hosted by Dr. Paul Thigpen, focuses on certain themes and passages from the Gospel of Luke. Here are some key highlights of his presentation, with room to take notes as you view the video to assist you in the group discussion.

The significance of the Temple

_____

_____

_____

Events surrounding the conception and birth of St. John the Baptist

_____

_____

_____

The meaning of Gabriel's message to Mary

_____

_____

_____

The significance of Mary's response to the angel

_____

_____

_____

_____

_____

Mary's visit to Elizabeth

_____

_____

_____

_____

_____

_____

| The Visitation of St. Elizabeth to the Virgin Mary, 1503 (oil on panel), Albertinelli, Mariotto (1474-1515) / Galleria degli Uffizi, Florence, Italy / Bridgeman Images

Catechism Connections

These readings from the Catechism of the Catholic Church (CCC) will deepen your understanding of this session's presentations and discussions. The numbers identify the relevant paragraphs in the Catechism.

✤ St. John the Baptist: CCC 523, 717–20.

✤ The Annunciation and Visitation: CCC 484–86, 494–95.

✤ The Immaculate Conception: CCC 490–93, 722.

Small Group Discussion

DIGGING DEEPER

1. To fulfill his promises of a Messiah, why doesn't God simply choose a descendant of King David to take his throne, anointing him to rule the people with justice? Why does God himself become a Man to establish the Kingdom?

_____

_____

_____

_____

2. God promised through the prophets to send a messenger to prepare the way for the Messiah (Jesus Christ). How exactly was St. John the Baptist to accomplish that task of preparation?

_____

_____

_____

_____

3. The Old Testament Ark of the Covenant has been seen as a foreshadowing, or *type*, of Mary because of the parallels that are pointed out in the study notes and the video presentation. But there are other parallels as well. Consider how the ancient Ark of the Covenant contained the stone tablets of the Ten Commandments given by God to Moses; a golden urn of the manna that appeared each morning in the wilderness to feed the ancient Israelites on their journey; and the budding staff of Aaron, their first high priest (see Heb 9:3–5). Compare each of these sacred items in the first Ark with the holy Child in the womb of Our Lady, known as the new Ark. What parallels can you find between them?

_____

_____

_____

_____

4. More of Mary's words and actions are recorded in this chapter than in all the rest of Scripture. What do they tell us about her character? What virtues does she display?

_____

_____

_____

_____

5. How is Luke's great theme of divine mercy woven into this chapter of his account? How is God's mercy being demonstrated in the events recorded here?

_____

_____

_____

_____

| *The Ark of the Covenant passes over the Jordan (1896-1902) / James Tissot / Wikimedia Commons*

LIFE APPLICATION

1. In the events of this first chapter of Luke, God shows himself faithful to fulfill his promises to his people. In what ways has God shown himself faithful to you?

_____

_____

_____

_____

2. In these events God also surprises his people by acting on their behalf in unexpected ways. In what ways has he surprised you by what he has done in your life?

_____

_____

_____

_____

3. When Mary learned that her elderly relative Elizabeth was pregnant, she hurried off to help her, even though she had to travel some distance to reach her. When we sense that God wants us to help someone—even if only in a small way—are we prompt to respond?

_____

_____

_____

_____

Life Application Video

After breaking from your small group discussion, gather to watch the second video, a pastoral reflection from Fr. Jeffrey Kirby, STD.

Voices of the Saints

Mary opened to us the unspeakable abyss of God's love for us. Through her the old enmity with the Creator is destroyed. Through her, our reconciliation with Him is strengthened, peace and grace are given to us, men are made the companions of angels, and we, who lived in dishonor, are made the children of God. . . . So with Gabriel, the great archangel, let's exclaim to her, "Hail, full of grace!"

—*St. John of Damascus, Second Homily on the Dormition*

How Then Shall We Live?

Review silently the following summary of Fr. Kirby's reflection to prepare for answering the questions in "Living It Out."

Luke's account of these events clearly illustrates an important truth: God has a plan, and his plan is patient, kind, and slow—qualities that our fallen world often fails to appreciate. (These are qualities that sometimes we ourselves fail to appreciate.)

God had a powerful plan for Mary, Zechariah, Elizabeth, and John the Baptist. Look at how intricate and specific were his workings in Gabriel's appearances to Zechariah and Mary, and Our Lady's visit to her kinswoman Elizabeth. God worked through each of these events, linking them all together, molding and shaping with tenderness and gentleness, so that each one played a part in fulfilling his plan—not just in the infancy of Jesus Christ, but throughout his entire life.

What plan is God working out in *our* lives? What intricate details is he coordinating in the plan he has for each one of us? Do we recognize these details? St. Luke recognized them in salvation history and in his own life. He recounted by divine inspiration the very work and ministry of Jesus Christ, and he followed him as a friend and disciple, as we are called to follow him.

Do we make an effort to see God's work? Are we trying to discern his will and our mission? Those who do not have faith wonder, "Where is God?" But those of us who seek to have faith know that there is nowhere in which God is *not*. God is working in us, always, among his people. Do we have the eyes of faith? Are we observing closely so that we can see God's activity in our lives?

In life, we can be just spectators,

Way of St. James, Camino de Santiago, sign shells marks for pilgrims to Compostela Cathedral, Galicia, Spain, © Gena Melendrez, Shutterstock

or people who just talk about Jesus Christ—or we can truly choose to follow him and to see his work in our lives and in the state of affairs around us.

Living It Out

On your own, spend three to five minutes praying, discerning, and writing down the specific ways that God might be calling you to make changes in your life. Share and discuss afterwards only if you feel comfortable doing so.

Consider this week how God is calling you to …

❧ Act on his behalf, even in a small way.

❧ Identify specific, concrete evidence that he is at work in your life.

❧ Help someone else to grow in confidence in his plan for his or her life.

Words To Know

Ark of the Covenant: A large chest made of acacia wood and overlaid with gold, built at God's command to house the stone tablets on which the Ten Commandments were engraved. It was carried by the ancient Israelites through the wilderness and into the Promised Land, and was eventually housed in the Temple in Jerusalem built by Solomon.

Canticle: A sacred song of praise and thanksgiving to God. The canticles appearing in the first chapter of Luke, prayed by Zechariah, Mary, and Simeon, are known as the three evangelical canticles: the *Benedictus*, the *Magnificat*, and the *Nunc dimittis*, now sung daily in the liturgy of the Divine Office.

Christ: From the Greek term *Christos*, meaning "the Anointed One." See *Messiah* below.

Covenant: A solemn agreement between people, or between God and his people, that binds them to one another. God's covenants promise his people blessings and call them to live according to his gracious law as a condition for those blessings.

Fiat: Latin for "Let it be." Mary's assent to God's message through Gabriel is known as her *fiat*: "Let it be to me according to your word" (Lk 1:38).

Immaculate Conception: The conception of the Virgin Mary, in which—through a unique grace and privilege of God—she was preserved from all stain of original sin from the first moment of her existence. This grace was given through the merits of her Son, Jesus Christ.

Levitical priesthood: The descendants of Moses' brother, Aaron, of the tribe of Levi, who were appointed by God to serve as sacred ministers to the Israelites. They were entrusted with leading public worship, including the various sacrifices commanded by God; teaching and preserving God's law; and acting as judges in certain matters.

Messiah: From the Hebrew term *Mashiach*, meaning "the Anointed One." In ancient Israel, kings and other people appointed to high office customarily received a ritual of anointing (the pouring of oil on their heads) as a sign that God had chosen them for the position. Multiple prophecies in the Old Testament promised that God would send the Jewish people a great king and deliverer, sometimes called "the Anointed One." In the New Testament, the Greek term *Christos* ("Christ") has the same meaning. The messianic prophecies were fulfilled in Jesus Christ.

Shekinah: A Hebrew term for "dwelling, settling, habitation." Though this noun form of the word is not found in Scripture, it occurs frequently in the later literature of Jewish rabbis to refer to the glorious and abiding presence of God. Manifestations of the *Shekinah* in the Old Testament include such occasions as the pillar of cloud guiding the Israelites in the wilderness; the cloud atop Mount Sinai where Moses met with God; and the cloud of glory settling on the Tabernacle and later filling the Temple.

Tetrarch: The governor of the fourth part of a province (a tetrarchy). The term is also used loosely in the sense of a petty prince, the ruler of a small district. Herod Antipas, son of Herod the Great, was the tetrarch of Galilee, before whom Jesus appeared briefly while on trial.

Type: In biblical interpretation, a foreshadowing. More specifically, a person, thing, action, or event in the Old Testament that the Holy Spirit portrays as a foreshadowing of the future. For example, Noah's ark is a type of the Church; the Passover lamb, a type of Christ; the Ark of the Covenant, a type of Mary. Other spiritual types can be discerned as well: St. Paul, for example, presents human marriage as a type of Christ's union with the Church (see Eph 5:21–33).

Closing Prayer

Hail, Mary, full of grace; the Lord is with thee. Blessed art thou amongst women, and blessed is the fruit of thy womb, Jesus. Holy Mary, Mother of God, pray for us sinners, now and at the hour of our death. Amen.

Christ and four saints, altar panel designed by Burne-Jones, Rooke, Thomas Matthews (1842-1942) / Private Collection / Photo © Bonhams, London, UK / Bridgeman Images

BIRTH
AND
CHILDHOOD

And the child grew and became strong, filled with wisdom;
and the favor of God was upon him.

LUKE 2:40

SESSION READING
LUKE 2:1–52

Introduction

Only the Gospels of Matthew and Luke provide an infancy narrative—a record of events surrounding Jesus' birth. Matthew's infancy narrative is told from the perspective of Joseph, to whom Mary is engaged. Luke tells the story from Mary's perspective.

Luke's second chapter begins with the story of Jesus' birth in Bethlehem. His account includes details that help us see God's concern for the poor and lowly. It also reveals certain aspects of Mary's character.

Next, Luke tells how Mary and Joseph fulfill several Jewish religious laws and customs that have to do with childbirth. Jesus is named and circumcised on the eighth day of his life. Forty days after Jesus' birth, Mary and Joseph bring Jesus to the Temple for the prescribed religious rites of ritual purification for a mother and presentation of a child to God. In the Temple, more about Jesus' unique identity and destiny is revealed through an encounter with two strangers, Simeon and Anna.

After the Holy Family returns home to Nazareth, the story leaps forward twelve years. They journey to Jerusalem to celebrate the great Passover feast, and the young Jesus gets separated from Mary and Joseph. They finally find him in the Temple, which he knows to be his true Father's house.

Prayer to Prepare for Study

Lord, my God, bestow upon me an understanding that knows You, diligence in seeking You, wisdom in finding You, a way of life that is pleasing to You, perseverance that waits trustfully for You, and confidence that I shall embrace You at the last. Amen.

—Prayer of St. Thomas Aquinas before study

Study Notes

These notes provide insights to help you understand and reflect upon the biblical text.

✤ A Gospel *infancy narrative* is an account of Jesus' birth and the events surrounding it. Only the Gospel accounts of Matthew (chapters 1–2) and Luke (chapters 1–2) contain infancy narratives.

✤ Luke records the birthplace of Jesus Christ as Bethlehem of Judea. Although a small town, it is steeped in salvation history. The city is the resting place of the great Old Testament matriarch Rachel (Gn 48:7). King David was born and later anointed king there by the prophet Samuel (1 Sm 16:1–13). The prophet Micah foretold that Bethlehem would be the birthplace of the Christ (Mi 5:2). The name Bethlehem is Hebrew for "City of Bread," and Jesus is in fact "the bread of life" (Jn 6:35). Note also that Jesus is laid in a manger, a feeding trough (Lk 2:7, 12). This imagery foreshadows Our Lord's institution of the Eucharist during his last celebration of the Passover (commonly known as "the Last Supper" or "the Lord's Supper"; Lk 22:14–20).

✤ Luke refers to Jesus as Mary's "firstborn son." This term does not imply that there were other children born to Mary, with Jesus only the first. Luke is employing a specific term used in the Jewish religious Law recorded in the Book of Exodus. Moses says there that "every firstborn of man among your sons you shall redeem" (Ex 13:13)—that is, he belongs to God, and you must buy him back from God, so to speak, by offering an animal sacrifice in his stead. This sacrifice is to be offered only days after the son is born. If, according to the Law, "firstborn" referred only to a child with younger siblings, how could the parents comply? They couldn't know so soon whether another child would ever be coming, unless there had been a multiple birth. Clearly, then, to call a child "firstborn" with regard to the Law does not necessarily imply younger siblings. Jesus is Mary's firstborn, and he is Mary's only Child.

✤ Luke notes the role of angels and shepherds in the story of Jesus' nativity. Not simply Gabriel, but a host of angels celebrate the birth of the Son of God, and vigilant shepherds in their night watch are invited to go and adore the newborn Messiah and Lord (2:10–12). The angelic praise recorded in this Gospel is the basis of the *Gloria* hymn that is sung in Sunday Masses outside of penitential seasons: "Glory to God in the highest, and on earth peace to people of good will" (2:14).

| *The Presentation of Jesus in the Temple, Bellini, Giovanni (c.1430-1516) / Galleria Querini-Stampalia, Venice, Italy / Bridgeman Images*

✤ Circumcision is the sign of God's covenant with Abraham. It is intended to mark the very part of the body through which God will fulfill his promise to Abraham that he will give him a son and make him the father of many nations. Luke records that Jesus is circumcised on the eighth day in fulfillment of the ceremonial law (Lv 12:3; Lk 2:21–22). This act recognizes Jesus as a son of Abraham. It is also the first blood that Jesus will shed on our behalf.

❧ In the ceremony of circumcision, a child receives his name. Typically, the child's father chooses the name, and so it is with Jesus. Joseph may be the one to *announce* the Child's name that day, but Joseph has not chosen the name himself, for Joseph is only his foster father. God the Father, Jesus' true Father, has chosen the name *Jesus* and instructed the angel to reveal it to Mary (2:21).

❧ Already in the infancy narrative of St. Luke, Jesus is given several titles: the name "Jesus" itself (which means "God is salvation" or "God saves"), as well as "Son of the Most High," "Son of God," "Dawn from on High," "Savior," the Greek title "Christ" (which in Hebrew is "Messiah"), and "the Lord." Each of these is full of meaning in salvation history and indicates a fulfillment of prophecy and the mission of the long-awaited Savior of humanity.

❧ In the Law of Moses, the mother of a newborn son is designated as ritually unclean, confined to her house for forty days after the birth and unable to take part in public religious rites. When that forty-day period is complete, she presents herself in the Temple for a purification ceremony (Lv 12:1–7). Mary and Joseph bring the Child to the Temple for this rite (Lk 2:22–24).

❧ If Mary is all-pure, why would she need to submit to this rite of purification? The religious law requiring the ceremony has to do with ritual purity, not moral purity. Giving birth to a child is not an immoral act, but in the Law, because of the flow of blood involved, it renders a woman ceremonially unclean, just as the menstrual blood flow does (Lv 12:1–5).

❧ St. Francis de Sales suggests that even though she is not bound by this law, she obeys it in order to avoid scandal: "Thus she comes today to the Temple to remove all suspicion from men who might have wondered about her. She comes also to show us that we ought not to be satisfied with avoiding sin, but that we must avoid even the shadow of sin" (*Sermon for the Feast of the Purification*).

❧ St. Alphonsus Liguori concludes that her great humility compels her to join other mothers in fulfilling the Law, as an act of solidarity with them: "Her humility and obedience make her wish to go like other mothers to purify herself" (*The Glories of Mary*).

❧ A lamb is normally prescribed as the sacrifice for the ceremony of the mother's purification after giving birth. But if the family is poor, they can offer two turtledoves instead (Lv 12:6–8). This is in fact the offering given by Mary and Joseph

| Fresco cycle in the Scrovegni Chapel, 1304 - 1306 (fresco), Giotto di Bondone (c.1266-1337) / Scrovegni (Arena) Chapel, Padua, Italy / Mondadori Portfolio/Electa/Sergio Anelli / Bridgeman Images

when they go to the Temple to perform that obligation (2:24). With this detail, then, Luke indicates the poverty of the Holy Family. Their simplicity is a strong reminder to Christian families of every generation to live modestly and avoid extravagance.

✤ The exalted role of prophets in the Old Testament has become diminished in the time of Jesus, but prophets continue to give teachings and counsel. When Jesus is presented in the Temple, we meet two prophets: Simeon (2:25–27) and Anna (2:36–38). They are elderly, symbols of the Old Testament and of wisdom, and both recognize Jesus as the redemption and glory of Israel, and God's revelation to the Gentiles (2:32, 38). Simeon and Anna are regarded as some of the last prophets of the Old Covenant, with John the Baptist regarded as the very last prophet of that covenant (16:16). Each of these three bear witness to Jesus' identity as the One promised by God. All the prophets throughout salvation history were united in the one task of preparing for the promised Savior, and Simeon, Anna, and John the Baptist have the immense honor of finally proclaiming that the Savior has come and is Jesus of Nazareth.

✤ Simeon tells Mary, "Behold, this child is set for the fall and rising of many in Israel, and for a sign that is spoken against (and a sword will pierce through your own soul also), that thoughts out of many hearts may be revealed" (2:34–35). Note how Simeon's prophecy foreshadows the vocal (and eventually violent) opposition of Christ's adversaries.

✤ Simeon's prophecy also stresses Mary's participation in the saving work of her divine Son. Mary spiritually suffers with her Son in his mission; this is the first of her sorrows known traditionally as the "Seven Sorrows of Mary." As disciples, all Christians are called to some degree of suffering, which has redemptive value when joined to Christ's own suffering.

✤ Three canticles found in the Gospel of Luke now appear in the Liturgy of the Hours, which is prayed every day in the Church. The name for each canticle comes from the first word (or words) in its Latin translation. The Canticle of Zechariah (1:67–79), called the *Benedictus*, is always prayed at *Lauds* (Morning Prayer). The Canticle of Mary (1:46–55), called the *Magnificat*, is always prayed at *Vespers* (Evening Prayer). The Canticle of Simeon (2:29–32), called the *Nunc Dimittis*, is always prayed at *Compline* (Night Prayer).

✤ Joseph has no recorded words in the canonical Gospels. He is a righteous man of faithful obedience to God and hard work. Luke's account relies on Joseph, but Joseph does not hold the focus of the narrative; he yields that position to Jesus and Mary. In this way, Joseph is a great example of humility and perseverance. He is the highest model of Christian fatherhood, and also of various other roles of influence and responsibility (mentors, employers, teachers, coaches, and similar roles).

✤ Luke tells us that when Jesus is twelve years old, he accompanies his parents to Jerusalem for the celebration of the Passover, the feast that re-presents the Old Testament events through which God ransomed his people from slavery as described in the Book of Exodus (Ex 12). According to ancient Jewish custom, religious instruction for a boy intensifies after he turns twelve.

| *Jesus Among the Doctors, 1862 (oil on canvas), Ingres, Jean Auguste Dominique (1780-1867) / Musee Ingres, Montauban, France / Bridgeman Images*

✤ After the celebration, Jesus remains in Jerusalem without his parent's knowledge. Mary and Joseph are not concerned at first, because they assume that Jesus is traveling with his extended family. When Mary and Joseph realize that Jesus is not in the caravan, they return to Jerusalem and look for Jesus for three days before they find him in the Temple. For three days, Mary feels the loss of her Son, and these early three days of sorrow begin to prepare her for her own mission. Years from now she will grieve again for three days for the loss of her Son while he is in the tomb (2:46; 24:7).

✤ When Jesus is found, he is in the Temple with the elders (2:46–47). Luke records this story as the culmination of his account of Jesus' childhood. After so much has been said and witnessed about him, now Jesus speaks for himself. It is significant that his first recorded words in Luke's Gospel are within the Temple, and they show a strong self-understanding, filial boldness towards God, and a sense of unquestioned mission: "How is it that you sought me? Did you not know that I must be in my Father's house?" (2:49).

✤ As a final summary of Our Lord's childhood (2:52), Luke tells us in one brief sentence that his human nature grew in all four essential aspects: wisdom (mentally), stature (physically), and in favor with God (spiritually) and man (socially).

To prepare for small group discussion, turn ahead now to this session's "Digging Deeper" and "Life Application" sections.

Rome to Home

During the years of Jesus' hidden life in the house at Nazareth, Mary's life too is "hid with Christ in God" (Col 3:3) through faith. For faith is contact with the mystery of God. Every day Mary is in constant contact with the ineffable mystery of God made man, a mystery that surpasses everything revealed in the Old Covenant. From the moment of the Annunciation, the mind of the Virgin Mother has been initiated into the radical "newness" of God's self-revelation and has been made aware of the mystery. She is the first of those "little ones" of whom Jesus will say one day: "Father, … you have hidden these things from the wise and understanding and revealed them to babes" (Mt 11:25).

—St. John Paul II, *Redemptoris Mater, 17*

Opening Prayer

Let the words of my mouth and the meditation of my heart be acceptable in your sight, O LORD, my rock and my redeemer!

—Psalm 19:14

Teaching Video

This first video, hosted by Dr. Paul Thigpen, focuses on certain themes and passages from the Gospel of Luke. Here are some key highlights of his presentation, with room to take notes as you view the video to assist you in the group discussion.

Matthew's and Luke's infancy narratives

_____

_____

_____

_____

_____

| *Cherubim, Vatican Holy Water Font, Rome, Italy, Photographer Craig Mace*

Events at Bethlehem

_____

_____

_____

_____

God's solidarity with the poor and lowly

_____

_____

_____

_____

Mary as a woman of contemplation

_____

_____

_____

_____

| *Anno Domini or the Flight into Egypt, 1883, Long, Edwin Longsden (1829-91) / © Russell-Cotes Art Gallery and Museum, Bournemouth, UK / Bridgeman Images*

Jesus' naming, circumcision, and presentation in the Temple

_____

_____

_____

_____

Simeon and Anna

_____

_____

_____

_____

Finding Jesus in the Temple

_____

_____

_____

_____

Catechism Connections

These readings from the Catechism of the Catholic Church (CCC) will deepen your understanding of this session's presentations and discussions. The numbers identify the relevant paragraphs in the Catechism.

✤ Titles of Jesus: CCC 430, 436–37, 441–43, 446–48

✤ Christ's soul and human knowledge: CCC 471–74

✤ Mysteries of Jesus' infancy and hidden life as a Child: CCC 522–34

Small Group Discussion

DIGGING DEEPER

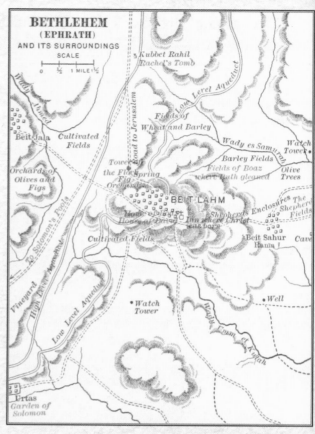

1. Why is it necessary that Jesus be born in Bethlehem? How do the circumstances surrounding Jesus' birth highlight Luke's theme of God's identification with the poor and the forsaken?

_____

_____

_____

_____

_____

The Holy Land in Geography and in History. [With maps and plans.] p. 167, by Maccoun, Townsend. Original held and digitized by the British Library / Wikimedia Commons

2. Simeon and Anna play important roles in this chapter. Who are they? How does Simeon's prophecy help to reveal Jesus' mission? What important events do his words foreshadow?

_____

_____

_____

_____

3. In this chapter, Jesus is given many titles. How do the titles given to Jesus reveal his mystery and his mission?

_____

_____

_____

_____

4. The shepherds play an important role in the birth of Jesus. In addition to being the first to greet him, they are also the first to tell the world of the newborn Messiah. What other shepherds have played an important role in salvation history (Gn 4:4; 30:25–43; Ex 2:11–3:6; 1 Sm 16:11–13; Am 1:1)? How is the theme of "shepherding" continued in Jesus' ministry? (See Jn 10:11; Lk 15:3–7.)

| *Angels announcing Christ's birth to shepherds, 1639, Flinck, Govaert (1615-60) / Louvre, Paris, France / De Agostini Picture Library / Bridgeman Images*

5. What does it mean that Jesus "increased in wisdom and in stature, and in favor with God and man" (2:52)? Does this mean that he is not fully God?

LIFE APPLICATION

1. God has demonstrated in Jesus Christ a special concern for the poor and lowly of the world. In what concrete ways might you be able to show a similar concern for those in need?

_____

_____

_____

_____

2. Jesus has many names and titles in Scripture and Tradition. Which ones have meant the most to you in your personal devotional life, and why?

_____

_____

_____

_____

3. Sorrow is inescapable in this life, as Mary knew well. In what ways has God brought good out of the sorrows in your life to make them redemptive? How might Mary, Our Lady of Sorrows, be a source of consolation to you?

_____

_____

_____

_____

| _Our Lady of Sorrows, 1509-1511, central panel of altarpiece from Mother of God church, by Quentin Massys (1466-1530), oil on panel, 171x151 cm / De Agostini Picture Library / G. Dagli Orti / Bridgeman Images_

Voices of the Saints

What shall I say? And how shall I describe this birth to you? For this wonder fills me with astonishment. The Ancient of Days has become an Infant. He who sits upon the sublime and heavenly throne, now lies in a manger. And He who cannot be touched, who is simple, without complexity, and without a body, now lies subject to the hands of men. He who has broken the bonds of sinners, is now bound by an infant's bands. But He has decreed that what lacks honor shall become honorable, disgrace shall be clothed with glory, and total humiliation shall be the measure of His goodness.

—*St. John Chrysostom*

Life Application Video

After breaking from your small group discussion, gather to watch the second video, a pastoral reflection from Fr. Jeffrey Kirby, STD.

How Then Shall We Live?

Silently review the following summary of Fr. Kirby's reflection to prepare for answering the questions in "Living It Out."

In the birth of Jesus Christ, so beautifully portrayed in the Gospel of Luke, we see the perfection of what it means to be a human being. We can discern in him a way of life: how to think, pray, feel, act, and love. In times when we aren't sure what to do, or what virtue we're called to exercise, Jesus can be our teacher, inspiration, and guide.

We must look to Bethlehem, to the God-Man Jesus Christ, the One who has come to save us and show us how to live. And when we find him, we are at rest—just like Simeon, who for years and years "awaited the consolation of Israel" until he encountered the infant Jesus in the Temple. When we find him, we are filled with joy, just like the shepherds who gathered by the manger.

We are not the sum total of our sins. Our dignity is not based on our utility or appearance, our wallets or status. We turn to the God made Man, and he shows us our identity as children of God, unveiling the power of holiness and the glory of love. In Jesus Christ, we do not search alone for the answers to our questions, because Jesus Christ, the Answer, is searching for us. He has come to seek and to save the lost. He has come to show us the Father, and to reveal to us how we are called to live and how we are empowered to love.

Will we let this saving truth into our hearts? Will we look to Jesus Christ as the Way, the Truth, and the Life? Will we look to him, and no other, to know what it means to be a human being and a child of God?

Living It Out

On your own, spend three to five minutes praying, discerning, and writing down the specific ways that God might be calling you to make changes in your life. Share and discuss afterwards only if you feel comfortable doing so.

Consider this week how God is calling you to …

✦ Look to Jesus as your model for responding to a particular individual or situation in your life.

✦ Identify something in your life that you are tempted to make a false source of your dignity (such as personal appearance, abilities, possessions, popularity, or status).

✦ Provide comfort and support to someone who is suffering or in difficulty and who needs to be affirmed as a child of God.

| *The Lady with the Ermine (Cecilia Gallerani), 1496 (oil on walnut panel), Vinci, Leonardo da (1452-1519) / © Czartoryski Museum, Cracow, Poland / Bridgeman Images*

Words to Know

Infancy narrative: A Gospel account (in Matthew and Luke) of Jesus' birth and the events surrounding it.

Liturgy of the Hours: The official cycle of the Church's daily prayer (also known as the Divine Office). It consists of hymns, antiphons, psalms, Scripture selections, readings from the Church Fathers, commentaries on Scripture and the Christian life, writings of the saints, and traditional Catholic prayers.

Ritual impurity/uncleanness: In some ancient religions, the designation of a person or object as disqualified from having contact with, or participation in, what is holy, such as sacred objects, places, or ceremonies. Ritual impurity is not the same thing as moral impurity; it may be temporary and can result from a natural activity or condition, such as childbirth or certain kinds of illness.

Seven Sorrows of Mary: Also called the Seven Dolors of Our Lady, these are seven occasions in the life of the Blessed Mother when she was filled with sorrow: when hearing Simeon's prophecy in the Temple; at the loss of the Child Jesus in Jerusalem; on the Way of the Cross (or *Via Dolorosa*), the path down which Jesus carried his cross to Calvary; at the crucifixion of Jesus; at his descent from the Cross, when his body was taken down; and at his entombment.

Closing Prayer

O Jesus, Prince of Peace and King of the Universe, You chose to humble Yourself and come into the world, not as a powerful ruler, but as a helpless Infant; grant us the grace of humility and gentleness before You and our brothers and sisters. Amen.

—From a traditional novena to the Infant Jesus of Prague

Man of Sorrows (oil on canvas), Dyce, William (1806-64) / Private Collection / Bridgeman Images

BAPTISM

AND

TEMPTATION

The heaven was opened, and the Holy Spirit descended upon him
in bodily form, as a dove, and a voice came from heaven:
"Thou art my beloved Son; with thee I am well pleased."

LUKE 3:21–22

SESSION READING

LUKE 3:1–4:13

Introduction

Luke's account leaps ahead again; now Jesus is about thirty years old. His cousin John the Baptist begins his ministry to prepare the way of the Lord. John urges the people to turn from their sins and calls for a baptism of repentance: the long-promised Messiah is coming.

Jesus himself comes to be baptized, not because he is sinful, but to act in solidarity with the sinners he came to save, and to cleanse the waters, making them fit for Christian Baptism. After He emerges from the water, praying, the Holy Spirit descends on him in the form of a dove, and God the Father speaks from heaven: "Thou art my beloved Son; with thee I am well pleased."

Before continuing his narrative, Luke provides Jesus' genealogy. He traces his ancestry all the way back to Adam, the first man, to show that Jesus is a brother to all people, and the Savior of all.

Next Luke tells how Jesus is sent by the Spirit into the wilderness to engage in combat with Satan. After Our Lord has fasted and prayed for forty days, the Devil tempts him to compromise his mission. But Jesus responds with the Word of God, overcoming each temptation.

Prayer to Prepare for Study

Lord, my God, bestow upon me an understanding that knows You, diligence in seeking You, wisdom in finding You, a way of life that is pleasing to You, perseverance that waits trustfully for You, and confidence that I shall embrace You at the last. Amen.

—Prayer of St. Thomas Aquinas before study

Study Notes

These notes provide insights to help you understand and reflect upon the biblical text.

- ⚜ After the infancy narrative, Luke gives a three-part series of instruction: He tells about the ministry of John the Baptist (3:1–18), the baptism of Jesus (3:21–22), and the genealogy of Jesus (3:23–38). These three parts of his account set the stage for Jesus' ministry and establish his credibility as the long-awaited Christ.

- ⚜ Luke details the Roman and Jewish leadership of Jesus' day (3:1–2). He gives the names of the most universal (Tiberius Caesar) and the most local of leadership figures (Pilate, Herod, Philip, Lysanias, along with the high priests Annas and Caiaphas). This information, reflecting Luke's biographical focus (1:1–4), indicates the historical reality of the events recorded in the Gospel and places the ministries of both John the Baptist and Jesus within a specific time period.

- ⚜ We know from secular historians of this period that the tetrarch Philip (3:1) was actually the half-brother of this Herod (Herod Antipas); they were born to different wives of their father, Herod the Great (1:5). It is important to note that the Greek word used here is *adelphos,* commonly translated in English as "brother." This is only one example of how the word (in both its masculine and feminine forms) was commonly used to refer to relatives other than biological children of the same father and mother. So the Church's teaching that Jesus was Mary's only son is not contradicted by references in the Gospels to Jesus' "brothers" and "sisters" (*adelphoi, adelphai;* Mt 13:55–56; Mk 6:3).

| *John the Baptist rebuking Herod, Fattori, Giovanni (1825-1908) / Galleria dell' Accademia, Florence, Italy / Bridgeman Images*

✤ John is moved by "the word of God" while he is "in the wilderness" (3:2). The spiritual importance of the wilderness is highlighted throughout the Bible. In order for God's word to reach the human heart, in order for the heart to receive all that God desires to give, the heart must be willing to accept solitude and silence, sometimes rejection or isolation, so that it can be disposed to receive and live all that God desires to impart. John is an example of this docility, and he becomes the model for all those who will later seek to live the Christian life through ascetic discipline (hermits, monks, nuns).

✤ In his ministry, John announces a baptism of repentance for the forgiveness of sins (3:3). This message serves as the focus of his work and leads to his eventual martyrdom. In the Bible, repentance is a holistic act in which sinners not only acknowledge guilt from offenses they have committed, but also firmly desire to amend and turn their lives around. This is the radical summons given by John. It is presented as an immediate prelude to the ministry of Jesus Christ, who alone can remove and absolve sin. John is preparing Israel and the world for the coming of Jesus Christ.

❦ The baptism of John (3:3) is a Jewish devotional practice known in that time for ritual purification. It is a symbolic action, and it is not the Christian Sacrament of Baptism, as even John himself will testify: "I baptize you with water; but he who is mightier than I is coming, the thong of whose sandals I am not worthy to untie; he will baptize you with the Holy Spirit and with fire" (3:16). The Christian Sacrament of Baptism is given later by Jesus as a part of the New Covenant. It carries a power that is not contained in John's baptism of repentance.

❦ Luke cites the prophet Isaiah (Is 40:3–5) as a summary of the work of John the Baptist, who will cry out and call on all people of good will to prepare for the Christ. This particular reference to Isaiah is significant because chapter 40 begins the second section of the prophetic book. This second section is a review of salvation history: the deliverance of the Jews from exile and the bliss experienced in the Promised Land. With this citation, Luke indicates that this passage of Isaiah is a blueprint for what will happen through the Christ, who will restore God's people from the exile of sin and return to them the hope of eternal joy. Also important to Luke's Gentile audience is Isaiah's declaration that "all flesh shall see [the salvation of God]" (Is 40:5)—not just the Jews.

❦ As a Gentile, writing to a primarily Gentile audience, Luke stresses some important teachings of John the Baptist that would appeal to non-Jews. In particular, Luke notes how John tells the Jews: "Bear fruits that befit repentance, and do not begin to say to yourselves, 'We have Abraham as our father'; for I tell you, God is able from these stones to raise up children to Abraham" (3:8). And Luke observes that tax collectors (a group rejected for their collaboration with the Roman Gentiles) and soldiers (most likely Gentiles) ask the Baptist what they need to do to repent. John addresses both groups by calling for specific actions, such as refusing to cheat or falsely accuse others (3:10–14). This portion of the teachings of John is recorded only by Luke.

❦ John's preaching also reminds us that along with God's mercy is his justice. The chastisement of divine "fire" is essential to his message (3:9, 17).

❦ John makes his appeal for repentance to everyone, including Herod the tetrarch. Herod has divorced his wife and married his still-living half-brother's wife in violation of the Law of Moses (Lv 18:16, 20:21). So the Baptist denounces the tetrarch in defense of marriage and calls on Herod to repent. In response, Herod has John imprisoned in the dungeon of his fortified hilltop palace beside the Dead Sea (3:20). A man who had spent so much of his life out in the wilderness would no doubt have found life in Herod's dungeon intolerable.

❦ The ancient Jewish historian Josephus suggests that Herod also had other reasons to imprison John: He feared that such a popular and influential religious leader might lead a political rebellion. In any case, for Luke, the imprisonment of John sets the stage for the beginning of Jesus' public ministry.

✤ Luke's account of Jesus' baptism is a simple narrative. After he is baptized, Jesus is in prayer (3:21). Only Luke mentions this detail. And during Jesus' prayer, the heavens open up, the Spirit descends like a dove, and the voice of the Father is heard: "Thou art my beloved Son; with thee I am well pleased" (3:22). This is the clearest manifestation of the Holy Trinity in Jesus' early ministry. The Spirit appears as a dove, since that bird is a symbol of peace and reconciliation, which will be the work of the Beloved Son. The dove is seen earlier in salvation history with Noah and the great flood (Gn 8:11).

✤ The words from heaven, and the descent of the Holy Spirit, echo two important messianic passages from the Old Testament. In Psalm 2:7, God addresses the Anointed One (Messiah), the coming King, and says, "You are my son." In Isaiah 42:1, God speaks of "my chosen, in whom my soul delights; I have put my Spirit upon him."

| *The Baptism of Christ (oil on canvas), Tintoretto, Jacopo Robusti (1518-94) / S. Silvestro, Venice, Italy / Bridgeman Images*

✤ Though the description of this event includes a prominent reference to the Holy Spirit, Luke has already, in the first chapters of the book, noted his activity seven times before: John will be filled with the Spirit (1:15); the Spirit comes upon Mary at the Annunciation (1:35); Elizabeth is filled with the Spirit when Mary visits (1:41); Zechariah is filled with the Spirit when he prophesies (1:67); the Spirit is upon Simeon and has revealed to him that he will see the Messiah, and he has inspired him to come into the temple that day (2:25–27); John says that the Messiah will baptize his followers in the Holy Spirit (3:16). Clearly, the work of the Holy Spirit is one of the great themes of Luke's Gospel.

✤ In the ancient world, to be banished from one's family and tribe was a terrible punishment. People were known by their family. Foreigners were approached with suspicion because no one knew their family (and, by extension, their intentions). Luke is well aware of the importance of family and ancestry, so he provides a genealogy of Jesus (3:23–38). It is only one of two genealogies of the Christ, with the other being provided by Matthew in his Gospel (Mt 1:1–17). At points, the two genealogies seem inconsistent. However, Luke apparently takes the unprecedented move in biblical history of following the family line of a woman, Mary; while Matthew follows that of a man, Joseph, the legal father of Jesus.

✤ Luke goes even farther back in the generations by tracing Jesus' family line, not just to Abraham, the patriarch of the Jewish people (as Matthew does), but all the way to Adam, the first man, the father of the entire human race, both Jews and Gentiles.

✦ Luke describes Adam as "the son of God" (3:38). This is not a false divinization of Adam, but a statement of truth: As the first man, Adam was the created son of God, made in his image. Jesus Christ, on the other hand, is the only-begotten Son of God, coeternal with God the Father and God the Holy Spirit. Luke addresses Adam in this way to show the universality of God's fatherhood over humanity. He is balancing the Jewish claim to be sons of God through Abraham by asserting the sonship of all through Adam (and through the work of Jesus Christ, by which they can be adopted into God's family; Rom 8:23; Gal 4:4–7; Eph 1:5).

| *The Annunciation and Expulsion from Paradise, c. 1435 (tempera on panel), Giovanni di Paolo di Grazia (1403-82) / National Gallery of Art, Washington DC, USA / Bridgeman Images*

✦ We should also note that the Apostle Paul, Luke's mentor, once called Jesus Christ the "last Adam" who brings life to the world, in contrast with the first Adam, who brought death to the world (1 Cor 15:45–49). Seen in this light, Luke's genealogy of Christ takes us from the "second Adam" back to the "first Adam."

✦ After Our Lord's baptism, the Holy Spirit once again figures prominently: Jesus is led by the Spirit into the wilderness for forty days to be tempted by the Devil (4:1–2). The number forty is significant in the Bible, since it indicates a time of formation and preparation for a forthcoming mission. The rains of Noah's flood lasted forty days (Gn 7:4, 12, 17); the Israelites spent forty years in the desert (Ex 16:35); Jesus appears to his disciples for forty days between his resurrection and his ascension (Acts 1:3). In all these episodes, and in multiple others throughout the Bible, the number forty is prominent as a time of strengthening for a specific work.

✦ Luke recounts that while Jesus is in the wilderness, he eats nothing (4:2). In this time of preparation, the Lord willingly fasts and prays to get ready for his mission. His example shows us the importance and value of fasting in our own efforts to know and follow the will of God.

✦ In ancient times the wilderness was considered a place where someone might encounter not just God, but also Satan. It was viewed as the Devil's own territory: the desolate place abandoned by human beings, where the dead were buried (outside the city) and the demons haunted the earth. So Jesus goes out into the wilderness precisely so that he can do battle with the Devil, on the demon's own turf. Centuries later, when the monastic movement began in the deserts of North Africa and the Middle East, the monks saw themselves as advancing into the Enemy's territory as Jesus had done—not just when he went to be tempted, but also when he exorcised a demon-possessed man who lived in the tombs in the wilderness (8:27).

✤ Not surprisingly, then, Luke indicates that even though no other human beings are with Jesus, he is not completely alone in the wilderness. The Devil visits Our Lord and chooses a time and place of vulnerability to tempt him to abandon his saving mission (4:2). Satan is a real personal being, a fallen angel, and not merely a personification of human sinfulness or a fictional character from ancient times. This ancient Enemy of the human race seeks the downfall of Jesus, as he also seeks our fall from grace.

✤ The Devil tells Jesus, *"If you are the Son of God …"* (4:3, 9). Perhaps Satan doesn't yet fully know Jesus' divine identity, and the conditional statement is sincere. On the other hand, he may well know who Jesus is, but is trying to insinuate subtly into Jesus' mind a doubt about his identity, just as the Devil did with Eve. Of course, Satan is quickly presented evidence that Jesus is the Christ, the Son of God, as he resists the temptations and shows his love and faithfulness to God the Father. In this perseverance, Jesus demonstrates that he is the Beloved Son. Unlike Adam in the Garden of Eden, or the nation of Israel in the desert, he does not abandon God for the passing things of this world.

✤ Throughout the temptations, Jesus uses the Sacred Scriptures against the Devil (4:4, 8, 12). In particular, he uses the Book of Deuteronomy, which can be considered the "last will and testament" of Moses before he died. It was a full summary of the Law with the firm command to choose God above all things. In this exchange with the Devil, Jesus is showing himself as the fulfillment of the Law of Moses. He himself is the definitive last will and testament, as well as the new beginning.

✤ Jesus' use of the Sacred Scriptures shows us how important it is to know, study, live, and apply the Bible in our daily lives as the children of God (2 Tm 3:16). The Bible is a living word that cuts to our core (Heb 4:12) and can guide us as a light to our feet (Ps 119:105).

✤ Luke notes that in the temptations, the Devil himself uses the Bible (4:10–11). He cites the Sacred Scriptures in his attempts to convince Jesus to abandon his mission. This detail of the account shows how the Bible can be misinterpreted, abused, and used for evil purposes. It shows how much the Church and the world need a Magisterium, a Christ-appointed teaching authority, to interpret, guide, correct, affirm, and explain the Bible to humanity.

✤ Since no other human beings accompanied Jesus in the wilderness, he himself must have recalled this experience to his disciples. That he would do so suggests that he considered it essential for them (and for us) to know about it.

✤ Luke concludes his account of Our Lord's wilderness experience with the chilling observation: "And when the Devil had ended every temptation, he departed from him until an opportune time" (4:13). When was that opportune time? St. Augustine comments on this text: "Satan will return. He will enter Judas and make him betray his master" (*Homily 284.5*). The temptations in the wilderness, Augustine observes, were of the seductive sort. But the later temptations will take the form of ferocious, brutal violence against him.

To prepare for small group discussion, turn ahead now to this session's "Digging Deeper" and "Life Application" sections.

Rome to Home

With Baptism we become *children of God in his only-begotten Son, Jesus Christ*. Rising from the waters of the Baptismal font, every Christian hears again the voice that was once heard on the banks of the Jordan River: "You are my beloved Son; with you I am well pleased" (Lk 3:22). From this comes the understanding that one has been brought into association with the beloved Son, becoming a child of adoption (Gal 4:4–7) and a brother or sister of Christ. In this way the eternal plan of the Father for each person is realized in history: "For those whom he foreknew he also predestined to be conformed to the image of his Son, in order that he might be the first-born among many brethren" (Rom 8:29).

—*St. John Paul II, Christifideles Laici, 11*

Opening Prayer

Let the words of my mouth and the meditation of my heart be acceptable in your sight, O Lord, my rock and my redeemer!

—Psalm 19:14

Teaching Video

This first video, hosted by Dr. Paul Thigpen, focuses on certain themes and passages from the Gospel of Luke. Here are some key highlights of his presentation, with room to take notes as you view the video to assist you in the group discussion.

Wilderness as the place of encounter with God

_____

_____

_____

_____

| *View of the Judean desert in winter.*
© *Shutterstock*

The ministry of John the Baptist

_____

_____

_____

_____

The baptism of Jesus

_____

_____

_____

_____

Why Jesus goes into the wilderness

_____

_____

_____

_____

Satan's strategies in temptation

_____

_____

_____

_____

| _The Temptation of Christ, 1854 (oil on canvas), Scheffer, Ary (1795-1858) / National Gallery of Victoria, Melbourne, Australia / Bridgeman Images_

How Jesus responds

_____

_____

_____

_____

Catechism Connections

These readings from the Catechism of the Catholic Church (CCC) will deepen your understanding of this session's presentations and discussions. The numbers identify the relevant paragraphs in the Catechism.

⚜ Baptism of Jesus: CCC 535–537, 1223–1225

⚜ Jesus' temptations in the desert: CCC 538–540

⚜ John the Baptist: CCC 717–720

⚜ Foreshadowings of Baptism in the Old Covenant: CCC 1217–1222

Small Group Discussion

DIGGING DEEPER

1. John is sent by God into the wilderness, where he is prepared for the work that God has called him to do. The theme of being sent into the wilderness or the desert for preparation and for encounter with God is a recurring theme in the Bible. What other major figures in salvation history were sent into the wilderness by God? (See Gn 12:1–9; 32:13–32; Ex 3:1–6; 1 Kgs 19:4–18.)

_____

_____

_____

_____

2. While he is preaching, John baptizes the people with a baptism of repentance. This act is a precursor to Christian Baptism. Christian Baptism is also prefigured in other events in the Bible. What events in the Old Testament are "types" (foreshadowings) of the Sacrament of Baptism? (See CCC 1217–1222; Gn 1:1–2; 7:1–5; Ex 14:15–22; Jo 3:7–17.)

_____

_____

_____

_____

3. Jesus, as the Son of God, is sinless. Why, then, is he baptized by John? Does he need to be baptized? How does the Father respond to Jesus' baptism? (See CCC 535–537.)

_____

_____

_____

_____

4. How does the temptation of Jesus in the desert by the Evil One reveal the kind of Messiah that he will be?

_____

_____

_____

_____

5. In the reading assigned for this session, how does Luke show that Jesus is the "New Adam"?

_____

_____

_____

_____

LIFE APPLICATION

1. As we recount the event of the Lord's baptism and mission, how do we understand our own baptism and the mission that we have been given?

_____

_____

_____

_____

2. How do we live the graces of our baptism in our marriages, families, neighborhoods, and work places? How do people see the grace of God in us?

_____

_____

_____

_____

3. What new resolutions can we make so that the graces of our baptism can be lived more deeply?

_____

_____

_____

_____

Voices of the Saints

Don't let temptations frighten you; they are the trials of the souls whom God wants to test when he sees they have the necessary strength to sustain the struggle, thus weaving the crown of glory with their own hands.

—*St. Pio of Pietrelcina, Letter, 1920*

| *Little girl on ceremony of child christening in church, © Mylu, Shutterstock*

Life Application Video

After breaking from your small group discussion, gather to watch the second video, a pastoral reflection from Fr. Jeffrey Kirby, STD.

How Then Shall We Live?

Silently review the following summary of Fr. Kirby's reflection to prepare for answering the questions in "Living It Out."

St. Luke recounted for us the story of the Lord's baptism and the beginning of his ministry. We should ask ourselves what we have done with our own baptisms. Are we living the baptismal way of life?

The Scriptures declare that with our reception of the Sacrament of Baptism we have died in Christ. We have died to our sins, our wayward passions, the passing trends of this world, and all things that can cause harm to ourselves or to others. We have died in Christ, so that we might rise with him to newness of life. In the newness of life, God can bring to full flourishing the fruits of his Spirit, such as peace, patience, kindness, love, self-control, joy, goodness, chastity, gentleness, generosity, faithfulness, and modesty.

When Jesus was baptized in the Jordan, God the Father acknowledged his divine Son, and the Spirit was made manifest. This divine Trinity—Father, Son, and Holy Spirit—brought us into the family of God when we were baptized.

Do we fully understand the mission that has been given to us? We see the Lord enter the desert after his own baptism. We are also called to the desert, and we don't need sand to have a desert. It is in the desert of our hearts that we choose to die to ourselves and to live in Jesus Christ. It is in this desert that we die to impatience and are reborn to patience; where we die to lust and are reborn to chastity; where we die to anger and are reborn in peace. We cannot avoid the desert if we want to cooperate with the graces of Baptism and live the way of the Lord Jesus.

The Lord received his baptism so that we might know what to do to be reborn and follow him. The Lord shows us how to live a new life, and he has given us the grace to do it.

| *Israel Desert View, © Tiia Monto, 2016, Wikimedia Commons*

Living It Out

On your own, spend three to five minutes praying, discerning, and writing down the specific ways that God might be calling you to make changes in your life. Share and discuss afterwards only if you feel comfortable doing so.

Consider this week how God is calling you to …

⚜ Deepen in the understanding of your baptism.

⚜ Examine how you have been or have not been living the baptismal way of life.

⚜ Look up the date of your baptism and celebrate it as your birthday into eternal life.

Words to Know

Adelphos: The Greek word for "brother" that also can refer to other relatives, such as a half-brother or cousin, an acquaintance, or even a member of the spiritual "family" of God (Lk 3:1; Mt 5:22–24; Acts 21:20).

Promised Land: The land of Canaan, which God promised to give to the descendants of Abraham (Gn 12:7).

Theophany: A manifestation of God (Father, Son, or Holy Spirit) to human beings, usually through the senses. Examples: God's appearance to Moses in the burning bush; the Blessed Trinity's manifestation at the baptism of Jesus.

Closing Prayer

Come, O Spirit of fortitude, and give fortitude to our souls. Make our hearts strong in all trials and in all distress, pouring forth abundantly into them the gifts of strength, so that we may be able to resist the attacks of the Devil. Amen.

| *The Temptation in the Wilderness, illustration for 'The Life of Christ', c.1886-94 (w/c & gouache on paperboard), Tissot, James Jacques Joseph (1836-1902) / Brooklyn Museum of Art, New York, USA / Bridgeman Images*

Christ the Consolator / Carl Bloch / Restored Traditions

SESSION 5

MISSION
OF
MERCY

*And Jesus returned in the power of the Spirit into Galilee, and a report
concerning him went out through all the surrounding country.*

LUKE 4:14

SESSION 5 | SELF STUDY

Introduction

After Jesus defeats the Devil in the wilderness, he returns to Galilee to begin his public ministry. He begins by teaching in the synagogues throughout the cities and towns of the region, where his ministry is well received. But in his hometown of Nazareth, he encounters violent opposition.

In the synagogue there, he declares that he fulfills the messianic prophecy in the Book of Isaiah, which foretells his ministry accurately and powerfully. But when the overfamiliarity of his old neighbors causes them to doubt his mission and authority, he warns them that in times past, when the Chosen People have rejected God's prophets, he has bypassed them and worked among the Gentiles instead. His warning infuriates them, and they try to throw him off a cliff.

Jesus passes through the mob unharmed and goes on to another town of Galilee, Capernaum, which becomes the center of his ministry. His words and deeds there sum up his three years of ministry ahead: He preaches the good news of the kingdom of God, heals the sick, and casts out demons. Many people receive him gladly, but the opposition in Nazareth is a sign of things to come.

Prayer to Prepare for Study

Lord, my God, bestow upon me an understanding that knows You, diligence in seeking You, wisdom in finding You, a way of life that is pleasing to You, perseverance that waits trustfully for You, and confidence that I shall embrace You at the last. Amen.

—Prayer of St. Thomas Aquinas before study

Study Notes

These notes provide insights to help you understand and reflect upon the biblical text.

❖ Luke reports that after the temptations, Jesus is led back to Galilee by the power of the Spirit (4:14). This is a pivotal shift in Luke's Gospel. So much of the narrative up to this point has been setting the stage, and now Jesus begins his public ministry. Once again, much has been said about him, but now he will speak publicly for himself. Going to the synagogue of Nazareth, his hometown, Jesus proclaims a messianic passage of Isaiah (61:1–2, 58:6). After reading it, he announces: "Today this scripture has been fulfilled in your hearing" (4:21). For Luke, this pronouncement begins Jesus' public ministry and gives it a clear direction and purpose.

❖ The first appearance of Jesus in his public ministry is marked by confusion and rejection, as the people ask: "Is not this Joseph's son?" (4:22). It is significant that the Lord's public ministry begins with a rejection in his own hometown. As Jesus explains: "Truly, I say to you, no prophet is acceptable in his own country" (4:24). In response to the people of Nazareth, Luke writes, the Lord references the widow of Zarephath and Naaman the Syrian (4:25–27). Both of these figures in the Old Testament were Gentiles, and both were greatly favored by God (1 Kgs 17:8–24; 2 Kgs 5:1–14). Luke records these teachings in light of his focus on the Gentiles.

✤ Jesus leaves Nazareth and goes to Capernaum. The port city of Capernaum becomes one of the focal points of Jesus' ministry in the region of Galilee, and in many respects "a second home" to him. It is the hometown of Peter and Andrew, and Jesus will frequently go and rest there.

✤ The account of the Lord's initial visit to Capernaum appears to be one long day (4:31–44). The narrative is told in a type of slow motion in order to indicate what a day in the life of the Lord looks like and what his specific work and teachings are.

✤ In his day at Capernaum, the Lord works two miracles showing his power over unclean spirits afflicting body and soul. These are the first recorded miracles of Jesus in Luke's Gospel, and they are ordered in such a way as to show the Lord's authority and to give credibility to his teachings.

✤ The day begins with Jesus going to the synagogue of Capernaum and teaching. In the synagogue, the Lord encounters a demon as he did in the wilderness (though not necessarily Satan himself this time). Unlike the Lord's temptations in the desert, in which he was largely responding to the Enemy's assault, here Jesus takes the offensive against dark forces and performs an exorcism. It's significant that the first miracle of Jesus recorded by Luke is an exorcism. The Devil is mentioned twenty-three times in Luke's Gospel, as the Evangelist wants to emphasize Jesus' divine identity and his manifest authority over unclean spirits. In the encounter in Capernaum, the demon knows who Jesus is: "What have you to do with us, Jesus of Nazareth? Have you come to destroy us? I know who you are, the Holy One of God" (4:34). In many respects, this encounter draws the battle lines for the work of redemption and clearly indicates who the combatants are in the battle.

The Man Possessed of a Devil in the Synagogue, illustration for 'The Life of Christ', c.1884-96 (w/c & gouache on paperboard), Tissot, James Jacques Joseph (1836-1902) / Brooklyn Museum of Art, New York, USA / Purchased by Public Subscription / Bridgeman Images

✤ The demon calls Jesus "the Holy One of God." This is a title rich in biblical history, since many servants of God have been called by this title, including the high priest Aaron (Ps 106:16) and the prophet Elisha (2 Kgs 4:9). The title, however, takes on a higher meaning when it's applied to Jesus as he shows his power in exorcising unclean spirits.

✤ When the demon calls Jesus the "Holy One of God," the Lord rebukes and silences it (4:35). This shows the Lord's power over the unclean spirit. The silencing also has several other meanings: First, the title itself is holy and should not be spoken by unclean spirits. Second, the Lord's presence as the Messiah should be made known solely by self-proclamation. Third, the timing of the Lord's revelation is significant since he has a mission to complete before it's consummated in his passion, death, and resurrection. This silencing occurs again later in the day when the Lord is healing the sick (4:41).

✤ St. Athanasius notes that Our Lord's silencing of the demon should also teach us never to listen to demons, even when they seem to be speaking truth. Whatever truth they may speak, he insists, will sooner or later be mixed with error. Jesus wants to keep the demons from "sowing their own wickedness in the midst of the truth" (*Life of St. Anthony*, 26).

Good and Evil: the Devil Tempting a Young Woman, 1832 (detail of 89709) (oil on canvas), Orsel, Andre Jacques Victor (1795-1850) / Musee des Beaux-Arts, Lyon, France / Peter Willi / Bridgeman Images

✤ In the New Testament, St. James teaches that the demons have knowledge of God's identity, but it does not save them, since they are opposed to him (Jas 2:19). This is a significant reminder, since many people know Jesus, or know about him, but they don't respond to this divine knowledge. It's essential to note that knowledge of God must be acted upon, obeyed, integrated, and lived in daily life if grace is to bring about our salvation and lead us into a holy life.

✤ In the encounter between the Lord and the demon in Capernaum, the possessed man is thrown down but "no harm" is done to him (4:35). The Devil will oftentimes use fear or confusion to seduce and retain souls. Here the Lord shows the work of exorcism, and by extension the work of redemption, in freeing the human person from the assaults of the Devil and sin and bringing him unharmed to a life of freedom and grace.

✤ After the exorcism, Luke tells us, everyone is amazed, and they say to one another, "What is this word? For with authority and power he commands the unclean spirits, and they come out" (4:36). The people are beginning to understand the newness of what the Lord is doing, and word spreads about him.

✤ The Lord's day in Capernaum continues, and so he leaves the synagogue after the exorcism and visits the home of Simon Peter. The chief apostle's mother-in-law has a high fever, and they ask him for help (4:38). The Lord rebukes the fever and heals her (4:39). This is the Lord's second miracle reported in Luke's Gospel, and it shows once again that he has authority over unclean spirits afflicting body and soul.

✤ The reference to Peter's "mother-in-law" does indicate that the chief apostle married, but he may have been widowed at this point. Given the level of surrender and the demands involved in his vocation as an apostle, some scholars believe that when Peter began following the Lord, Peter's wife was deceased. This seems to be confirmed by Luke's silence about her. If she were still alive, it would seem that Luke would have mentioned her in the account of the healing of her mother. In the Apostle Paul's later statement that Cephas (Peter) is "accompanied by a wife" (1 Cor 9:5), the Greek word can also be translated as "woman" or "sister." Luke has told us that certain devout women accompanied Our Lord and the Apostles to minister to them (8:3).

✤ In any case, the reference to St. Peter's mother-in-law does not undermine the Church's discipline of clerical celibacy, since the charism of celibacy (or continence) was observed from apostolic times. It is reflected in the very life of Jesus Christ and the Apostles, who surrendered all things to follow him.

✤ After St. Peter's mother-in-law is healed, Luke tells us that "immediately" she rises and serves them (4:39). This exemplifies the call of the Christian disciple. Whatever is received is meant to be given. As this woman is healed and served, so she rises and begins to serve others.

✤ As the Lord and the Apostles eat supper, Luke tells us, the sun is setting, and many people bring their sick to him (4:40). The Lord's evening is filled with compassion and healings. Luke reports that the Lord lays his hands "on every one of them" (4:40). The act of "laying on of hands" is a visible sign of the action of God and the giving of invisible grace. The same action forms part of the sacraments (such as Confirmation, the Anointing of the Sick, and Holy Orders), as well as various blessings.

✤ Jesus ends his day in Capernaum as he began it, exorcising unclean spirits (4:41).

✤ In various places in the Gospels, the Lord retreats to pray at night. After the long day in Capernaum, however, it seems his human nature needs sleep. Luke does not indicate that the Lord prays that evening, but when it is day, he departs and goes "into a lonely place" (4:42). Jesus will continue his mission of prayer. This incident is an example and a summons to all Christian believers: Prayer must surround everything that is done in God's name.

✤ Our Lord's time of prayer, however, is interrupted by people seeking him out and trying to have him stay in Capernaum. The Lord responds that he must move on to other cities and proclaim the good news of the kingdom of God. In this way, Luke begins his account of the Lord's public ministry beyond his day in Capernaum.

To prepare for small group discussion, turn ahead now to this session's "Digging Deeper" and "Life Application" sections.

Rome to Home

Notwithstanding the great joy that marked the beginning of Jesus' ministry, in the synagogue of Nazareth you [Mary] must already have experienced the truth of the saying about the "sign of contradiction" (see Lk 4:28ff). In this way you saw the growing power of hostility and rejection which built up around Jesus until the hour of the Cross, when you had to look upon the Saviour of the world, the heir of David, the Son of God dying like a failure, exposed to mockery, between criminals. Then you received the word of Jesus: "Woman, behold, your Son!" (Jn 19:26). From the Cross you received a new mission. From the Cross you became a mother in a new way: the mother of all those who believe in your Son Jesus and wish to follow him.

—*Pope Benedict XVI, Spe Salvi, 50*

| *Monument to Pope Pius VIII by Pietro Tenerani (1866) / Rome, Italy, photo / Photographer Craig Mace*

Opening Prayer

Let the words of my mouth and the meditation of my heart be acceptable in your sight, O LORD, my rock and my redeemer!

—Psalm 19:14

Teaching Video

This first video, hosted by Dr. Paul Thigpen, focuses on certain themes and passages from the Gospel of Luke. Here are some key highlights of his presentation, with room to take notes as you view the video to assist you in the group discussion.

Three types of ministry essential to Jesus' mission

_____

_____

_____

Luke's emphasis on the Holy Spirit

_____

_____

_____

Jesus in the synagogue at Nazareth

_____

_____

_____

The response of the people at Nazareth

_____

_____

_____

_____

Jesus' ministry in Capernaum

_____

_____

_____

_____

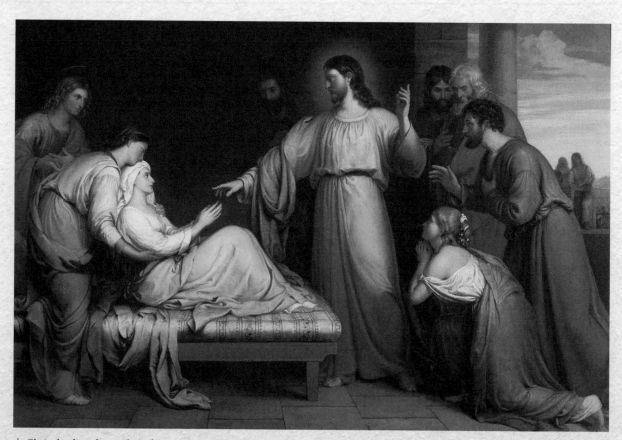

| _Christ healing the mother of Simon Peter, Bridges, John (fl.1818-54) / Private Collection / Photo © Agnew's, London / Bridgeman Images_

Catechism Connections

These readings from the Catechism of the Catholic Church (CCC) will deepen your understanding of this session's presentations and discussions. The numbers identify the relevant paragraphs in the Catechism.

❖ The signs of the kingdom of God: CCC 547–550

❖ Jesus and prayer: CCC 520, 2599–2602

❖ Proclaiming the kingdom of God: CCC 541–546

Small Group Discussion

DIGGING DEEPER

1. Why do the people in the synagogue at Nazareth change their minds and go from accepting Jesus to rejecting him and attempting to stone him?

2. Jesus notes that "no prophet is acceptable in his own country" (4:24). In this statement, he is identifying with the Old Testament prophets who were rejected by Israel. Why did the people of ancient Israel and Judah reject the prophets sent by God? What is the result of this rejection of the prophets? What is the result of rejection of Jesus and his teachings? (See Zec 7:12–14; Jer 7:24–28; 11:9–13; Neh 9:26–27; 2 Chr 24:17–22.)

3. Several times in Luke's fourth chapter, Jesus acts with authority and power, especially through his words. Describe these instances and explain how they reveal who Jesus is.

_____

_____

_____

_____

_____

4. In the synagogue in Nazareth, Jesus reads from the prophet Isaiah and announces that the Scriptures are fulfilled "today." What four groups of people needing ministry are mentioned in this passage? In his ministry, how will Jesus fulfill the words of Isaiah? How do these words indicate the kind of Messiah that Jesus will be? (See Is 58:6; 61:1–2; CCC 547–550.)

Jesus Teaching in the Synagogue, illustration for 'The Life of Christ', c.1886-94 (w/c & gouache on paperboard), Tissot, James Jacques Joseph (1836-1902) / Brooklyn Museum of Art, New York, USA / Bridgeman Images

_____

_____

_____

_____

5. The study notes point out that the Devil is mentioned twenty-three times in the Gospel of Luke and that Luke wants to emphasize Jesus' power over the Evil One and unclean spirits. Why is it important that we understand who the Devil is? Why is it important to understand Jesus' power over the Devil? (See CCC 550.)

_____

_____

_____

_____

LIFE APPLICATION

1. How have we accepted the mission of mercy in our own lives? Do we frequently go to the Sacrament of Confession?

_____

_____

_____

_____

2. In what ways have we sought to live the mission of mercy entrusted to us?

_____

_____

_____

_____

3. Who are we called to reach out to and forgive today?

_____

_____

_____

_____

Voices of the Saints

Do not fear, because the Lord is great, that perhaps he will not condescend to come to one who is sick, for he often comes to us from heaven, and is accustomed to visit not only the rich but also the poor and the servants of the poor. And so now he comes, when called upon, to Peter's mother-in-law. "And he stood over her and rebuked the fever, and it left her, and immediately she arose and ministered to them." As he is worthy of being remembered, so, too, is he worthy of being longed for, worthy, too, of love for his condescension to every single matter that affects men, and his marvelous acts. He does not disdain to visit widows, and to enter the narrow rooms of a poor cottage. As God he commands; as Man he visits.

—*St. Ambrose, Concerning Widows, X, 60*

Life Application Video

After breaking from your small group discussion, gather to watch the second video, a pastoral reflection from Fr. Jeffrey Kirby, STD.

How Then Shall We Live?

Silently review the following summary of Fr. Kirby's reflection to prepare for answering the questions in "Living It Out."

St. Luke powerfully illustrates the life-changing mission of mercy that the Lord Jesus began and continued throughout his public ministry. Truly, the Lord is Mercy itself, and the whole of his work among us can be summarized in that simple word: mercy. But how is this supposed to help us? Are we just dealing with consoling or inspiring stories that give us a kind of "warm fuzzy" and that's all? Or is there something more? Are we just spectators, or should we be doing something?

In life, we cannot give what we do not have. Are we, then, making ourselves available to receive, live, and integrate the Lord's mercy in our own lives and experience? Or are we just hearing an encouraging truth, finding it consoling, and moving along and living our lives? Is the message of mercy true, but not really helping us?

| *Christus Consolator, 1851 (oil on canvas), Scheffer, Ary (1795-1858) / Minneapolis Institute of Arts, MN, USA / Bridgeman Images*

Do we realize that not only are we called to receive the mission of mercy, but we are also called to go forth and continue that mission of mercy? Do we each realize that we are all commissioned and sent as missionaries of mercy to those around us? Yes, even to our spouses, our families, neighbors, fellow parishioners, coworkers, and all we meet (and this includes even a server at a restaurant or a gas station attendant). Do we share and extend the mission of mercy to others?

This is the message of mercy that Luke recounts and the mission of mercy that we are called to receive. Then, in gratitude and humility for what we have received, we are called to go forth in this mission and to extend and give this mercy to others, so that what we say is not only true, but helpful to those around us.

Living It Out

On your own, spend three to five minutes praying, discerning, and writing down the specific ways that God might be calling you to make changes in your life. Share and discuss afterwards only if you feel comfortable doing so.

Consider this week how God is calling you to …

* Reflect on dark times when you needed and received God's profound mercy.

* Prepare for and make a good sacramental Confession.

* Identify people to whom you have extended your mercy and pray for them.

Words to Know

Apostle: Literally, "one sent out" on a mission, who represents the sender with authority. Jesus first appointed twelve apostles to continue his ministry as the foundation of the Church, and there were later other apostles as well, such as Matthias (who took the place of Judas) and Paul of Tarsus.

Disciple: Student; follower.

Synagogue: A local assembly place where Jewish communities pray, worship, and study Scripture.

Closing Prayer

Grant us, O merciful God, to desire eagerly, to discover wisely, to acknowledge sincerely, and to fulfill perfectly the mission of mercy you have given us, to the praise and glory of Your holy Name. Amen.

—Based on a prayer in the *Raccolta*

Sermon on the Plain by Makapo6 (Макаров) (http://ru-oldrussia. livejournal.com/11583.html) [Public domain], via Wikimedia Commons

SESSION 6

CALL

OF THE

APOSTLES

All night he continued in prayer to God. And when it was day, he called his disciples, and chose from them twelve, whom he named apostles.

LUKE 6:12–13

SESSION READING

LUKE 5:1–6:49

Introduction

Luke's account now follows Jesus as his public ministry receives increasing popularity, and scrutiny, throughout the towns and villages of Galilee. He cures a leper with just a touch. He heals a paralyzed man and restores a man's diseased hand to perfect health. Those who suffer from various illnesses flock to him, and he heals them all.

Luke also begins to provide substantial records of Our Lord's teaching. Jesus speaks about the Sabbath, fasting, judging others, almsgiving, loving enemies, and bearing good fruit. He declares a series of blessings similar to the well-known Beatitudes recorded in Matthew's Gospel—but with an accompanying series of sobering woes.

Jesus also stirs up more controversy when he forgives a man his sins, heals on the Sabbath, and allows his disciples to pick grain to eat on the Sabbath. The opposition to his ministry is intensifying.

In addition to all these authoritative words and gracious deeds, Our Lord lays the foundations for the Church he will establish to continue his mission of mercy after his earthly life comes to a close. Luke tells us specifically about the calling of Peter, James, John, and Matthew (Levi). These four are among the twelve who are chosen from among his many disciples to become Apostles.

| *Jesus instructing the Apostles, Fresco by Fra Angelico, San Marco, Florence, Wikimedia (circa 1395–1455) [Public domain], via Wikimedia Commons*

Prayer to Prepare for Study

Lord, my God, bestow upon me an understanding that knows You, diligence in seeking You, wisdom in finding You, a way of life that is pleasing to You, perseverance that waits trustfully for You, and confidence that I shall embrace You at the last. Amen.

—Prayer of St. Thomas Aquinas before study

Study Notes

These notes provide insights to help you understand and reflect upon the biblical text.

✣ After Luke describes Jesus' day in Capernaum, he begins to narrate the call of the first Apostles. Simon (whom Jesus will later name Peter, meaning "Rock") is called first. The encounter between Jesus and Simon occurs because Jesus needs to move out from the shore so that the large crowd can see and hear him. As they are on board, Jesus asks Simon to lower his nets (5:4). Simon tells Jesus that they have fished all night with little success, but he does as Jesus asks (5:5). So many fish are caught that the nets almost tear, and additional fisherman are needed to unload the catch.

✣ Several of the Church Fathers teach that the fish represent the multitude of peoples (Jewish and Gentile) who will be called to follow Jesus. We should note, then, that only Luke's Gospel contains this story of the fish in connection to the call of Simon Peter, James, and John, reflecting Luke's emphasis on the call to the Gentiles. St. Augustine comments, "The apostles received from Jesus the nets of the Word of God. They cast them into the world as if into a deep sea. And they caught the vast multitude of Christians that we now marvel to see" (Sermon 248.2).

✣ After witnessing the miracle, Simon falls to his knees and asks the Lord to depart from him (5:8). He realizes his sinfulness and weakness. This has been described as a "first conversion" in the spiritual life. It is one of the few requests that the Lord does not honor. The Lord calls Simon to himself. He immediately follows, as do his coworkers, James and John. The three of them will serve as the Lord's inner circle and be with him at key moments of his life, such as the Transfiguration (9:28–36) and in the Garden of Gethsemane (Mt 26:36–37).

✣ The Apostles leave everything and follow Jesus (5:11). Luke emphasizes this response of faith and obedience, and he echoes it throughout his Gospel. The person who hears Jesus and wants to follow him must be willing to leave everything.

✣ The account of Jesus' public ministry is now more sporadic in Luke's Gospel (5:12–39). Different scenes are brought together in order to emphasize certain truths or lessons. Some time after Peter, James, and John follow the Lord, Jesus is approached by a leper. In order to approach him, the leper breaks with the ceremonial law that requires lepers to stay away from crowds. Jesus does not rebuke the leper, but honors his request for a cure. After the Lord heals the leper, he tells him to go and show himself to a priest as required by

| *Saint Peter (Simon bar Jona, ?-65) 1st pope, after a medallion of the Basilica of Saint Paul Outside the Walls (-Rome) / Bridgeman Images*

the Mosaic Law (Lv 13:45–46, 49; 14:2–9; Nm 5:2–3). Here, while Luke is showing deference to the Law of Moses by recounting the story, he is also showing how Jesus is fulfilling the Old Testament ceremonial law (Rom 10:4; Eph 2:15).

✤ Throughout Luke's Gospel, Jesus silences the demons that announce his identity, and he asks people not to tell anyone what he has done (4:35; 5:14). Their silence on the matter will allow Jesus the time to preach without hindrance in all the towns and villages. If people don't obey his instruction, Jesus is surrounded by large crowds and not able to move about freely (5:15). Whenever this happens, Jesus removes himself and seeks solitude in order to pray (5:16).

✤ The healing of the leper is followed by the healing of a paralytic. Both healings are examples of God's compassion and care for humanity. In the healing of the paralytic, since the man's friends cannot get him closer to Jesus, they go up on the roof and lower the paralytic down in front of Jesus. Our Lord is moved when he looks upon the faith of the paralytic's friends, and he says to the paralytic, "Man, your sins are forgiven you" (5:20). This shows us that we can exercise our faith on behalf of those who are weak in faith, through intercession and other means.

✤ Jesus' claim to forgive the paralytic's sins outrages the scribes and Pharisees. They immediately question Jesus' authority to absolve the sins of others. This is a power that belongs to God alone. By claiming the power to forgive sin, Jesus is implicitly asserting his divinity.

✤ Jesus' response is a rarity in the Gospels. He works a miracle of healing, not in response to the sufferer's faith, but as an answer to the scribes' and Pharisees' disbelief. With the command "Rise, take up your bed and go home," he heals the paralytic man in their presence (5:24–25). In doing this, Jesus demonstrates his divinity and thus his power to forgive sin.

✤ The healing of the paralytic is one of the most dramatic scenes in Luke's Gospel. It shows that every miracle and physical healing performed by Jesus illustrates a more powerful spiritual truth. The miracles and healings are in service to the conversion of hearts and the redemption of humanity. In the Gospels and in the life of the Church, miraculous physical healings are a gift to the few. But they testify to and confirm the power of the Lord to bring salvation and the forgiveness of sins, which is available to all.

✤ After recounting the call of Simon Peter, James, and John, and the two stories of healing, Luke returns to the call of discipleship. Jesus encounters Levi, a tax collector, at the customs post. The Lord tells him, "Follow me" (5:27). Levi leaves everything and follows him. In celebration, Levi hosts a banquet, and many criticize Jesus for attending the event.

✤ In Jesus' day, tax collectors are Jews who work for the Roman occupying force in collecting taxes for the Emperor. The tax collectors are not paid for this work, so they often overtax their fellow Jews. This overtaxing is not modest, but frequently severe. Tax collectors became very wealthy and are protected by Rome's military. While their fellow Jews suffer in poverty, the tax collectors live comfortable lives surrounded by a great fortune.

| *The Chief Priests Ask Jesus by What Right Does He Act in This Way, illustration from 'The Life of Our Lord Jesus Christ', 1886-94 (w/c over graphite on paper), Tissot, James (1836-1902) / Brooklyn Museum of Art, New York, USA / Purchased by Public Subscription / Bridgeman Images*

✤ Because of this state of affairs, tax collectors are outcasts in Jewish society and viewed as collaborators with the Roman authority and traitors to their people. The term "tax collector" is a synonym for "public sinner." So people are shocked that Jesus will eat at the home of a tax collector (who comes to serve as one of his Apostles). The people complain that Jesus eats with sinners. Luke records Jesus' answer: "Those who are well have no need of a physician, but those who are sick; I have not come to call the righteous, but sinners to repentance" (5:31–32). This declaration illustrates Luke's emphasis on God's mercy in response to our repentance and the universal call to follow Jesus.

✤ After the call of Levi, Jesus begins to address various matters of Jewish spiritual life. This address serves as a prelude to his Sermon on the Plain (see below). The first challenge issued to Our Lord by scribes and Pharisees following Levi's banquet is the criticism that Jesus and his disciples do not fast. The observation is made that John the Baptist's disciples fast and the disciples of the Pharisees fast, but Jesus' disciples do not (5:33). Jesus places the question within the context of a wedding and asks if anyone would fast at such a celebration (5:34). He indicates that his disciples will fast when he is taken away from them, and it will be a new fasting by the power of the Spirit (5:38). As with the temptations of Jesus in the wilderness (4:1–13), Luke emphasizes the meaning and importance of fasting. This statement is also an implicit reference to Christ as the Bridegroom (implying that the Church is his Bride).

| *Christ with Apostles overlooking Jerusalem, Enrique Simonet [Public domain], via Wikimedia Commons*

✤ After the debate on fasting, Jesus is challenged about the Sabbath. Because the Sabbath is central to the ceremonial law of the Old Covenant, the Lord's response to these challenges is perhaps one of the most revealing statements of his public ministry. He announces, "The Son of man is lord of the Sabbath" (6:5). In declaring himself "the lord of the Sabbath," he is revealing his divine identity, since no one but God has authority over the Sabbath.

✤ Two other challenges to Jesus' practice appear in chapter 6. One is a complaint that the disciples pick grain to eat on the Sabbath (6:2), and the other is a rebuke that Jesus heals a man with a withered hand on the Sabbath (6:10). In response to both challenges, Jesus claims authority over the Sabbath and returns the Sabbath observance to its original place, which was one of both service to humanity and worship of God. In his response, Jesus compares himself to King David (6:3–4), claiming a regal-priestly authority. The scribes and Pharisees are enraged by Jesus' claims, and they begin to ask themselves what they can do to him (6:11).

✤ After addressing fasting and the Sabbath, Jesus lays the groundwork for his Sermon on the Plain (see below). In preparation, he spends the night in prayer, calls the disciples together, and chooses twelve of them as Apostles (6:12–13). The Apostles will be his immediate coworkers and will share more intimately in his ministry of leading, teaching, and sanctifying the community of disciples and the entire world. Throughout time, the bishops, as the successors of the Apostles, continue this apostolic work. With a teaching office established, then, Jesus is ready to give his sermon.

✤ Unlike Matthew, who presents the better-known Sermon on the Mount (Mt 5:1–7:28), Luke is less concerned to draw the parallel between Jesus and Moses, so his account of the principal teachings of the Lord is less structured. It is sometimes called the Sermon on the Plain (6:17–49).

✤ The Sermon on the Plain includes the Beatitudes and "woes" (6:20–26). We must note that even though Luke's Gospel is "the Gospel of mercy," we still find in this account Jesus' warning about God's judgment in the "woes," which are not recorded in the other Gospels.

✤ The Sermon on the Plain also includes the admonishment to "turn the other cheek" (6:27–36); the "Golden Rule" (6:31); the warning about judging others (6:37–38); the parable of "the blind leading the blind" (6:39); the status of a teacher (6:40); the call for self-accusation (6:40–42); the principle of good trees and bad trees bearing fruit according to their nature (6:43–45); and the final admonishment: "Why do you call me 'Lord, Lord,' and not do what I tell you?" (6:46). This last admonishment is followed by the story of the two foundations of rock and sand (6:47–49).

✤ Luke intends for the Sermon on the Plain to be heard by all people, and his narrative of the sermon is broad, not restricted within the system and understanding of the Mosaic Law as Matthew presents it. Luke sees the sermon as a summary of how a disciple of Jesus Christ is called to live.

To prepare for small group discussion, turn ahead now to this session's "Digging Deeper" and "Life Application" sections.

Rome to Home

Our hearts ring out with the words of Jesus when one day, after speaking to the crowds from Simon's boat, he invited the Apostle to "put out into the deep" for a catch: *"Duc in altum"* (Lk 5:4). Peter and his first companions trusted Christ's words, and cast the nets. "When they had done this, they caught a great number of fish" (Lk 5:6). *Duc in altum!* These words ring out for us today, and they invite us to remember the past with gratitude, to live the present with enthusiasm, and to look forward to the future with confidence: "Jesus Christ is the same yesterday and today and forever" (Heb 13:8).

—*St. John Paul II, Novo Millennio Ineunte, 1*

Opening Prayer

Let the words of my mouth and the meditation of my heart be acceptable in your sight, O Lord, my rock and my redeemer!

—Psalm 19:14

Teaching Video

This first video, hosted by Dr. Paul Thigpen, focuses on certain themes and passages from the Gospel of Luke. Here are some key highlights of his presentation, with room to take notes as you view the video to assist you in the group discussion.

Jesus' plan to offer redemption beyond his earthly ministry

The church was God's plan
Calls his disciples/apostles → the foundation of his church

JH Farm   Israel   Giving → visitation
        Am Society Ed (Mormon   monastery
                        the bes)   mobile

Typical characteristics of rabbis and disciples

Disciples watched their Rabbi closely
① called to intimacy w/ Jesus ② called to
abandon everything

How Jesus fits the common pattern of a rabbi and disciples

How Jesus departs from the common pattern of a rabbi and disciples

_____

_____

_____

_____

Jesus chooses twelve disciples to become Apostles

_____

_____

_____

_____

What we know about the Apostles

_____

_____

_____

| _Giving of the Keys to St. Peter, from the Sistine Chapel, 1481 (fresco), Perugino, Pietro (c.1445-1523) / Vatican Museums and Galleries, Vatican City / Bridgeman Images_

How the apostolic ministry will be continued after the lifetime of the Twelve

[handwritten: The Call of matthew Carvagio, painter]

Catechism Connections

These readings from the Catechism of the Catholic Church (CCC) will deepen your understanding of this session's presentations and discussions. The numbers identify the relevant paragraphs in the Catechism.

⚜ The Apostles' mission: CCC 551, 858–860

⚜ Preferential love for the poor: CCC 2443–2448

⚜ Poverty of heart: CCC 2544–2547

⚜ The law of the gospel: CCC 1965–1970

Small Group Discussion

[handwritten: The Twelve: The Lives of the Apostles After Calvary By C Bernard Ruffin]

DIGGING DEEPER

1. As the study notes point out, Jesus' call to the Apostles is twofold: He calls them to follow him, and he calls them to leave everything behind. What is each of the Apostles' response to this twofold call? (See 5:9–11, 27–29.)

Vineyards at sunset in autumn harvest. Ripe grapes in fall, © Deyan Georgiev, Shutterstock

2. How do Jesus' exchanges with the Pharisees regarding the Sabbath (6:1–11) reveal his divine authority?

_____

_____

_____

_____

3. Explain how the account of Jesus' calling Peter follows a pattern similar to the Lord's call of Moses at the burning bush and the call of the prophet Isaiah. (See Lk 5:6–11; Ex 3:1–21, 4:1–17; Is 6:1–13.)

Each were called + each obeyed

_____

_____

_____

| *The burning thorn bush, © Markus Gann, Shutterstock*

4. In Luke 5:33–39, Jesus relates parables about patching garments and putting wine into wineskins. What is the deeper meaning of these somewhat confusing parables?

Old Covenant

Old wineskin — why the disciples & they would burst

_____

_____

_____

_____

5. The Sermon on the Plain includes a universal call to holiness for all followers of Jesus. It is also the beginning of the radical teachings noted in question 4. What are some of the radical teachings included in this sermon? Why are these ideas so radical? (See CCC 1965–1970.)

_____

_____

_____

_____

LIFE APPLICATION

1. Do I understand the importance of the Apostles (and their successors, the bishops) to the Church and the world?

_____

_____

_____

_____

2. Do I realize that I, too, have been called and sent into the world to share the Good News according to my state in life?

_____

_____

_____

_____

3. How have I sought to present and give to others the truths of faith in a way that will help them to live better as children of God?

_____

_____

_____

_____

Voices of the Saints

In loving our enemies, there shines forth in us some likeness to God our Father who, by the death of his Son, ransomed from everlasting damnation, and reconciled to himself, the human race, who before were his most persistent enemies. Let the closing passage of this exhortation and injunction be the command of Christ our Lord, which we cannot, without utter disgrace and ruin, refuse to obey: "Pray for those who spitefully abuse you and persecute you, so that you may be the children of your Father who is in heaven."

—*St. Pius V, Catechism of the Council of Trent, IV, 9, xix*

| *The Council of Trent, 4th December 1563 (oil on canvas), Italian School, (16th century) / Louvre, Paris, France / Bridgeman Images*

Life Application Video

After breaking from your small group discussion, gather to watch the second video, a pastoral reflection from Fr. Jeffrey Kirby, STD.

How Then Shall We Live?

Silently review the following summary of Fr. Kirby's reflection to prepare for answering the questions in "Living It Out."

Luke beautifully recounts the call of the Apostles by the Lord Jesus. It's the beginning of the Lord's constitution of the Church. He begins by calling and then forming his Apostles after his own heart. He will entrust them with a portion of his ministry while he is with them, and then entrust the entire Church—the people, doctrine, sacraments, and the care for humanity—to them and their successors. Plainly put, the Apostles (and their successors throughout time, whom we called bishops) are a big deal!

We rely on the apostolic ministry in order to know what is true doctrine, what are the valid sacraments, and how to care for humanity in the proper way. The bishops, successors of the Apostles, need the support and prayers of the People of God. The priests of the Church are their coworkers, and the deacons are their immediate assistants in the care of the sick and poor.

The deacons, priests, and bishops of the Church continue the work of the Apostles, given to them by Jesus Christ, of blessing, teaching, sanctifying, and shepherding the Church and humanity.

Listen again to the account from Luke of the call of the Apostles, and let it sink in. The Lord prayed for and commissioned them, as he prayed for and commissioned our local bishop and our local pastor. Let's recognize the work and ministry of our shepherds, and let's support them and show them our love.

| *European bishops' procession into Notre Dame of Paris cathedral (photo) / Godong/UIG / Bridgeman Images*

Living It Out

On your own, spend three to five minutes praying, discerning, and writing down the specific ways that God might be calling you to make changes in your life. Share and discuss afterwards only if you feel comfortable doing so.

Consider this week how God is calling you to …

- ✤ Seek to understand better the Church's teachings about an area of life where you struggle in your discipleship (showing mercy, marriage and family, life issues, and so on).

- ✤ Pray for your bishop and local priests and deacons.

- ✤ Extend a word of kindness or support to your pastor or another priest.

Words To Know

Beatitudes: Promises of blessing made by Jesus to his disciples who obey his teaching, found in Mt 5:3–12.

Rabbi: Literally, "my master" or teacher; respectful form of address used for religious teachers by their disciples.

Sermon on the Mount: The teaching of Jesus presented in Mt 5:1–7:29, beginning with the Beatitudes (see above) and ending with the parable of the house built on rock.

Sermon on the Plain: The teaching of Jesus presented in Lk 6:17–49, which contains beatitudes similar to those in Matthew's Gospel (see above), along with "woes" not found in Matthew; parables; and other moral instructions.

Twelve, the: The twelve disciples chosen by Jesus as Apostles: Peter (Simon); Andrew; James; John; James, son of Alphaeus; Levi (Matthew); Philip; Bartholomew (Nathaniel); Simon "the Zealot"; Thomas (Didymus); Jude (Judas, Thaddeus); and Judas Iscariot.

Closing Prayer

Raise us up, we ask You, O Lord, by the apostolic assistance of blessed Peter, Your apostle, so that the weaker we are, the more mightily we may be helped by the power of his intercession. Being perpetually defended by this same holy apostle, may we neither yield to any sin, nor be overcome by any adversity, through Christ our Lord. Amen.

—Adapted from a prayer in the *Raccolta*

*Magdalene in the House of Simon the Pharisee,
by Giuseppe Tortelli, oil on canvas / Mondadori
Portfolio/Electa/Adolfo Bezzi / Bridgeman Images*

SESSION 7

THE
SINFUL
WOMAN

And he said to the woman, "Your faith has saved you; go in peace."

LUKE 7:50

SESSION READING
LUKE 7:1–50

Introduction

Luke tells how Our Lord's mission of mercy continues to transform the lives of those who come to him in faith. He heals the slave of a centurion—a Roman Gentile who recognizes that Jesus has divine authority. He raises from the dead the only son and support of a grieving widow.

The disciples of John the Baptist come to Jesus inquiring whether he is indeed the Messiah. In that very hour, Jesus is preaching the good news of the kingdom of God, healing the sick, and casting demons out of their victims. He reminds them that such words and deeds are signs of his messianic identity; they fulfill the prophecies of Isaiah. When they leave, Jesus gives high praise to John and his mission.

The chapter concludes with the story of a sinful woman who comes to Jesus for forgiveness, presenting a beautiful and powerful portrait of a life made new. Jesus is dining in the home of a Pharisee when she arrives, showing to Our Lord a tearful repentance and a humble faith. The smug self-righteousness of the host is a clear contrast with the penitential sorrow of the woman. Jesus forgives the woman and sends her home in peace.

Prayer to Prepare for Study

Lord, my God, bestow upon me an understanding that knows You, diligence in seeking You, wisdom in finding You, a way of life that is pleasing to You, perseverance that waits trustfully for You, and confidence that I shall embrace You at the last. Amen.

—Prayer of St. Thomas Aquinas before study

Study Notes

These notes provide insights to help you understand and reflect upon the biblical text.

✤ In his public ministry, Jesus shows his power over sin and death—in particular, when he heals the Gentile centurion's slave (7:1–10), raises the dead son of the widow of Nain (7:11–17), identifies his messianic works (7:22–23), and forgives the sinful woman (7:36–50).

✤ In the encounter with the Roman centurion, whose slave is about to succumb to a fatal illness, the pagan officer's history of kindness to the Jewish community in Capernaum earns their efforts to get Jesus' attention (7:4–5). Jesus is moved by the faith of a Roman, a non-Jew, who has utter confidence that the Lord can heal his slave. Jesus exclaims, "I tell you, not even in Israel have I found such faith" (7:9). Luke records this saying to emphasize the universal need for Jesus Christ and his universal openness to all people, especially the Gentiles. Once again, Luke misses no opportunity to demonstrate God's mercy toward the Gentiles as well as the Jews.

| *Christ and the Widow of Nain, c.1550-55 (oil on canvas), Caliari, Paolo (Veronese) (1528-88) / Private Collection / Photo © Christie's Images / Bridgeman Images*

✤ We see not only the centurion's faith, but also his strong humility. The military leader does not feel worthy to approach Jesus directly. He does so through intermediaries (7:3). Through his example, we can see that humility is essential for faith.

✤ The Gentile centurion's words (7:6–7) became the basis of the prayer now said at every Mass: "Lord, I am not worthy that you should enter under my roof; but only say the word, and my soul shall be healed."

✤ Luke notes the Lord's immense compassion in his encounter with the Jewish widow and her dead son in Nain. The dead son has probably been the woman's sole support, both in family and in sustenance. Without the young man, the widow is not only bereft and lonely, but financially desperate. This time, Jesus doesn't wait for her to approach him—she may not even know who he is. He comes across her son's funeral procession, feels deep compassion for her, tells her not to weep, and raises her son from the dead with a simple command (7:14).

✤ Only Luke records this story. Perhaps because of his close relationship with Mary, Jesus' mother, Luke is more sensitive to widows who have lost their only sons. If so, it's quite natural that he would have included this event in his account of the Lord's public ministry.

✤ As Jesus works powerful signs and miracles, John the Baptist—still in prison for defending marriage against Herod—sends messengers asking whether Jesus is the Christ (7:18–20).

Jesus does not directly answer the question but lists all the deeds he is doing (7:21–23) that fulfill the prophecy about the Messiah (Is 35:4–6). In this way, Jesus answers the question and provides prophetic testimony that he is the Christ. Luke wants all of humanity, both Jews and Gentiles, to hear Jesus' answer and to know the wonderful things he has done. It's an invitation for all people to accept Jesus Christ.

✦ When the messengers come from John the Baptist, Jesus speaks about the prophet. He attests that John is the promised "Elijah," the one to come and prepare the way for the Christ (7:24–28). It's worth noting here that even though some claim that, based on these words, John was in fact Elijah reincarnated, Jesus' meaning is clarified when we recall the angel Gabriel's prophecy to Zechariah that John will come "in the *spirit* and *power* of Elijah" (1:17).

✦ In the time of Jesus, the Pharisees (7:39) are a Jewish sect who insist on a scrupulous observance of the ancient Law of Moses. They teach that every Jewish person is obligated to follow, not just the divine commandments in Scripture, but also a large body of oral tradition and interpretation of those commandments. Their concern is to avoid transgressing God's law under the influence of pagan practices or through moral and ceremonial laxity.

✦ As we make our way through Luke's Gospel, we'll see more and more evidence that the Pharisees as a whole are among Jesus' strongest opponents. Ironically, their theological beliefs are closer to his than those of other Jewish religious parties of the day. Nevertheless, they consider him lax when he teaches that God's principles of justice and mercy supersede and sometimes even contradict their interpretations of the Law. In addition, many Pharisees oppose him because they envy his popularity and influence over the people.

✦ The lawyers, sometimes called scribes or scholars of the Law, are a professional class of copyists and notaries of the Law of Moses who by the time of Jesus have become influential interpreters of it. In doctrine and practice, they are usually allied with the Pharisees, so they, too, tend to be skeptical and suspicious of Jesus. Luke notes that the Pharisees and the lawyers as a whole have rejected John's baptism of repentance, and in doing so, they have rejected God's purpose for themselves.

✦ In response to Jesus, the tax collectors acknowledge the righteousness of God, while the Pharisees and scholars of the Law reject his message (7:29–30). Jesus compares them to children not dancing

| *Aaron with the Scroll of the Law, 1875 (oil on canvas), Solomon, Simeon (1840-1905) / Southampton City Art Gallery, Hampshire, UK / Bridgeman Images*

to music or people not moved to mourn by a funeral song (7:31–32). In saying these things, the Lord is saying how lifeless and without joy the lives of the scholars and Pharisees have become. Luke records these teachings as a summons to live life fully in Jesus Christ and to hold on to the joy that comes from loving God.

✦ A Pharisee invites the Lord to dinner in his home. The Pharisees, as strict observers of the Law, should be the first to welcome Jesus. Yet they approach him with suspicion and skepticism. A woman of sin, most likely a prostitute, approaches Jesus at this dinner. She understands what Jesus is offering and seeks his pardon. The Lord affirms her and contrasts her acts of love for him with the Pharisee's failure to offer him even the basics of hospitality: The host has given him no water to wash his feet, yet the woman has wet his feet with her tears and wiped them with her hair. The host hasn't given him the customary kiss of greeting, but she hasn't stopped kissing his feet. The host hasn't anointed his head with oil, but she has anointed his feet with ointment (7:44–46).

✦ Only Luke's Gospel records the scene of the sinful woman, and Luke narrates this encounter to show the call of mercy to repent and change our lives through acts of love and service. The woman stands as a stunning example of God's mercy and a reminder to us of our need for God's mercy so that we can love him and our neighbor accordingly.

✦ In commenting on this incident, St. Ambrose reminds us that when we love those who are most in need, we too are kissing the feet of Christ, because whatever we do for the least of his brothers and sisters, we do for him (Mt 25:40).

To prepare for small group discussion, turn ahead now to this session's "Digging Deeper" and "Life Application" sections.

Rome to Home

Especially through His lifestyle and through His actions, Jesus revealed that love is present in the world in which we live—an effective love, a love that addresses itself to man and embraces everything that makes up his humanity. This love makes itself particularly noticed in contact with suffering, injustice and poverty—in contact with the whole historical "human condition," which in various ways manifests man's limitation and frailty, both physical and moral. It is precisely the mode and sphere in which love manifests itself that in biblical language is called "mercy."

—*St. John Paul II, Dives in Misericordia, 3*

Opening Prayer

Let the words of my mouth and the meditation of my heart be acceptable in your sight, O LORD, my rock and my redeemer!

—Psalm 19:14

Teaching Video

This first video, hosted by Dr. Paul Thigpen, focuses on certain themes and passages from the Gospel of Luke. Here are some key highlights of his presentation, with room to take notes as you view the video to assist you in the group discussion.

Various reasons why people come to watch and hear Jesus

_____

_____

_____

_____

The Pharisee's failure to show customary hospitality to Jesus

_____

_____

_____

_____

The sinful woman's situation and actions

_____

_____

_____

_____

Simon's response to the woman

_____

_____

_____

_____

The parable of the two debtors

_____

_____

_____

_____

The woman's reward

_____

_____

_____

_____

Catechism Connections

These readings from the Catechism of the Catholic Church (CCC) will deepen your understanding of this session's presentations and discussions. The numbers identify the relevant paragraphs in the Catechism.

⚜ Jesus and prayer: CCC 2609–2610, 2616

⚜ The centurion's words become ours before Communion: CCC 1386

⚜ Jesus and the leaders of Israel: CCC 574–576, 587–591

⚜ Jesus' raising the dead as a sign of his resurrection and ours: CCC 994

⚜ Christ the physician: CCC 1503

⚜ Only God forgives sin: CCC 1441

Small Group Discussion

DIGGING DEEPER

1. Why is Jesus moved with such compassion when he encounters the widow of Nain? Why would it be shocking to those watching the funeral to see Jesus touch the funeral bier? (See Nm 19:11–19, Dt 26:12.)

_____

_____

_____

_____

2. Why does John the Baptist send his followers to Jesus to ask him, "Are you he who is to come" (7:20)? Doesn't he know who Jesus is? How does Jesus answer John? (See CCC 547–549, Is 35:4–6.)

_____

_____

_____

_____

3. How is Jesus' encounter with the centurion a lesson in faith and in persevering prayer? (See CCC 2616, 1386.)

_____

_____

_____

_____

| *Woe unto You, Scribes and Pharisees, illustration from 'The Life of Our Lord Jesus Christ', 1886-94 (w/c over graphite on paper), Tissot, James (1836-1902) / Brooklyn Museum of Art, New York, USA / Purchased by Public Subscription / Bridgeman Images*

4. The study notes point out that the Pharisees are typically Jesus' strongest opponents. Why are the Pharisees even more upset with Jesus after his encounter with the sinful woman at Simon's house?

_____

_____

_____

_____

5. What does the story about the sinful woman teach Simon, and us, about the connection between love and forgiveness? What do her actions teach us about how we should respond to Jesus' mercy?

_____

_____

_____

_____

SESSION 7 | GROUP STUDY

LIFE APPLICATION

1. In our time of darkest sin, where do we turn for encouragement and consolation?

_____

_____

_____

_____

2. Do we realize the amazing mercy of God and regularly turn to him for forgiveness?

_____

_____

_____

_____

3. Do we judge others rashly and without compassion? Do we forget to see the sinner as our brother or sister?

_____

_____

_____

_____

Voices of the Saints

Show your wound to the Physician, then, so that he may heal it. Even if you don't show it to him, he knows it, but he waits to hear your voice. Wash away your scars by tears. This is what that woman in the Gospel did, and it wiped out the stench of her sin; in this way she washed away her fault, when washing the feet of Jesus with her tears.

St. Ambrose, On Repentance, II, viii, 66

Life Application Video

After breaking from your small group discussion, gather to watch the second video, a pastoral reflection from Fr. Jeffrey Kirby, STD.

How Then Shall We Live?

Silently review the following summary of Fr. Kirby's reflection to prepare for answering the questions in "Living It Out."

Luke's Gospel is truly the Gospel of mercy. In our lesson today, the "Beloved Physician" recounts our Lord's encounter with the sinful woman. It's an endearing episode that should fill each of us with great consolation and hope.

The Lord is kind and merciful! And he desires our freedom and salvation. In our most difficult hour, our darkest hour, the hour in which we realize that we have committed a grave sin (or been an accomplice to a grave sin), when even we ourselves are surprised and shocked by our sin, the Lord calls us out of that darkness into his own wonderful light. But will we turn to him?

We have to imitate that sinful woman. We have to approach the Lord and confess our sins. We have to seek out the Sacrament of Confession and let our sins go. We have to surrender them and allow ourselves to be free and happy in Jesus Christ.

In addition, we have to be gracious in our judgment of the sins of others. Do we give others the benefit of the doubt that they are trying their best? Isn't that benefit of the doubt what we often hope for from others? And as followers of Jesus Christ, shouldn't we best exemplify this kindness and compassion towards others?

Italy, Turin, painting of St John of Nepomuk Hearing the Confession of the Queen of Bohemia / De Agostini Picture Library / G. Dagli Orti / Bridgeman Images

Do we make rash judgments? Are we willing to write other people off? The Lord is not. He loves, and love is patient and kind; it bears all things, hopes all things, endures all things. Love never fails. That's what the Lord showed the sinful woman, and that's what he wants to show us and have us show to others.

Living It Out

On your own, spend three to five minutes praying, discerning, and writing down the specific ways that God might be calling you to make changes in your life. Share and discuss afterwards only if you feel comfortable doing so.

Consider this week how God is calling you to …

- ⚜ Examine your conscience and identify the things that are weighing you down.

- ⚜ Prepare for and make a good sacramental Confession.

- ⚜ Ask other people for their forgiveness, and generously extend your forgiveness to others.

| *Jesus and the Centurion (oil on canvas), Veronese, (Paolo Caliari) (1528-88) / Prado, Madrid, Spain / Bridgeman Images*

Words to Know

Centurion: An officer of the ancient Roman imperial army in command of a division known as a century, containing a hundred soldiers.

Parable: A short fictitious story that illustrates a moral or spiritual principle.

Pharisees: A Jewish sect in the time of Jesus whose members insist on a scrupulous observance of the ancient Law of Moses. They teach that every Jewish person is obligated to follow, not just the divine commandments in Scripture, but also a large body of oral tradition and interpretation of those commandments.

Scribes: A professional class of copyists and notaries of the Law of Moses who by the time of Jesus have become influential interpreters of it. Also known as lawyers or scholars of the Law.

Closing Prayer

Have mercy on me, O God, according to your merciful love; according to your abundant mercy, blot out my transgressions. Wash me thoroughly from my iniquity, and cleanse me from my sin! For I know my transgressions, and my sin is ever before me. Create in me a clean heart, O God, and put a new and right spirit within me. Amen.

—Adapted from Ps 51:1–3, 10

The Raising of Jairus' daughter, 1871 (oil on canvas), Polenov, Vasilij Dmitrievich (1844-1927) / Museum of the Academy of Fine Arts, St Petersburg / Bridgeman Images

CHILD, ARISE!

Jesus on hearing this answered him,
"Do not fear; only believe, and she shall be well."

LUKE 8:50

Introduction

Much of Luke's eighth chapter is devoted to Our Lord's teaching as great crowds assemble to watch and listen to him. But it begins with an interesting note—consistent with Luke's concern for women—that among his faithful followers are several women he has healed or delivered from demons. These women play an essential role in the ministry because they provide financial support to Jesus and the Apostles.

Our Lord's first teaching in this passage, the parable of the sower, helps his faithful disciples understand why some people ignore or even oppose Jesus' ministry. The second parable, about the lamp that must not be hidden, exhorts them to be open in their witness to him and fruitful in their labors.

The next miracle reported shows that as the Son of God, Jesus has authority to command even the elements of nature—in this case, a storm on the sea. The miracle becomes the occasion for the disciples' faith to be tested and then strengthened.

Three miracles that bring new life and hope to those in desperate circumstances finish out the chapter. Jesus casts out a host of unclean spirits from a demon-possessed man; heals a woman with a debilitating chronic illness; and raises a young girl from the dead.

Prayer to Prepare for Study

Lord, my God, bestow upon me an understanding that knows You, diligence in seeking You, wisdom in finding You, a way of life that is pleasing to You, perseverance that waits trustfully for You, and confidence that I shall embrace You at the last. Amen.

—Prayer of St. Thomas Aquinas before study

Study Notes

These notes provide insights to help you understand and reflect upon the biblical text.

✤ As a Gentile, and not restricted by Jewish notions of gender roles, Luke is comfortable in describing the role that women play in Jesus' public ministry (8:1–3). Only Luke's Gospel mentions the work of these holy women. This is the first reference to Mary Magdalene (8:2).

✤ After noting the role of women in Jesus' public ministry, Luke records the parable of the sower (8:4–8). In this parable, the Lord identifies four possible locations of the seed: along the path, on the rocks, among the thorns, or on good soil. The seed on the path is trodden upon and eaten by birds; the seed in the rocks withers because it has no moisture; the seed in the thorns is choked by the thorns; but the seed in the good soil grows and yields a hundredfold.

✤ The parable is explained by the Lord (8:11–15) and indicates the kind of reception various people give to the Word of God. It's a reminder to Christian disciples to receive the Word with generosity and to nourish it with good soil.

✤ Luke quotes Jesus explaining that the parables are given so that "seeing they may not see, and hearing they may not understand" (8:10). Luke emphasizes that the Lord's teaching about the Kingdom is a mystery that no one can control or fully comprehend. The Lord teaches in many parables, which are often followed by multiple miracles affirming their spiritual lessons.

✤ St. Cyril of Alexandria notes on this passage: "We might say that parables are the images not of visible objects, but rather of spiritual objects that are understood by the mind. The parable points out to the eyes of the mind what cannot be seen with the eyes of the body" (*Commentary on Luke*, Homily 41).

✤ After presenting the parable of the sower and explaining the purpose of the parables, the Lord observes that no one lights a lamp and then covers it with a vessel or places it under a bed. Rather, lamps are lit and then placed on tables to give light (8:16).

The Sower, illustration for 'The Life of Christ', c.1886-94 (w/c & gouache on paperboard), Tissot, James (1836-1902) / Brooklyn Museum of Art, New York, USA / Bridgeman Images

The Lord offers this observation as a further emphasis on the importance of receiving the Word and living it out faithfully.

✤ As Luke recounts Jesus' public ministry, he explains a scene in which the Lord's mother and "brothers" come to see him. Since the crowds are so thick, word is sent to Jesus that his family is present and wants to see him. The Lord responds, "My mother and my brethren are those who hear the word of God and do it" (8:21).

- This statement is often misunderstood as a reproof to the Lord's mother and family. The words of the Lord, however, can be understood in exactly the opposite way: Those who are waiting to see him—Mary of Nazareth and his kinsmen—are family to him in ways higher than mere blood or marriage. They all—especially his mother—are with him in spirit and will understand his mission. By extension, then, anyone else who is with him in spirit is also his family. Rather than dismissing his biological family, then, Jesus is affirming them and broadening this family with new members. This reality is affirmed by the presence of Mary with the Apostles in the upper room after the Lord's passion, death, and resurrection (Acts 1:13–15).

- It's important to note the reference to the Lord's "brethren" in the passage (8:19). The Church has always held that Mary was perpetually a virgin. This is not an assumption based on some negative attitude toward sexuality; rather, it simply affirms the historical reality. Mary's virginity was preserved because her body was sacred; it had carried the Son of God.

- Given Mary's perpetual virginity, how should we understood the reference to "brethren" of the Lord? As we observed in the study notes for Session 4, the Greek word here, commonly translated in English as "brothers," is often used to refer to relatives other than biological children of the same father and mother. So "brother" can also mean a cousin or a young uncle. It's also possible that Joseph was a widower when he married Our Lady, and the "brethren" who are mentioned are actually legal half-brothers of the Lord. Either way, the perpetual virginity of Mary is the consequence of her vocation as the Mother of God and of the all-holiness of God.

- Luke is now giving sporadic accounts of Jesus' public ministry. After the scene with the Lord's family, the Evangelist describes a series of four important events in his ministry. They show his power and authority over both the powers of nature and the unclean spirits of soul and body: the calming of the storm (8:22–25); the exorcism of a demon-possessed man (8:26–39); the raising of a dead girl to life (8:40–42, 49–56); and the healing of a woman with a chronic illness (8:43–46).

- In the calming of the storm, Jesus and the Apostles board a boat and are crossing the Sea of Galilee. (Though traditionally called a "sea," it is more properly termed a lake.) The Lord is tired, and he falls asleep (8:23). Scenes such as this one show the humanity of Jesus Christ and remind us that the Lord was fully human, like us in all things except sin (Heb 4:15).

- While the Lord sleeps, a great squall arises; to this day, the Sea of Galilee is known for its sudden storms. The boat transporting the Lord and the Apostles is being swamped, and they are in danger (8:23). The Apostles awaken Jesus. He immediately rebukes the storm, then asks them, "Where is your faith?" (8:25).

- The Lord calls the Apostles to trust him. The story is a powerful one. It reminds every disciple that even when the storm seems overwhelming and dangers abound, the Lord is present, and he has power over the storms of nature and of life.

Christ Stilling the Tempest, illustration for 'The Life of Christ', c.1886-94 (w/c & gouache on paperboard), Tissot, James Jacques Joseph (1836-1902) / Brooklyn Museum of Art, New York, USA / Bridgeman Images

✦ After the Lord has calmed the storm, he and the Apostles continue across the sea to Gerasa, the land of the Gerasenes (8:26). It's significant that the Lord would go there, since the city is on the eastern shore of the Sea of Galilee, where the population is predominantly Gentile. In total, the eastern side of the Sea of Galilee contains at this time ten Greek communities known as the *Decapolis* (literally, "the ten cities").

✦ The Gentile identity of the local population is discernible in the presence of herds of pigs (8:32). According to Jewish ceremonial law, pigs are unclean, and no practicing Jew would herd or even come close to pigs (Lv 11:7–8).

✦ The Lord goes to this and other Gentile regions to proclaim the Good News of the Kingdom. Immediately upon his arrival here, he is met by a demoniac (8:27). Note the response of spiritual darkness to spiritual light. As the Lord brings the Good News, the demon—who has horribly treated the man, leaving him isolated, naked, and homeless among the tombs of his city—manifests itself to the Lord. It shouts, "What have you to do with me, Jesus, Son of the Most High God? I beseech you, do not torment me" (8:28).

- The demon addresses Jesus as "Son of the Most High God," revealing his divine identity. As the demon reveals Jesus' identity, the Lord in turn asks the demon its name. It responds, "Legion" (8:30). This indicates that the man is subject to many demons. The name of the demon implies that demonic forces have a stronghold in the Gentile regions, where the people worship false gods, practice astrology, perform occult rituals, and engage in other pagan spiritual customs of the Greco-Roman world that open doors to demonic activity in their lives.

- The Lord performs an exorcism and sends the demons into the pigs. The presence of the demons causes such a stir in the unclean animals that they run off the cliff and drown themselves (8:33). This incident shows the strong power of the demons and the chaos that is caused by their presence. In contrast, after the demon leaves the man, he is no longer afraid, but sits peacefully with Jesus, dressed and in his right mind (8:35).

- Some modern biblical interpreters claim that demons don't exist, and that Jesus was simply accommodating a common superstition of the time when he performed exorcisms on people with serious mental disorders. Such an interpretation cannot account for the circumstances of the exorcism Luke reports here. A mental illness cannot be cast out of a man into a herd of pigs.

- The people of the region, in hearing what Jesus has done, are afraid and ask the Lord to leave (8:37). The Lord will never stay where he is not welcome. This is an important lesson for Christian believers. If a believer says "Jesus is lord" but then acts in a contrary manner, the believer is not welcoming the presence of the Lord. And the Lord will not stay, for he remains only where he is welcome.

- The freed man asks the Lord if he can come with him (8:38). The Lord declines. In the heavily Jewish regions where he has ministered, he has commanded silence about his miraculous power and divine identity. But here in a largely pagan area, Jesus tells the Gerasene man to go and tell how much God has done for him (8:38–39). In one sense, the Lord sends the man out as a missionary. This incident is a great reminder to all Christians: We are to go out and tell the world what God has done in our lives.

- As the Lord returns from Gerasa, a crowd is waiting for him (8:40). In the crowd is Jairus, the leader of the local synagogue and the father of a very sick child, a twelve-year-old girl (8:41–42). The Jewish leader asks the Lord for help. Jairus is one of the most important men in the city, and this petition to Jesus could cost him his moral authority in the community. But Jairus is desperate for his child to be healed. He sets aside his pride and his preconceived notions

Gadarene Swine (gouache on paper), Uptton, Clive (1911-2006) / Private Collection / © Look and Learn / Bridgeman Images

about Jesus and asks for his help. This is a strong reminder to Christian disciples today. No matter what our positon in society might be, we are always called to show honor to the Lord and to seek his help.

❧ The Lord agrees to intervene, and the crowd moves toward Jairus' house. On the way, however, Jesus encounters a woman who has suffered from bleeding for twelve years (8:43), as long as the life of Jairus' daughter.

❧ Luke tells us she has "spent all her living upon physicians," but none could help her (8:43). Recall that Luke himself is a physician, so he may be a little sensitive about this matter. In fact, the Gospel of Mark notes that not only have the doctors failed to help the woman, but they have made her worse (Mk 5:26)! But understandably, Luke decides to leave out that particular detail.

❧ In touching the cloak of the Lord, the ill woman violates the Jewish ceremonial law. A woman who bleeds this way is ritually unclean and is forbidden to touch others (Lv 15:19–30). But the woman is desperate for help. She is suffering and knows the Lord can help her, so she risks everything to touch the edge of the Lord's cloak (8:44).

❧ After the woman touches the Lord, he asks, "Who touched me?" Peter responds, "Master, the people are crowding and pressing against you" (8:45). Of course, the Lord knows who has touched him, just as he knows that power has gone out from him (8:46). But Jesus wants to speak with the woman, and he wants her to show the Apostles and the crowd the boldness of her faith.

❧ The woman approaches the Lord with "trembling" and falls at his feet (8:47). She testifies to what she has done and the healing she has received. The Lord hears her words and affectionately calls her "daughter." Then he says that her faith has healed her, and he sends her home in peace (8:48).

❧ In this scene between Jesus and the sick woman, we see a marvelous exchange. Normally, under Jewish ceremonial law, what is unclean—such as a leper, a bleeding woman, or a dead body—defiles what is clean when the two come into contact. In this providential exchange, however, the clean purifies the unclean. The Lord is not affected by what is unclean. As the fulfillment of the Law and the One through whom all things have been created, he makes the unclean to be clean again.

❧ Jairus is present for this woman's healing, and when the Lord addresses her as "daughter," his heart must certainly be stirred. But as the scene is concluding, Jairus is told by a messenger that his daughter is dead (8:49). The Lord hears this news and calls Jairus to greater faith (8:50). Sometimes, it's when things look completely bleak, or we don't understand what God is doing, that he calls us to greater faith in him and in his divine providence.

❧ Despite the mournful news, however, the woman's healing is an immediate and undeniable demonstration of Jesus' power. So it can serve as a boost to Jairus' faith that Our Lord can cure his little girl.

❧ Jesus goes to the home of Jairus, where the public mourning has already begun. Jesus takes three of the Apostles and the child's parents with him into the house, leaving everyone else outside. The people laugh at Jesus when he tells them the child is only sleeping (8:52–53). In Scripture, death is sometimes spoken of as "sleep" (Ps 13:3; 1 Cor 15:51). Jesus is emphasizing that the girl's death is like a brief nap from which he will rouse her.

✤ Our Lord probably leaves the mourners outside because they are noisy and distracting. Then, too, these particular mourners are skeptical and irreverent in their laughter. In ancient Jewish culture, women were hired as professional mourners to weep and wail loudly for the deceased. Though the custom may seem staged and artificial to us, they considered it a sign of respect for the dead.

✤ Jesus touches the dead body of the child and tells her, "Child, arise!" (8:54). The girl comes back to life and rises from her bed (8:55). The Lord is manifesting his power over death, as well as making the ritually unclean body clean again.

✤ Luke includes the endearing detail that the Lord tells the child's parents to feed her (8:55). Perhaps he wants them to have clear evidence that she is truly alive again; if she can eat, she cannot be a mere ghost or apparition. Using the same logic, after his resurrection Jesus will ask for something to eat, to prove his bodily resurrection (24:41–43).

✤ Though Jesus has instructed the man of Geresa to tell everyone what has happened, he orders Jairus and his wife *not* to tell anyone what has happened (8:56). Our Lord is now back among the Jewish people, where reports of his miracles can hinder his movement and ministry.

✤ This scene in Luke's Gospel also shows the growing importance of Peter, James, and John and their status as an "inner circle" among the Twelve. These three will become the "key three" of the Apostles. Peter will be the chief Apostle (the first pope). James will be the first Apostle to die a martyr. John will be a mystic, one of the four Evangelists, and the last Apostle to die. He will serve as the great bridge between the first generation and the second generation of Christians. On account of this mission, John will be the only Apostle not to die a martyr.

To prepare for small group discussion, turn ahead now to this session's "Digging Deeper" and "Life Application" sections.

Rome to Home

Jesus, seeing the crowds of people who followed him, realized that they were tired and exhausted, lost and without a guide, and he felt deep compassion for them (Mt 9:36). On the basis of this compassionate love he healed the sick who were presented to him (Mt 14:14), and with just a few loaves of bread and fish he satisfied the enormous crowd (Mt 15:37). What moved Jesus in all of these situations was nothing other than mercy, with which he read the hearts of those he encountered and responded to their deepest need. When he came upon the widow of Nain taking her son out for burial, he felt great compassion for the immense suffering of this grieving mother, and he gave back her son by raising him from the dead (Lk 7:15). After freeing the demoniac in the country of the Gerasenes, Jesus entrusted him with this mission: "Go home to your friends, and tell them how much the Lord has done for you, and how he has had mercy on you" (Mk 5:19).

—*Pope Francis, Misericordiae Vultus, 8*

Opening Prayer

Let the words of my mouth and the meditation of my heart be acceptable in your sight, O Lord, my rock and my redeemer!

—Psalm 19:14

Teaching Video

This first video, hosted by Dr. Paul Thigpen, focuses on certain themes and passages from the Gospel of Luke. Here are some key highlights of his presentation, with room to take notes as you view the video to assist you in the group discussion.

Jairus' status and desperation

_____

_____

_____

_____

The woman with the flow of blood

_____

_____

_____

_____

Jairus' situation worsens

_____

_____

_____

_____

[handwritten: ⅓ parable, ⅓ teaching, ⅓ how to live out the law]

[handwritten: How Rabbi's taught]

[handwritten: 12 = totality. Perfect Government]

Jesus' response to the little girl's death

_____

_____

_____

_____

The professional mourners

_____

_____

_____

_____

Jesus raises the girl from the dead

_____

_____

_____

_____

The Raising of Jairus's Daughter, 1871 (oil on canvas), Repin, Ilya Efimovich (1844-1930) / State Russian Museum, St. Petersburg, Russia / Bridgeman Images

Jesus tells the family not to spread the news of what he has done

_____

_____

_____

_____

Catechism Connections

These readings from the Catechism of the Catholic Church (CCC) will deepen your understanding of this session's presentations and discussions. The numbers identify the relevant paragraphs in the Catechism.

⚜ Mary, ever-virgin: CCC 499–501

⚜ Parables: CCC 546

⚜ The signs of the kingdom of God: CCC 547–549

⚜ Bearing fruit: CCC 1131, 1724, 2074

⚜ Jesus hears our prayer: CCC 2616

Small Group Discussion

DIGGING DEEPER

1. In the parable of the sower, Jesus describes the seed falling in four different places: along the path, on rock, among thorns, and on good soil. The implication is that we are responsible to respond to God's word, and to foster growth so that we can bear much fruit, just like the seed that fell on good soil. How do we foster that growth? (See CCC 1131, 1724, 2074.)

_____

_____

_____

_____

Parables → Earthly story w/ a heavenly meaning

2. Luke chapter 8 reports several parables. Some of them are so hard to understand that Jesus must interpret them for the disciples. What exactly is a parable? Why did Jesus speak in parables? Why does he explain the parables to his disciples? (See CCC 546; Glossary, "Parables".)

Idea of Relics & touching things

3. When Jesus heals the woman with the hemorrhage, he doesn't allow her to slip away quietly. Rather, he calls attention to her. Why? (See Lv 15:19–30.)

Her boldness of faith

He was a Gentile & they needed to know the power of God

4. After he frees the Gerasene demoniac, Jesus tells the man, "Return to your home, and declare how much God has done for you" (8:39). This is the opposite of what he has previously told the leper (5:14–15) and the parents of the girl he raised from the dead (8:56). Why does Jesus tell the demoniac to speak of God's goodness, while he tells the others to keep silent?

St Gertrude

Church triumphant
Church militant - us, fighting a spiritual war every day
Church suffering - those in purgatory

Faith opens up heaven

5. How do the healing of the woman with the hemorrhage and the raising of Jairus' daughter from the dead highlight the link that exists between faith and salvation? (See CCC 2616.)

Salvation & healing (link betwn)

unlock heaven's door

The Red Tent (bk)

St Catherine Laboré — The miraculous medal — 1830

LIFE APPLICATION Pray for blessings - bless her, bless God

1. Do I understand the power of God in our world today? Do I believe in miracles and rely on God's providence?

8:15 - noon
Tues 5:30-7:30
St Michael
JP II blood & hair
1st Class relic

2. How do I challenge the cynicism and skepticism of our culture as it affects my heart and those around me?

3. Do I allow myself to be amazed, uplifted, and inspired by the work of God among his people?

Life Application Video

After breaking from your small group discussion, gather to watch the second video, a pastoral reflection from Fr. Jeffrey Kirby, STD.

LUKE: THE GOSPEL OF MERCY

SESSION 8 | GROUP STUDY

Voices of the Saints

Those who hear the word of God and do it are thus called the mother of our Lord, because daily in their actions or words they bring him forth, as it were, in their inmost hearts. They are also his brothers when they do the will of his Father, who is in heaven.

—*St. Bede the Venerable, Catena Aurea: St. Luke*

How Then Shall We Live?

Silently review the following summary of Fr. Kirby's reflection to prepare for answering the questions in "Living It Out."

Luke tells us how Jesus raises from the dead the daughter of Jairus, a synagogue official. The man approaches Jesus while his daughter is yet alive, asking the Lord to heal her. It's an intense scene, full of human drama and intrigue: Why is this Jewish religious leader, so fearful of losing his daughter, turning to Jesus for a cure? But it's also a scene full of expectation and hope: Will Jesus bring this little girl back to life?

At times, we too may find ourselves in situations of intense drama, facing fearful challenges. When we do, where do we turn? Where do we expect to find a reason for hope? Contemporary people seem to look for solutions in all kinds of places: the medical sciences, money, power, social influence. These aren't necessarily bad in themselves, but they draw us quickly into a dark place when we make idols of them—when we rely only on them, forgetting about God and his divine providence.

Luke recounts this raising from the dead of Jairus' daughter in order to encourage us in our own discipleship. He wants us to recognize God's love and care for us. The Gospel writer emphasizes the power and the wisdom of God to show us, in this powerful miracle, the beautiful wisdom of God's providence.

What will we do with Luke's testimony?

Planting in the summer, © Produktownia, Shutterstock

Living It Out

On your own, spend three to five minutes praying, discerning, and writing down the specific ways that God might be calling you to make changes in your life. Share and discuss afterwards only if you feel comfortable doing so.

Consider this week how God is calling you to …

❧ Turn to God in a deeper way, naming the things that hurt or confuse you.

❧ Express your anxiety or struggles of faith to God in prayer.

❧ Make an act of faith, acknowledging your belief in God's providence, and accept his gift of peace.

Words to Know

Decapolis: Literally, "the ten cities." A district on the east and southeast coast of the Sea of Galilee containing ten cities inhabited primarily by Greek-speaking Gentiles, where Jesus went to minister.

Demoniac: A person possessed by a demon or demons.

Legion: The basic unit of the Roman imperial army, which typically contained about five thousand soldiers. When a demon tells Jesus that his name is "Legion," the implication is that a host of demons are present within the possessed victim.

Closing Prayer

Lord, you have said that all things are possible to the one who believes.
I believe; help my unbelief! Amen.

—Based on Mark 9:23–24

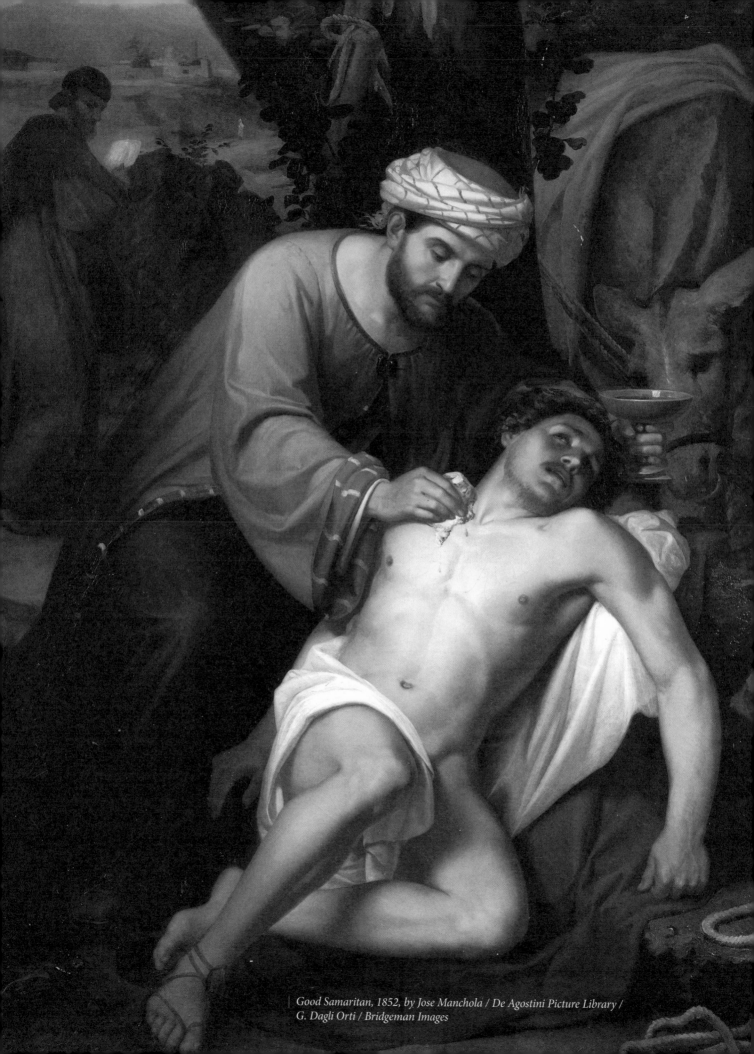

Good Samaritan, 1852, by Jose Manchola / De Agostini Picture Library / G. Dagli Orti / Bridgeman Images

SESSION 9

THE
GOOD
SAMARITAN

*"Which of these three, do you think, proved neighbor to the man who
fell among the robbers?" He said, "The one who showed mercy on him."
And Jesus said to him, "Go and do likewise."*

LUKE 10:36–37

SESSION READING
LUKE 9:1–10:42

Introduction

Luke tells us that people are amazed at Jesus, because his words have *authority*. As the account unfolds, we see that amazing authority displayed in multiple ways.

Jesus has only to speak a word—and the sick are healed, the dead return to life, the stormy sea is stilled, the food multiplies, the demons flee, sins are forgiven. Perhaps most strikingly, he has the authority to delegate his authority so that others can also work miracles.

Yet the authority of Christ manifests itself in still another way: His words have the power to transform lives. He teaches in memorable stories, such as the parable of the Good Samaritan (10:25–37). And he challenges his listeners with incisive observations: "What does it profit a man if he gains the whole world and loses or forfeits himself?" (9:25).

How does Jesus come to possess such authority? Luke tells us through Peter's declaration: He is "the Christ of God" (9:20). Then Luke's account of the Transfiguration (9:28–36) clarifies the matter further: God the Father speaks from heaven, saying, "This is my Son, my Chosen."

The almighty Creator has given his Son all authority in heaven and on earth (see Mt 28:18). No wonder, then, that the heavenly voice commands: "Listen to him!" (9:35).

Prayer to Prepare for Study

Lord, my God, bestow upon me an understanding that knows You, diligence in seeking You, wisdom in finding You, a way of life that is pleasing to You, perseverance that waits trustfully for You, and confidence that I shall embrace You at the last. Amen.

—Prayer of St. Thomas Aquinas before study

Study Notes

These notes provide insights to help you understand and reflect upon the biblical text.

✣ Luke reports the Lord's commissioning of the Apostles. He sends them out to share in his mission of mercy. In their mission, the Lord calls the Apostles to a spiritual poverty and simplicity of life; they must travel light in order to travel fast and far. After seeing how the Lord lives, and how he preaches and works miracles, the Apostles themselves are sent out to do as he does (9:1–6). Throughout the ages, the shepherds of the Church—the pope, bishops, priests, and deacons—continue this work on behalf of the Lord until he returns in glory.

✣ Jesus tells the Apostles that when the people of a town don't receive them, they are to shake the dust off their feet "as a testimony against them" (9:5). This symbolic action reflects a rabbinical custom of the time: When rabbis return home from travel in a Gentile land, they shake off from their feet the dust of the unbelieving pagans. The implication here is that those who don't receive the Apostles are unbelievers.

Jesus Discourses with His Disciples, illustration from 'The Life of Our Lord Jesus Christ', 1886-96 (w/c over graphite on paper), Tissot, James (1836-1902) / Brooklyn Museum of Art, New York, USA / Purchased by Public Subscription / Bridgeman Images

❧ Herod the tetrarch hears about Jesus and is perplexed (9:7). He has beheaded John the Baptist, and many have said that Jesus is John come back from the dead, or perhaps Elijah, or one of the other prophets of old. Herod doesn't understand who Jesus is, and Luke tells us that from this time on, Herod tries to see him (9:9).

❧ Herod Antipas is only a tetrarch (a "ruler of a quarter") at the time of Jesus. When his father Herod the Great died, the Roman Emperor divided up his kingdom, and Herod Antipas received only a portion of it. Herod Antipas is a "client king"—basically a puppet of the Emperor. He holds ceremonial power but very little real temporal power. Nevertheless, Herod is interested in meeting Jesus because of the stories about his miracles and signs (9:9).

❧ After the Apostles return from their mission, the Lord takes them to the city of Bethsaida, on the far side of the Jordan River, north of the Sea of Galilee (9:10). But the crowd follows them, so Jesus teaches and heals many. Keep in mind that Jesus has been apart from his close friends for some time, so he is withdrawing with them to a village some distance away where they can spend private time together. Nevertheless, when the throngs show up and thwart those plans, demanding his attention, he graciously welcomes them and cares for them. Once again, divine mercy is on display.

❧ Toward the end of the day, the Apostles ask the Lord to disperse the crowd so the people can go and find food and lodging, because the town is in a remote area (9:12). Instead, the

Lord tells the Apostles to feed the crowd. When they indicate that they have only five loaves and two fish (9:13), the Lord tells the Apostles to have the crowd of five thousand men (plus women and children) sit down (9:14).

✦ Assuming the traditional role of the head of the household at a meal, Jesus takes the loaves and fish, looks up to heaven, gives thanks, and breaks them (9:16). He gives them to the Apostles and tells them to distribute the food to the crowd. Everyone has enough food to be satisfied, and the Apostles collect what is left over: twelve baskets full, apparently, one for each of the Apostles (9:17).

✦ The Lord clearly works a miracle of food multiplication by feeding five thousand people with so few loaves and fish. He does it both as an act of charity for the people and as an occasion of spiritual formation for his Apostles. Having just returned from their own mission, they are being shown the power of God. This is the only miracle of Our Lord (other than his resurrection) that is reported in all four Gospels (Mt 14:13; Mk 6:30; Jn 6:1).

The Feeding of the Five Thousand (oil on panel), Patenier or Patinir, Joachim (1487-1524) / Monasterio de El Escorial, Spain / Bridgeman Images

✤ Note that Jesus doesn't feed the people directly himself. He gives the food to the Apostles, then has them distribute it. In a similar way, after he has ascended into heaven, he will give spiritual gifts and graces to the Apostles and their successors in the Church, the bishops, to be distributed to his people.

✤ This miracle is also a foreshadowing of the Eucharist, in which the Body and Blood of Christ is miraculously "multiplied" abundantly to feed his people, the Church. Luke's later account of the first Eucharist tells how Jesus takes, blesses (or gives thanks), breaks, and gives this spiritual food (22:19). That language is echoed here and also in Luke's account of the Eucharist celebrated by Our Lord at Emmaus after his resurrection (24:30).

✤ Once while Jesus is praying, he asks the disciples who people say that he is. After they respond, he asks them who they think he is (9:18–20). Only Peter answers, saying, "The Christ of God" (9:20). This is a pressing question that every person who encounters Jesus must be willing to consider carefully. The answer will determine whether we are disciples or just people in the crowd.

✤ In his public ministry, Jesus begins to warn the Apostles about his impending passion and death (9:22, 43–45). But they don't understand what he means; their thinking has been influenced too deeply by the popular expectations of a Messiah in their time. Until they experience the Lord's paschal mystery (his passion, death, and resurrection) and receive the Holy Spirit, they can't comprehend what the Lord is doing and its eternal significance.

✤ Luke's Gospel focuses heavily on the call to discipleship, so he records the Lord's exhortation that a person must be willing to deny himself and take up his cross to follow him. His followers must be willing to lose their lives if they are to be good disciples who receive the Lord's affirmation (9:23–27). These themes are central to Luke and his account of the Good News.

✤ Jesus' prophecy that "there are some standing here who will not taste death before they see the kingdom of God" (9:27) has been variously interpreted. Some commentators believe that he is referring to his upcoming transfiguration on the mountain (9:28–36), when Peter, James, and John will see a manifestation of the Kingdom in the glory of that event.

✤ Jesus reveals a portion of his glory to Peter, James, and John by taking them up to Mount Tabor to pray with him (9:28). In the Transfiguration that follows, Moses and Elijah appear,

| *The Transfiguration, 1594-95 (oil on canvas), Carracci, Lodovico (1555-1619) / Pinacoteca Nazionale, Bologna, Italy / Bridgeman Images*

representing the Old Testament Law and prophets. (St. Cyril of Alexandria refers to them here as Jesus' "bodyguard.") They come to Our Lord and speak with him about his impending departure, which will take place in Jerusalem (9:30). The term translated here as "departure" literally means "exodus," and may refer either to his departure from this life through death or to his departure from this world through his ascension.

✤ Jesus wants to reassure his "key three" Apostles that his upcoming death in Jerusalem will not be the end, but only the path he must take to glory. The dazzling brilliance of Jesus' face and clothing on the mountaintop are a visual manifestation of that glory, which will also be a characteristic of the glorified bodies of the saints in heaven after the resurrection (Mt 13:43; Phil 3:21; 1 Cor 15:43).

✤ The cloud that comes and overshadows Peter, James, and John is reminiscent of the *Shekinah* of the Old Testament (Ex 25:22; Lv 16:2), which manifests God's presence among his people. (See the study notes for Session 2.) God the Father affirms Jesus in proclaiming, "This is my Son, my Chosen; listen to him" (9:35). These words echo the affirmation the Father made when Jesus was baptized.

✤ Luke mentions three details about the Transfiguration not recorded by the other Evangelists. He indicates that the Transfiguration occurs while the Lord is praying (9:29), that the Apostles are "heavy with sleep" and see the Transfiguration when they become fully awake (9:32), and that Peter offers to build three shelters so that they can stay there (9:33).

✤ One of the temptations for Peter, James, and John is to stay on the mountain and enjoy the glory (9:33). But God wants them back down in the valley, getting ready for their part in the ministry of mercy. The Transfiguration is setting the stage for Jesus' journey to Jerusalem, where he will undergo his passion. The three Apostles must have their faith strengthened in anticipation of the difficult days ahead.

✤ As the Lord and the three Apostles descend the mountain, they are confronted with another demon-possessed person. Luke recounts these events in order to show clearly the battle that is being fought and the demons' growing realization of what the Lord is doing. In the crowd, a father asks for an exorcism of his son (9:38–39). The man indicates that he has asked the disciples to drive out the demon, but they could not (9:40).

✤ The Lord is frustrated by this inability and responds, "O faithless and perverse generation, how long am I to be with you and bear with you? Bring your son here" (9:41). This statement indicates the disciples' lack of faith. It presents an important challenge to every Christian: Do we believe in the Lord's power

Notre Dame Gargoyle, 2006 (photo) / Paris, France / © Max Koepke / Bridgeman Images

over evil? Are we confident that he has given us the power to resist the Devil's temptations as he resisted them in the wilderness (1 Cor 10:13)?

✤ As the Apostles witness the power of God, they argue over who will be the greatest among them (9:46). The Lord places a child in their midst and chides them: "He who is least among you all is the one who is great" (9:48). In this gesture, the Lord stresses the need for deference and humility, the true strength of the Christian disciple.

✤ In their conversation with Jesus, the Apostles tell him that they have seen another exorcist driving out demons in the Lord's name (9:49). The Apostles try to stop him because he isn't one of them, but the Lord tells them not to prevent him from doing it: Anyone who is not against them is for them (9:50). In this context, it's worth remembering the exorcised man of Geresa, whom the Lord sent to teach among his people (8:38–39). Jesus may be referring to this man or someone like him.

✤ Luke notes that Jesus has "set his face to go to Jerusalem" (9:51). His firm resolution contrasts sharply with the attitudes of many who want to follow him but make excuses: let me bury my father, or let me say farewell to my family (9:58–61). Luke emphasizes that Jesus is ready to begin his journey to Jerusalem and, in time, to suffer his passion.

✤ As the Lord heads to Jerusalem, he sends messengers ahead to find lodging in a Samaritan town where they will be passing through (9:52). But the people reject them because they are on their way to Jerusalem—that is, because they are Jews (9:53). The Apostles want revenge for this rejection, but Jesus refuses (9:55). This scene is found only in Luke's Gospel. It's an important demonstration of God's mercy, even to the Samaritans, who are adversaries of the Jewish people.

✤ Only Luke's Gospel records that in addition to sending the Apostles out (9:1–6), Jesus also sends out seventy disciples on a mission of mercy (10:1–2). The names of the seventy are not recorded, but since ancient times, commentators have speculated that they included early Christian disciples who appear in other scriptural passages, such as Barnabas (Acts 4:36), Sosthenes (1 Cor 1:1), Matthias, and Joseph Justus (Acts 1:23).

✤ The Lord gives them specific instructions regarding simplicity and poverty (10:2–12). He tells them not to rejoice over the power they have been given, but rather to rejoice that their "names are written in heaven" (10:17–20). In stressing the commission of the disciples, Luke is accentuating the universal call of everyone in the Church to mission and service.

✤ Luke records a special prayer that Jesus offers to the Father (also found in Mt 11:25–26). In the midst of his public ministry, Jesus gives thanks that God the Father has revealed himself to the childlike (10:21–22). In recording this prayer, Luke is emphasizing that God's revelation and faith are gifts. No one can earn or demand revelation. No spiritual pedigree or lineage will merit faith.

✤ Only Luke's Gospel contains the powerful story of the Good Samaritan (10:29–37). A lawyer approaches Jesus and asks what must be done to gain eternal life. Jesus asks the scribe how he would answer the question, and he answers that he must love God above all things and his neighbor as himself (10:25–28). Jesus confirms the answer, but the scholar goes on to ask who is his neighbor (10:29). Our Lord replies with the parable of the Good Samaritan.

✦ Between Judea and Galilee lies a central district called Samaria. Because of a complicated history with its inhabitants, the Samaritans, the Jews despise them as half-breeds and heretics, refusing to have any dealings with them. (See "Samaritans" in "Words to Know.")

✦ This story is a creative telling of the merciful work of redemption (10:25–37). The narrative is simple: A man falls victim to robbers and is left for dead. A priest passes by but doesn't help. A Levite passes by and ignores him. But a Samaritan comes by and helps the man. He places him on his own animal and takes him to an inn, where he gives coins to the innkeeper and tells him that he will pay the difference if he spends more money than the Samaritan has left with him.

✦ At one level, this parable illuminates the meaning of the commandment "Love your neighbor as yourself." It teaches us that anyone in need who crosses our path is our "neighbor," and we're called to show merciful compassion to others.

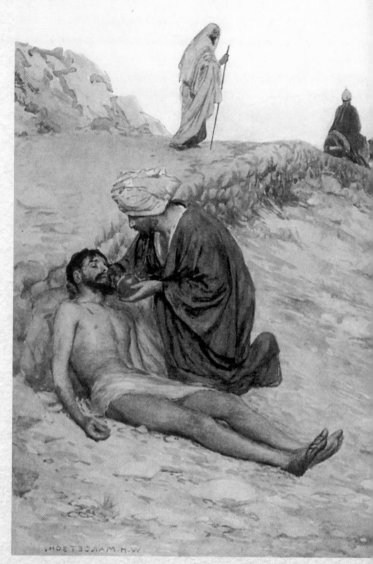

| *The Good Samaritan, Margetson, William Henry (1861-1940) (after) / Private Collection / © Look and Learn / Bridgeman Images*

✦ Yet there's another level of meaning here. Among the Church Fathers, the story was interpreted as an allegory of our redemption. Their interpretative details varied, but they offered several parallels: Humanity is the victim attacked by the demons, who are the thieves. They are wounded by sin and left for dead.

✦ The Old Testament provisions of the Law, the prophets, and the Temple are represented by the priest and Levite, who come by but can't save us. However, Christ (the Samaritan), the Son of God with a human nature (the Samaritan's beast of burden), comes and provides the sacraments (oil and wine) for humanity's wounds. He entrusts humanity to the Church (the inn), and for the care of wounded humanity, he leaves to the Church's shepherds (the innkeeper) the Old and New Testaments (or as some said, the sacraments), symbolized by the two coins. He promises to return (the second coming of Christ in glory). In this way, the story powerfully symbolizes the universal scope of the Church and an openness to the Gentiles.

✤ Only Luke's Gospel contains the story of Martha and Mary (10:38–42). The two sisters are hosting Jesus. Mary sits at his feet, while Martha is busy with the tasks of a hostess. Martha complains to the Lord that her sister should help her, but the Lord tells Martha she worries about too many things, and Mary has chosen the better part (10:41–42). This story is at the heart of the Church's vast spiritual tradition, clearly asserting the priority and preeminence of prayer (as well as religious and cloistered life). In this light, it's significant to note that Luke records this story right before the account of Jesus teaching the Apostles the Our Father (the Lord's Prayer).

To prepare for small group discussion, turn ahead now to this session's "Digging Deeper" and "Life Application" sections.

Rome to Home

The Church is called to carry out her mission in charity, not pointing a finger in judgment of others, but—faithful to her nature as a mother—conscious of her duty to seek out and care for hurting couples with the balm of acceptance and mercy; to be a "field hospital" with doors wide open to whoever knocks in search of help and support; even more, to reach out to others with true love, to walk with our fellow men and women who suffer, to include them and guide them to the wellspring of salvation. A Church which teaches and defends fundamental values, while not forgetting that "the Sabbath was made for man, not man for the Sabbath" (Mk 2:27); and that Jesus also said: "Those who are well have no need of a physician, but those who are sick; I came not to call the righteous, but sinners" (Mk 2:17). A Church which teaches authentic love, which is capable of taking loneliness away, without neglecting her mission to be a Good Samaritan to wounded humanity.

—*Pope Francis, Homily, October 4, 2015*

Opening Prayer

Let the words of my mouth and the meditation of my heart be acceptable in your sight, O Lord, my rock and my redeemer!

Psalm 19:14

Teaching Video

This first video, hosted by Dr. Paul Thigpen, focuses on certain themes and passages from the Gospel of Luke. Here are some key highlights of his presentation, with room to take notes as you view the video to assist you in the group discussion.

Manifestations of Jesus' authority

_____

_____

_____

_____

The history of hostility between Jews and Samaritans

_____

_____

_____

_____

Jesus' exchange with the lawyer

_____

_____

_____

_____

Important details about the characters in the parable of the Good Samaritan

_____

_____

_____

_____

_____

| The Good Samaritan, 1890 (oil on canvas), Gogh, Vincent van (1853-90) / Rijksmuseum Kroller-Muller, Otterlo, Netherlands / Bridgeman Images

Multiple levels of meaning in the parable

_____

_____

_____

_____

_____

_____

Catechism Connections

These readings from the Catechism of the Catholic Church (CCC) will deepen your understanding of this session's presentations and discussions. The numbers identify the relevant paragraphs in the Catechism.

❖ The priest as the Good Samaritan: CCC 1465

❖ The Transfiguration: CCC 444, 554–556, 697, 2583

❖ The Eucharist and the feeding of the five thousand: CCC 1335

❖ Taking up our cross: CCC 618, 1435

❖ The Holy Spirit and prayer in Christ's ministry: CCC 2600, 2603

Small Group Discussion

DIGGING DEEPER

1. In the parable of the Good Samaritan, how does Jesus show that holiness as described by the Old Covenant has now been replaced by the requirements of the New Covenant?

_____

_____

_____

_____

2. The feeding of the five thousand is the only miracle (other than Jesus' resurrection) that is included in all four of the Gospels. So it must be important to understand what this miracle means. Explain how the feeding of the five thousand is foreshadowed by the provision of manna to the Israelites, and how it foreshadows the Eucharist (see Ex 16:1–35, CCC 1335).

_____

_____

_____

_____

_____

The Multiplication of Loaves and Fishes (oil on panel), Francken or Franck, Ambrosius the Elder (1544-1618) / Koninklijk Museum voor Schone Kunsten, Antwerp, Belgium / © Lukas - Art in Flanders VZW / Photo: Hugo Maertens / Bridgeman Images

_____

_____

3. What is the difference between simply being an admirer of Jesus and being a follower of Jesus? Why is it so hard to follow Jesus? (See Lk 9:23–27, 57–62; CCC 618, 1435.)

_____

_____

_____

_____

4. How does the Transfiguration reveal each Person of the Holy Trinity? What is the significance of Moses and Elijah's appearance alongside Jesus? (See CCC 554–556, 697, 2583; Ex 24:15–18; 1 Kgs 19:1–14.)

_____

_____

_____

_____

5. How does the episode with Martha and Mary show the appropriate relationship between work and prayer?

_____

_____

_____

_____

LIFE APPLICATION

1. Do I realize my responsibility to care for fallen humanity?

_____

_____

_____

_____

2. How could I make practical changes in my life to be more attentive to those around me, especially those in need?

_____

_____

_____

_____

3. Do I have the humility to accept the care and concern of others when I am the one in need?

_____

_____

_____

_____

Life Application Video

After breaking from your small group discussion, gather to watch the second video, a pastoral reflection from Fr. Jeffrey Kirby, STD.

Voices of the Saints

In these two women, who were both well pleasing to the Lord, both objects of his love, both disciples… the two lives are symbolized: our present life, and the life to come; the life of labor, and the life of quiet; the life of sorrow, and the life of blessedness; the life of this world, and the life of eternity. These are the two lives we each have; ponder them more carefully…. In Martha is the image of things present, in Mary of things to come. What Martha is doing, we do now; what Mary is doing, we hope to do. Let us do the first life well, so that we may have the second life to the fullest.

—*St. Augustine, Sermons on Selected New Testament Lessons, 54*

How Then Shall We Live?

Silently review the following summary of Fr. Kirby's reflection to prepare for answering the questions in "Living It Out."

Jesus tells us about a man who is attacked while walking along the road to Jericho, then left injured on the roadside by robbers, till the Good Samaritan comes along and finds him.

So often, we want to see ourselves as the Good Samaritan. And all for the right reasons—there's nothing wrong with trying to be a Good Samaritan! But in the early Church, the Christian community saw itself as the man who was beaten up. For them, the parable was the story of fallen humanity, harassed and assailed by the Devil, who comes as a thief. So the Good Samaritan—who symbolizes Jesus Christ—comes and rescues humanity, since the priest and the Levite, symbols of the Old Covenant's Temple and Law, cannot heal or save humanity.

It is the Good Samaritan who comes to humanity's aid. After caring for us, the Good Samaritan entrusts us to "the inn," the "hotel," which is symbolic of the Church. So Christians are symbolized both by the injured man and by the inn: We move from lying on the roadside, a member of fallen humanity in need of healing, to serving in the inn, where we are called to heal.

The Good Samaritan leaves some coins with the innkeeper and promises to make up the difference if the innkeeper spends more money than the Good Samaritan had left. The coins represent the sacraments, and the innkeeper represents the pope and bishops. The money left there is his grace, and the Lord Jesus—always the Good Samaritan—leaves us his grace with the promise to make up the difference with even more grace if we need it.

What a powerful story, with a powerful lesson from the Lord Jesus!

| *Mother Teresa with a child (b/w photo) / Dinodia / Bridgeman Images*

Living It Out

On your own, spend three to five minutes praying, discerning, and writing down the specific ways that God might be calling you to make changes in your life. Share and discuss afterwards only if you feel comfortable doing so.

Consider this week how God is calling you to …

✦ Accept the ministry and loving kindness of the Good Samaritan in your life.

✦ Understand the nature and call of the Church in the midst of the world.

✦ Evaluate how you can be a more active member of the community of faith.

| *Christ Sending Out the Seventy Disciples, Two by Two, illustration for 'The Life of Christ', c.1884-96 (w/c & gouache on paperboard), Tissot, Joseph (1836-1902) / Brooklyn Museum of Art, New York, USA / Purchased by Public Subscription / Bridgeman Images*

Words to Know

Levites: In Jesus' day, descendants of the ancient tribe of Levi with special responsibilities to assist the priests in worship at the Temple.

Samaritans: Inhabitants of the district between Judea and Galilee. When the United Kingdom of Solomon divided into two kingdoms upon his death in the tenth century B.C., the Northern Kingdom (called Israel) included the area that came to be called Samaria after a capital city of that name was built. This city rather than Jerusalem became the center of Samaritan religious practice, and the northern kings eventually introduced idolatry as part of their worship. In the eighth century B.C., many of the Jews who had inhabited this area were deported by their Assyrian conquerors, and colonists from a number of Gentile lands were brought in to settle with those Jews who remained. In the time of Jesus, the Samaritans—who still practice a form of the old religion—are despised by the Jews as half-breeds and heretics.

Transfiguration: To transfigure is to transform—to give a new and exalted appearance with spiritual significance. In the transfiguration of Jesus, his divine glory is revealed when his appearance changes to exhibit a dazzling heavenly brilliance.

Closing Prayer

May [the Lord] support us all the day long, till the shades lengthen and the evening comes, and the busy world is hushed, and the fever of life is over, and our work is done. Then in His mercy may He give us a safe lodging, and a holy rest and peace at the last. Amen.

—Blessed John Henry Newman

NIHIL AD
PFECTIONE AOOVXIT
LEX

VITA ETERNA VT COGNOSCAMVS TE SOLV VERV DEVM

SESSION 10

THE
RICH FOOL

"But God said to him, 'Fool! This night your soul is required of you; and the things you have prepared, whose will they be?' So is he who lays up treasure for himself, and is not rich toward God."

LUKE 12:20–21

SESSION READING
LUKE 11:1–12:59

Introduction

Much of Luke's account in his eleventh and twelfth chapters is occupied with Our Lord's teaching. When the disciples ask him to teach them how to pray, he gives them the priceless gift of what we now call the Our Father (the Lord's Prayer), followed by an exhortation on perseverance in prayer. He encourages them not to worry, because God has an intimate concern for them. If they seek his kingdom, everything else will be provided.

These are all encouraging words. But the great majority of Jesus' teaching in this passage presents somber warnings: Whoever is not with Jesus is against him. When an unclean spirit leaves a person, he may return with seven spirits more evil than himself. Those who reject Jesus will suffer divine judgment.

Make sure the light you think you have within isn't actually darkness. Beware hypocrisy; everything now covered up will one day be exposed. Fear God rather than people. Those who blaspheme against the Holy Spirit will not be forgiven. Beware of greed. Be ready for Our Lord's return to judge the world.

| *Christ, The Lord of the World, by Paul Rubens shows a triumphant and risen Jesus Christ in heaven as the Lord and King of the World. Restored Traditions*

Even so, Jesus offers consolation to his disciples in the midst of so many warnings: "Fear not, little flock, for it is your Father's good pleasure to give you the kingdom" (12:32).

Prayer to Prepare for Study

Lord, my God, bestow upon me an understanding that knows You, diligence in seeking You, wisdom in finding You, a way of life that is pleasing to You, perseverance that waits trustfully for You, and confidence that I shall embrace You at the last. Amen.

—Prayer of St. Thomas Aquinas before study

Study Notes

These notes provide insights to help you understand and reflect upon the biblical text.

❧ The Apostles observe the Lord regularly retreating to a solitary place for prayer. On one occasion, after Jesus is done praying, the Apostles ask him to show them how to pray (11:1). In response to this request, Jesus gives the Apostles a format for prayer. This prayer has come to be called the "Our Father" or "the Lord's Prayer" and is revered by Christians of every tradition as the essential outline for all authentic Christian prayer. Tertullian, an early third-century Christian writer, describes it as a "summary of the whole gospel." St. Thomas Aquinas calls it the "most perfect of prayers."

❧ When the Apostles ask to be taught about prayer, they address Jesus in a relational term, calling him "Lord." The Apostles understand that prayer is about a relationship. It's not a quest for self-awareness, nor a journey of transcendental meanderings, but a relationship. This point must be emphasized because many current spiritual trends attempt to redefine "prayer" so that it becomes an absorption into a person's ego, or some form of Eastern mysticism, or some dubious practice of the New Age movement. Prayer, as seen in Luke 11:1, is about a relationship and a dialogue with God.

❧ Note that the Apostles ask the Lord to teach them. They realize that what they need, they cannot provide for themselves. They ask to be taught (11:1). This is the proper posture of a disciple, and one that every Christian should seek to imitate.

❧ The Lord's Prayer is recorded only in the Gospels of Luke (11:2–4) and Matthew (6:9–13). The two present slightly different versions. Luke's version is simpler but retains all the principal parts of Matthew's version. By ancient tradition, the Church always uses Matthew's version in the Holy Mass and other liturgies, as well as in her teaching and catechesis (such as in Part IV, Section Two of the *Catechism of the Catholic Church*).

| *Pater Noster, the Sermon on the Mount, by Domenico Morelli, Circa 1895, oil on canvas, Morelli, Domenico (1826-1901) / Galleria Nazionale d'Arte Moderna, Rome, Italy / De Agostini Picture Library / A. Dagli Orti / Bridgeman Images*

✦ The longer version in Matthew features all of the "seven petitions" as traditionally under-stood: (1) Our Father who art in heaven, (2) hallowed be thy name. (3) Thy kingdom come, (4) thy will be done on earth, as it is in heaven. (5) Give us this day our daily bread, (6) and forgive us our trespasses, as we forgive those who trespass against us, (7) and lead us not into temptation, but deliver us from evil.

✦ Early on in Christian history, common liturgical use concluded the Our Father with a *doxology,* or words of praise. In the first-century Christian text known as the *Didache,* we find: "For thine is the power and the glory forever." The fourth-century text called the *Apostolic Constitutions* adds to the beginning of that phrase "the kingdom," and this is the formula used by many Christians today in ecumenical prayer. Although neither of the biblical ver-sions of the prayer include this doxology, it can be used for private devotional purposes and appears (separated from the Our Father) in the Holy Mass during the Communion Rite.

✦ After teaching this prayer, the Lord provides an instruction on the nature of prayer and the need for perseverance. In the context of this teaching, Luke is the only Gospel writer to include the story of a friend who attempts to wake up another friend late at night to ask for bread so he can entertain unexpected guests (11:5–8). The story emphasizes trust in God's providence and the need for persistence in prayer.

| *The Importunate Neighbour. William Holman Hunt [Public domain], At the National Gallery of Victoria, via Wikimedia Commons*

✦ After speaking about prayer, Jesus exorcises an evil spirit. In response, some critics say that he receives his power from Beelzebul, the prince of demons. Others ask for a further sign of his power (11:15–16). The Lord responds firmly to the challenge and calls for a choice: Do they believe in his power or not? If they believe in his power, then the kingdom of God has come upon them (11:20).

✤ Jesus references the "finger of God" (11:20). The expression has deep roots in the Old Testament. At the time of the Israelites' liberation from Egypt, Pharaoh's court testified that "the finger of God" was upon Moses and Aaron (Ex 8:19). The "finger of God" wrote the Ten Commandments on the tablets on Mount Sinai (Ex 31:18). In addition, the ancient prophets received their inspiration by "the hand of the LORD" (Ez 37:1). This image can thus be seen as a symbol of God's authority and power.

✤ Jesus' opponents in the crowd say that he works his miracles through the demonic power of Beelzebul (11:15). This statement is extremely slanderous. It's not simply saying, "The man is evil," or "He traffics with evil spirits." Beelzebul was a false god of the Canaanites, an enemy people of ancient Israel. The cult of Beelzebul threatened the monotheism of the Israelites and caused great harm to God's people. For these reasons, as indicated in the sacred text, Beelzebul is considered the "prince of demons" (11:15). The accusation is blasphemous.

✤ The lines are now clearly drawn, and a choice must be made by the crowd: Will they accept the Lord's power as coming from the finger of God, or will they blasphemously denounce the Lord as subject to Beelzebul?

| *Finger of God, The Creation of Adam, from the Sistine Ceiling, 1510 (fresco) (detail), Buonarroti, Michelangelo (1475-1564) / Vatican Museums and Galleries, Vatican City / Alinari / Bridgeman Images*

✤ The Lord compares the consequences of denouncing him to the plight of a man fully armed (11:21–22) and a man freed from an evil spirit (11:24–26). The fully armed man has everything protected until someone stronger comes along, takes his armor, and divides up his plunder. The man who is freed from a demon sweeps his house and puts it in order, but the demon eventually returns with seven other evil spirits. In both cases, the Lord shows the weakness of humanity in defending itself against evil spirits, our urgent need of the Lord's power, and the newness of life he offers us by grace. The Lord soberly observes, "He who is not with me is against me, and he who does not gather with me scatters" (11:23).

✤ The intensity of these encounters lead one woman in the crowd to cry out, "Blessed is the womb that bore you, and the breasts that you sucked" (11:27). Jesus responds to her, "Blessed rather are those who hear the word of God and keep it" (11:28). This scene is recounted only in Luke's Gospel, and it's sometimes falsely interpreted as a rebuke to the Lord's mother.

✤ Jesus' words, however, represent not a rebuke but a reordering. Mary is not great solely because she has given birth to the Lord and nursed him (which is a great privilege indeed), but she is "blessed" because she has heard the word of God and obeyed it. Our Lady is the Lord's mother, not simply by birth, but by faith and obedience to God's word. Luke implies this interpretation earlier in the Gospel, when shortly after Gabriel's visit to Mary, he reports that she prays, "Henceforth all generations will call me blessed; for he who is mighty has done great things for me, and holy is his name" (1:48–49).

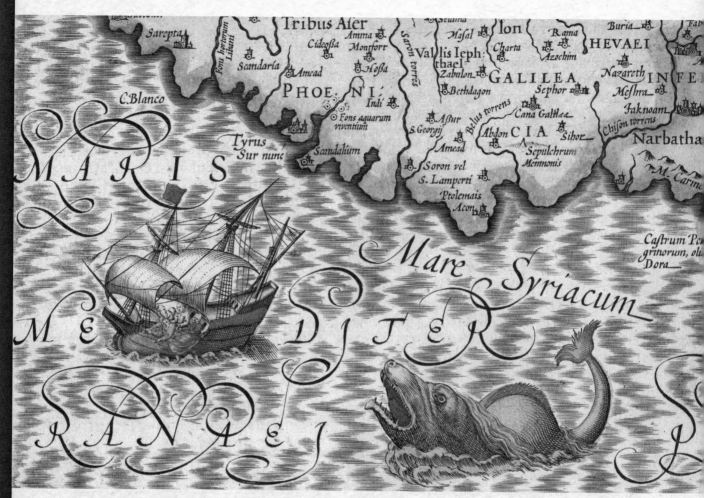

| *Jonah and the Whale, detail from p.347-8 (Terra Sancta) Mercator's "Atlas...", 1619 / British Library, London, UK / © British Library Board. All Rights Reserved / Bridgeman Images*

✤ After implicitly praising the faith of his mother, Jesus returns to those who ask for another sign (11:16). In response, Jesus calls as witnesses the Old Testament figures of Jonah and the Queen of the South. The prophet Jonah preached to the people of Nineveh, and they repented (Jon 3:1–10). The Queen of the South traveled a long distance to hear King Solomon's wisdom (1 Kgs 10:1–13). Yet something greater than Solomon and Jonah is present with them (11:31–32). Our Lord warns them that the Queen of the South and the people of Nineveh will stand in judgment of them. This warning concludes his response to the challenge made against his power and authority (11:15–16).

✤ Jonah was a popular biblical figure in the ancient Church, a favorite image in art and oral catechesis. Scenes of Jonah's life are found in the Roman catacombs, ancient Christian sarcophagi, statuettes, and mosaics. The prophet received such favor, not only because his story of being swallowed by a great fish was colorful, but because the Lord had spoken of him.

✤ The early Church saw Jonah's life as foreshadowing the life of Christ: His confinement in the fish's belly for three days, followed by his release, was a type of Our Lord's burial in the tomb and his resurrection on the third day (Mt 12:39–40). This was "the sign of Jonah" (Lk 11:29). In addition, various events in the prophet's life were used to teach about Christian discipleship, Baptism, conversion, and the Resurrection.

✤ The Lord mentions the Queen of the South (11:31), also known as the Queen of Sheba (1 Kgs 10:1–13). The ancient story of this monarch has inspired legends, literature, and sacred art throughout the history of Western civilization. Surprisingly, very little is known about her. She may have been Egyptian or Ethiopian.

| *The Visit of the Queen of Sheba to King Solomon (colour litho), Poynter, Edward John (1836-1919) (after) / Private Collection / The Stapleton Collection / Bridgeman Images*

✤ In summarizing the various teachings of the Lord, Luke is the only Gospel to include Jesus' warning about greed (12:13–15). Someone asks Jesus to intervene in a dispute between two brothers about an inheritance. Jesus asks, "Man, who made me a judge or divider over you?" (12:14). Then he warns everyone against greed, concluding with the reminder that "a man's life does not consist in the abundance of his possessions" (12:15). The inclusion of this warning reflects Luke's themes of sacrifice and discipleship.

✤ After speaking about Jonah and the Queen of the South, the Lord teaches using the imagery of light. He notes that the eye is the lamp of the body—that is, the instrument of vision for the body (11:34). Using bodily imagery to present spiritual truths, he declares that if the eye is unsound, then the body is dark; but if the eye is sound, then the body is full of light (11:34).

✤ The word translated here as "sound" is literally "single"; that is, the eye is focused, clear, not confused by seeing double. Beginning with the ancient Church Fathers, commentators on this passage generally interpret the "eye" to mean our perception and our mental and moral judgment. If we focus on what is good and practice right judgment, then our "whole body is full of light" (11:34)—that is, our conduct will also be right. The Lord cautions his hearers to keep away from darkness and calls on them to be light to the world (Mt 5:14–16). Our light, shining in the darkness, can lead others to the Lord.

✤ Jesus observes that a lamp must not be hidden, but rather placed on a lampstand (11:33). St. Ambrose comments on this passage that Christ is himself the Light (Lk 2:32; Jn 1:4–5, 9; 8:12). Our faith is the lamp that shines with his light, and we must not hide it.

✤ After these teachings, the Lord is invited to dinner (11:37). So much of Luke's Gospel is either on the road or at a meal. In the encounter, the Lord doesn't observe traditional Jewish washing customs, and his hosts are astonished. Their reaction leads Jesus to condemn hypocrisy and issue six "woes," three to the Pharisees (11:39–44) and three to the scribes (11:45–52). In the woes to these groups, the Lord is calling for purity of soul and integrity of action. He unmasks the false religiosity of the Pharisees and scribes and calls them (and us) to heartfelt obedience and worship of God.

✦ After this series of woes, the plot thickens. The Pharisees and scribes are now thinking of questions to ask the Lord that might trap him in saying something they can criticize or condemn (11:53–54). Their plotting is all part of the circumstances that require Jesus' journey to Jerusalem and preparation for his passion, death, and resurrection.

✦ This encounter leads the Lord to warn his disciples further about hypocrisy (12:1–3) and to urge fearlessness in their confession of him (12:4–12). In these admonitions, the Lord certainly understands the growing tension surrounding him and is seeking to strengthen his disciples for his impending passion and death. Knowing of the events that lie ahead, the Lord teaches, "I tell you, my friends, do not fear those who kill the body, and after that have no more that they can do. But I will warn you whom to fear: fear him who, after he has killed, has power to cast into hell; yes, I tell you, fear him!" (12:4–5). He is speaking, of course, about fearing God rather than other people.

✦ Luke's account of the Lord's admonition against greed leads to the parable of the rich fool (12:16–21). This story is told only in Luke's Gospel. The parable tells of a man who has a rich harvest and decides to tear down his old barn and build a larger one. The man is living extravagantly and has great plans for his future. Then God tells him that his life will be taken from him that very night. Jesus concludes, "So is he who lays up treasure for himself, and is not rich toward God" (12:21). The implication is that his selfishness has compelled him to hoard his wealth rather than perform corporal acts of mercy for those in need.

✦ After the parable, the Lord teaches clearly about trusting in Divine Providence (12:22–34): "For where your treasure is, there will your heart be also" (12:34). Even those who aren't rich can become too focused on worldly goods because of their anxiety about maintaining a livelihood.

✦ He also warns his listeners to stay vigilant (12:35–40): "You also must be ready; for the Son of man is coming at an hour you do not expect" (12:40). The Lord will return to judge the world at a time no one knows (Mt 24:36). But as the Church Fathers frequently remind us, the Lord also comes for each of us individually to judge us when we die. And few of us know when the hour of our death will be. So each one of us must be vigilant! Recall that these teachings are all given during the Lord's journey to Jerusalem. He is preparing his disciples to follow his sacrificial way of life.

✦ These admonitions are followed by the parable of severe and light beatings (12:47–48), which is unique to Luke's Gospel. Traditionally, this passage has been interpreted as a reference to purgatory, which is itself an expression of God's mercy. The same reality is described later in this chapter as a prison (12:57–59).

✦ After the parable, the Lord warns of the division that will come from following him (12:49–53).

He declares, "I came to cast fire upon the earth; and would that it were already kindled!" (12:49). In traditional Jewish thought, fire is typically a symbol of divine judgment (1 Kgs 18:38; 2 Chr 7:1; Ps 21:9).

✤ Jesus continues, "I have a baptism to be baptized with; and how I am constrained until it is accomplished" (12:50). The Greek word for "baptism" appearing here refers to an immersion; Jesus speaks of being submerged in and overwhelmed by mortal difficulty. But on the other side of that difficulty, his current constraints will be loosed; he will rise from the grave in triumph. In giving a prophecy of his impending passion and death, the Lord is once again preparing the disciples for what lies ahead.

✤ Beyond the disciples, the Lord addresses the "multitudes" and reminds them how signs are discerned in nature (12:54–56). If they can interpret the signs of nature, why can't they interpret the signs of the time? Jesus is asking them why they can't see who he is and the work he is doing.

✤ The Lord frequently uses analogies, observations, or experiences that any person can understand. In this way, he shows himself to be a good and patient teacher. In many respects, his example stands as a guiding principle for all Christian believers in their efforts to share the Good News. Each of us must express our faith in ways that others can easily grasp. Like the Lord, we must labor to be good teachers.

To prepare for small group discussion, turn ahead now to this session's "Digging Deeper" and "Life Application" sections.

Rome to Home

The breath of the divine life, the Holy Spirit, in its simplest and most common manner, expresses itself and makes itself felt in prayer. It is a beautiful and salutary thought that, wherever people are praying in the world, there the Holy Spirit is, the living breath of prayer. … Prayer is also the revelation of that abyss which is the heart of man: a depth which comes from God and which only God can fill, precisely with the Holy Spirit. We read in Luke: "If you then, who are evil, know how to give good gifts to your children, how much more will the heavenly Father give the Holy Spirit to those who ask him." The Holy Spirit is the gift that comes into man's heart together with prayer.

— *Pope St. John Paul II, Dominum et Vivificantem, 65*

Opening Prayer

Let the words of my mouth and the meditation of my heart be acceptable in your sight, O Lᴏʀᴅ, my rock and my redeemer!

—Psalm 19:14

Teaching Video

This first video, hosted by Dr. Paul Thigpen, focuses on certain themes and passages from the Gospel of Luke. Here are some key highlights of his presentation, with room to take notes as you view the video to assist you in the group discussion.

Consequences for those who reject God's mercy

_____

_____

_____

_____

The meaning of peace *the tranquility of right order*

_____

_____

_____

The consequences of disorder in our lives

_____

_____

_____

_____

The errors of the rich fool

You were made for something greater than your stuff

| *The Parable of the Rich Fool, Rembrandt [Public domain], via Wikimedia Commons*

How the rich fool could have used his wealth wisely

Luke 12. 22-23

The poor may also be too focused on earthly goods

Life is uncertain

Luke 12:22-23

Catechism Connections

These readings from the Catechism of the Catholic Church (CCC) will deepen your understanding of this session's presentations and discussions. The numbers identify the relevant paragraphs in the Catechism.

❧ The Lord's Prayer: CCC 2759–2865 (All of Part 4, Section 2, is dedicated to the Lord's Prayer.)

❧ Jesus teaches us to pray: CCC 2607–2615

❧ Divine Providence: CCC 302–305

❧ Jesus and the Law: CCC 579–582

❧ Covetousness: CCC 2514, 2534–2536

❧ Purgatory: CCC 1031, 1472

el dooner@gmail.com

Small Group Discussion

DIGGING DEEPER

1. In Luke 12:1–3, Jesus warns against the "leaven of the Pharisees, which is hypocrisy." In what ways are the Pharisees hypocrites? Why is hypocrisy dangerous to followers of Jesus?

Prayer it changes us, it doesn't change God

2. In Luke 11:5–8, Jesus tells the story of a man who persists in knocking on his neighbor's door until he answers the door. The lesson is that we must persist in our prayers. Does this mean that God is unwilling to answer our prayers?

armour against evil   *Ask for Gods will*

Rom 8:28

3. In the Lord's Prayer, Jesus teaches us to call God "Father." What does it mean to call God our Father? Why are we able to call God our Father? (See CCC 2779–2785.)

lack of trust

4. Jesus warns us about letting anxiety get in the way of our trust in God. Explain how anxiety can be just as damaging to our relationship with God as the covetousness of the rich fool.

anxiety-fear that paralyzes us; Be anxious for nothing;
Put your trust in God & he will take care of us
False Evidence Appearing Real (FEAR)
Perfect Love casts out Fear

E Fischer

Phillipians 4: 6-9

| Highrise buildings in Wall Street financial district, New York City, © Shaun Jeffers, Shutterstock

"Future" bread - the Coming of the Kingdom

5. What does it mean to ask God for our "daily bread" (11:3)? Does it simply mean to ask for food and provision for our bodies?

the Eucharist; the word of God

| *Shopping For Elderly Neighbour © SpeedKingz, Shutterstock*

LIFE APPLICATION

1. Do I try to live a life of simplicity: a life that is marked more by being a child of God than by having material things?

_____

_____

_____

_____

2. How attentive am I to the needs of my neighbor? Am I willing to give up the things I want in order to provide other people with the things they need?

_____

_____

_____

_____

3. Do I keep a healthy vigilance in my life, maintaining an awareness of God's judgment before me?

_____

_____

_____

_____

Voices of the Saints

"Our Father": At this name, love is awakened in us … and the confidence of obtaining what we are about to ask. … What would he not give to his children who ask, since he has already granted them the gift of being his children?

—*St. Augustine*

Life Application Video

After breaking from your small group discussion, gather to watch the second video, a pastoral reflection from Fr. Jeffrey Kirby, STD.

How Then Shall We Live?

Silently review the following summary of Fr. Kirby's reflection to prepare for answering the questions in "Living It Out."

The things of this world pass, and only the things of God remain. This was the tough lesson for the rich fool that Jesus describes for us in Luke's Gospel. The man wanted more and more, he was negligent of other more important things, and in the end—in his end—he lost everything, because his treasures were only of this earth.

Now, admittedly, the things of this world have a strong pull on our hearts. We are fallen and we think that by having a lot of things we gain power and control over things. But that's just an illusion. It's a lie. We don't have any power or control over anything in terms of life or death. We do, however, have power over what we will love, what we will value, and whether we will nurture the eternal things that will accompany us into eternal life.

The rich fool became a slave to his desire to possess things, and he lost his soul. He died as he had lived.

In our lives as Christian disciples, so strongly emphasized by Luke in his Gospel, we are called to approach the things of this world with a sense of both blessing and caution. We have to honor material things and use them as God intended: a means to provide basic human needs for our loved ones and ourselves and a means to help and console others who are not able to meet their basic human needs.

This is the challenge of the rich fool to each of us. It's a call to discipleship. It's a call for us to examine how we have lived and an opportunity to decide how we will choose to live now.

| *Christ Teacheth Humility, 1847 (oil on canvas), Lauder, Robert Scott (1803-69) / © Scottish National Gallery, Edinburgh / Bridgeman Images*

Living It Out

On your own, spend three to five minutes praying, discerning, and writing down the specific ways that God might be calling you to make changes in your life. Share and discuss afterwards only if you feel comfortable doing so.

Consider this week how God is calling you to …

❖ Examine how attached you might be to material things.

❖ Go through your belongings and give away what you don't truly need.

❖ Assess your tithe to the Church and donations of time and talent to others and seek to give more generously.

Words to Know

Apostolic Constitutions (Constitutions of the Holy Apostles): A fourth-century collection of eight treatises on Christian discipline, worship, and doctrine, most likely written in Antioch, Syria.

Beelzebul: The prince of demons. The name comes from a pagan Canaanite god; it means "prince-god." The ancient Israelites interpreted the word as "prince of demons" because they identified false gods with demonic spirits.

Covetousness: A disordered inclination or desire for pleasure or possessions, sometimes referred to as "greed" or "avarice." It is one of the seven capital vices ("deadly sins") and is forbidden by the ninth and tenth commandments (Ex 20:17).

Didache (or Teaching of the Twelve Apostles): A short but important first-century Christian work by an unknown author, probably written in Syria. Parts of it represent the oldest surviving Christian catechism.

Doxology: A liturgical prayer giving praise or glory to God.

Purgatory: "A state of final purification after death and before entrance into heaven for those who died in God's friendship, but were only imperfectly purified; a final cleansing of human imperfection before one is able to enter the joy of heaven" (CCC, "Purgatory," Glossary).

Sarcophagus (plural, Sarcophagi): A stone coffin. The word literally means "flesh eater."

Closing Prayer

Our Father who art in heaven, hallowed be thy name. Thy kingdom come, thy will be done on earth, as it is in heaven. Give us this day our daily bread, and forgive us our trespasses, as we forgive those who trespass against us, and lead us not into temptation, but deliver us from evil. Amen.

SESSION 11

THE CURE
ON THE
SABBATH

*Then the Lord answered him, "You hypocrites! … Ought not this woman,
a daughter of Abraham whom Satan bound for eighteen years, be loosed
from this bond on the sabbath day?"*

LUKE 13:15–16

SESSION READING
LUKE 13:1–14:35

Introduction

Our Lord's words of warning are becoming even more urgent now: "Repent or perish!" The barren fig tree will be cut down. Those turned away from the banquet of the kingdom of God will be left weeping and gnashing their teeth. Whoever exalts himself will be humbled. Because Jerusalem kills God's prophets, the city will be forsaken. Like salt gone bad, those who lose their spiritual savor will be thrown out. "He who has ears to hear, let him hear!"

Yet even in his dark warnings of divine judgment, glimmers of mercy and hope shine through. The vinedresser asks for another chance to help the fig tree bear fruit at last. The kingdom of God starts out tiny, but like a mustard seed it grows to become a great tree where many find refuge. Though the Kingdom is hidden and difficult to see, its powerful effects will be manifest, just as yeast leavens dough.

| *The Abandoned (oil on panel), Botticelli, Sandro (Alessandro di Mariano di Vanni Filipepi) (1444/5-1510) / Private Collection / Peter Willi / Bridgeman Images*

As Jesus approaches Jerusalem, the shadow of the Cross awaiting him lengthens, and his adversaries marshal their forces to oppose him. Once again, the Sabbath becomes a point of contention with them: Twice he heals on the Sabbath, and twice they condemn him for showing mercy. Clearly, true discipleship will cost his followers everything.

Prayer to Prepare for Study

Lord, my God, bestow upon me an understanding that knows You, diligence in seeking You, wisdom in finding You, a way of life that is pleasing to You, perseverance that waits trustfully for You, and confidence that I shall embrace You at the last. Amen.

—Prayer of St. Thomas Aquinas before study

Study Notes

These notes provide insights to help you understand and reflect upon the biblical text.

- ✠ The Lord's teaching about guilt and punishment that opens the thirteenth chapter of Luke is reported only in this Gospel (13:1–5). Jesus speaks about the Galileans who were killed by Pilate and the eighteen people killed by the collapse of the tower of Siloam. The passage apparently addresses current events, but we have no definite information about them. Jesus is observing that disasters happen, and we must be ready for them by repenting and being right with God now.

✦ At the same time, Our Lord is correcting the popular idea at that time that tragedy in someone's life results from that person's sin as a punishment from God (Job 4:7–9; Jn 9:1–3). Such an attitude makes people less merciful—less willing to help those suffering from tragedies—because they believe the person suffering is only getting what he deserves.

✦ The passage on guilt is followed by the parable of the fig tree (13:6–9). This parable clarifies the meaning of the teaching that precedes it. In the story, a fig tree fails to bear any fruit. The owner orders the gardener ("vinedresser") to cut it down. But the gardener asks for a year to cultivate it. If it doesn't bear fruit after the year, then it can be cut down. The grace of God is like fertilizer; if the tree doesn't respond to it, it will be cut down. This story illustrates the need for disciples to repent and regularly change their lives according to the gospel—one of Luke's central themes.

✦ The Sabbath law given by God commands that no work should be done on this day (Ex 20:8–11). But how is work defined? Is it work on the Sabbath to rescue a man or a beast who has fallen into a ditch? And are there other moral imperatives ("Love your neighbor as yourself") that take precedence over this law?

✦ The scribes and Pharisees of Jesus' day wrestle with such matters, and their positions are not always in agreement, even with regard to breaking Sabbath rules for the sake of mercy. They agree that the rules can be broken to save a human life. Some also allow for situations where someone's life might be in danger. But the particular scribes and Pharisees who so fiercely oppose Jesus apparently cannot tolerate his desire to extend mercy on the Sabbath even further—to anyone who needs a cure.

✦ The merciful healing of a crippled woman on the Sabbath (13:10– 13) is reported only in Luke, as is the healing on the Sabbath of the man with dropsy in the following chapter (14:1–6). Both stories show that God's laws are misinterpreted (or misapplied) when the interpretation or application is contrary to God's mercy and compassion. As St. Augustine points out, the woman isn't the only crippled person here. She is bent over in body, but Our Lord's critics are bent over in spirit, unable to see the truth.

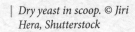

| *Dry yeast in scoop. © Jiri Hera, Shutterstock*

✦ In his teachings, the Lord compares the kingdom of God to both a mustard seed and leaven (yeast). Both images are easily recognizable and understood by his listeners (13:18–21). In describing the Kingdom this way, the Lord shows how it expands and grows. It's a consoling reminder that even if the believer's faith is small, and the number of believers is few, so long as the faith is sincerely grounded in Jesus Christ, the Kingdom will expand.

✤ "Through the parable of the mustard seed," writes the fourth-century Church Father St. John Chrysostom, "Jesus encourages the disciples to have faith and shows them that the preaching of the gospel will spread despite everything. They were the weakest of men, but because of the great power that was in them, the gospel has nevertheless been spread to all the world" (*Homily on St. Matthew*, 46).

✤ St. Cyril of Alexandria sees the yeast as the Word of God. When the Word comes into our hearts, it spreads throughout the soul to make us holy. The yeast image also seems to suggest that even a few believers can have a wider leavening effect on their society.

✤ Luke reminds us that Jesus is on his way to Jerusalem (13:22). Once again, this reminder gives us a specific context for everything the Lord is teaching and doing. He knows that his passion and death await him in the Holy City.

✤ After the Lord's analogies of the mustard seed and leaven, he tells the story of those who are locked out of the kingdom of God. The householder who shuts the door on them is Jesus himself. When those outside announce that they ate and drank in his presence and that he taught in their streets, the Lord will respond, "I tell you, I do not know where you come from; depart from me, all you workers of iniquity!" (13:27). The Lord then announces that many will come "from east and west, and from north and south" to sit at the table of the Kingdom.

✤ In this passage, Luke records the Lord's universal call to all men and women (Jew and Gentile alike). He cautions his Jewish listeners to enter through the narrow door or else they themselves will weep and gnash their teeth as they see Gentiles at the table of God's kingdom with the Jewish patriarchs Abraham, Isaac, and Jacob, and the prophets as well, while they themselves will be cast out (13:28–30).

✤ In response to the Lord's universal call, the Pharisees tell him to leave (13:31). They say that Herod wants to kill him. Only Luke records this warning to Jesus from the Pharisees. We know, however, that Herod actually wants to see Jesus and have him perform a miracle (9:9; 23:8). So the Pharisees may be saying this simply to get Jesus to leave. In any case, the Lord's reply powerfully states his firm resolve to carry out God's merciful plan, despite human opposition (13:31–33). His declaration that he will finish his course on "the third day" is an obvious reference to his resurrection (13:32).

✤ After this exchange, Jesus laments over Jerusalem and its rejection of him. He recalls the treatment of the prophets, and describes himself as a mother hen who seeks to gather her young under her wings, but his people are unwilling (13:34). This is one of only a very few times in Scripture when feminine imagery is used to describe God.

✤ It's important to note that this reference is a *simile*, a figure of speech comparing two essentially different things in order to show a particular similarity. This kind of statement is different from the revelation that God is Father, Son, and Holy Spirit, which is a declaration

| *Jesus Wept, illustration for 'The Life of Christ', c.1886-96 (gouache on paperboard), Tissot, James Jacques Joseph (1836-1902) / Brooklyn Museum of Art, New York, USA / Bridgeman Images*

of reality: God *is* Father (not "like" a father). But God is not a chicken. While God is spirit, and in one sense beyond gender, he nevertheless reveals himself as Father, and God the Son took on a real male human nature (including a male body) in Jesus Christ.

✦ A clear line of distinction must be drawn, then, between revelation and reality on one hand and a simile on the other. The reference to the mother hen is a simile. Incidentally, it is an effective simile, since the imagery used by the Lord is a familiar daily experience for most of his listeners.

✦ The entire fourteenth chapter of Luke's Gospel consists of events and lessons from Jesus' life that are not fully contained in any of the other Gospels.

✦ On a Sabbath after this series of teachings, the Lord is eating at the home of a prominent Pharisee (14:1). Recall that at this point the Pharisees are looking for reasons to accuse Jesus. Standing before him is a man with dropsy (an abnormal swelling of the body). The man's presence is probably not a coincidence; it has likely been arranged by the Pharisees. They already know that Our Lord doesn't hesitate to heal on the Sabbath, so they hope to accuse Jesus of violating the Law once more. Luke says that his adversaries "watched" him; the Greek word here means to scrutinize, to inspect scrupulously.

SESSION 11 | SELF STUDY

✦ Before healing the man, Jesus turns the tables on the scribes and Pharisees by asking them whether it is lawful to heal him (14:3). They remain silent, so Jesus miraculously heals him. Afterwards, reminding the scribes and the Pharisees that the ceremonial law is to be in service of the human being, Jesus says, "Which of you, having an ass, or an ox, that has fallen into a well, will not immediately pull him out on a sabbath day?" (14:5). In this act of healing and through his teachings, the Lord shows the religious leadership of his day the heart of true service to God and neighbor.

✦ Again Luke brings us to a table and to a context of eating and discussion. This incident is followed by two parables about the conduct of guests and hosts (14:7–11, 15–24). In between them is sandwiched a straightforward admonition to his host to show mercy by inviting to meals people who cannot repay the favor (14:12–14). The admonition serves us as a reminder, not just to be generous, but to consider the motives of our generosity. Do we give only because we look to be repaid in some way?

✦ In the first parable, Jesus teaches that guests are to show humility by taking the lower place at a table. The Church Fathers frequently emphasize that humility is essential to the Christian life, the soil in which all the other virtues grow. "If you should ask me what are the ways of God," St. Augustine writes, "I would tell you that the first is humility, the second is humility, and the third is still humility. Not that there are no other precepts to give, but if humility does not precede all that we do, our efforts are fruitless."

The Wedding Meal at Yport, 1886 (oil on canvas), Fourie, Albert-Auguste (b.1854) / Musee des Beaux-Arts, Rouen, France / Bridgeman Images

✤ This parable, along with the words to Jesus' host, challenge the existing customs of his day in order to nurture environments in which people can more richly experience the mercy and compassion of God. Luke stresses this message as a part of the disciple's way of life, which can be summarized this way: Be humble. Don't exalt yourself. Be merciful. Serve the poor.

✤ The second parable (14:15–24) maintains the dining context but focuses on the life to come. When Jesus speaks of a reward at the resurrection of the righteous, one of the guests at the table says, "Blessed is he who shall eat bread in the kingdom of God" (14:15). In biblical language, eating bread in the kingdom of God refers to enjoying the happiness of heaven, which is pictured as a banquet (Is 25:6; Mt 22:1–14).

✤ Jesus responds with a parable about a great banquet. The host has invited many guests, but when the time for the feast arrives, and a servant is sent to gather them, those who received invitations begin making excuses to be absent. So the host tells the servant to gather instead from the streets those who are poor, sick, or injured. Even these don't fill up the banquet hall, so the host sends the servant to fill the hall with guests from far away. In the end, those guests who were first invited are the ones who fail to take part in the feast.

✤ As St. Cyril of Alexandria points out, the host of the banquet is God the Father; the servant is Jesus himself, the Son of God who "emptied himself, taking the form of a servant, being born in the likeness of men" (Phil 2:5–7). The parable clearly warns Jesus' listeners that if they refuse his invitation to come to the banquet of mercy that God is spreading for them, their places in heaven will be taken by the very people they despise: the poor, the afflicted (whom they assume are being punished for their sins), and the Gentiles.

✤ The host's command to the servant to "compel people to come in" (14:23) has in earlier ages been used to justify coerced conversions to the Christian faith. But as some commentators have noted, we "compel" others to come to God's banquet, not by coercion, but by our Christian way of life, which they find compelling, and by our prayers.

✤ From these two accounts, Jesus launches into a full summary of discipleship (14:25–33). He begins with a startling statement, "If any one comes to me and does not hate his own father and mother and wife and children . . . , yes, and even his own life, he cannot be my disciple" (14:26). Is Our Lord calling his followers to hate their families and themselves?

✤ This is one of the statements traditionally known as the "hard sayings" of Jesus. We must keep in mind that in this declaration, he is using *hyperbole*—a figure of speech that employs extravagant exaggeration—to make an important point. It's a common way of speaking in the ancient Near East, so his listeners are familiar with it and know he isn't speaking literally.

✤ At the same time, we must recognize that Jesus employs hyperbole precisely to indicate the intensity of his point. Our love for him should become so all-consuming that any other love, even our love for those closest to us, fades by comparison. No other love must ever take priority over our love for Jesus.

✤ This "hard saying" must have been a great consolation to St. Perpetua, whose experience helps us understand the meaning of Jesus' words. She was a young North African noblewoman who died as a martyr in the year 203. The Roman imperial authorities sentenced her to be thrown to the wild beasts in the amphitheater because she refused to deny her Christian faith.

✤ Her prison journal records that she had to give up her infant child when she was cast into the dungeon, and her aged father came to her repeatedly before the magistrates to beg her to renounce Christ and save her life. He was utterly distraught, crying out with pitiful entreaties, tearing out his beard, throwing himself face down on the ground, beaten mercilessly by the soldiers. Perpetua felt deep sorrow for him, but she stood fast in her love for Christ, refusing her father's pleas.

| *St Perpetua comforting her father, 1857, by Antonio Ridolfi (1824-1900), oil on canvas, 131x97 cm. / De Agostini Picture Library / F. Lensini / Bridgeman Images*

✤ Now just imagine what some of the pagans watching these events would have thought. Some of them may have admired her courage and been inspired to become Christians themselves. But in the eyes of those who didn't understand, such a determined love for Christ must have seemed like hatred for everyone else she held dear.

✤ Next Luke records several other points of Our Lord's instruction. Alluding to the cross he himself will bear to Calvary, Jesus warns that his disciples will have their own crosses to bear as they follow him. These words should be a comfort to all Christians who are bearing a burden of adversity: We carry our crosses in his footsteps; he has walked this way of pain before us, and he is with us.

✤ Jesus also teaches that the disciple must imitate the contractor who assesses resources before attempting to build a tower, or a military commander who evaluates the enemy's strength in deciding whether to fight or sue for terms of peace. Jesus exhorts the disciples to do likewise. They must recognize what is being

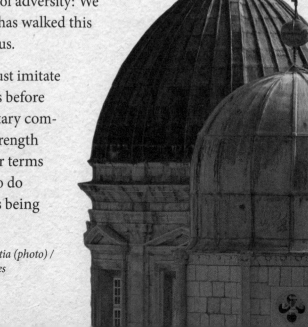

| *Bell Tower, Dubrovnik, Dubrovnik-Neretva, Croatia (photo) / Peter Langer/Design Pics/UIG / Bridgeman Images*

asked of them, and they must be generously willing to give everything. In keeping with one of Luke's prominent themes, he records Jesus' command: "So, therefore, whoever of you does not renounce all that he has cannot be my disciple" (14:33).

❧ The chapter concludes with a warning about salt that loses its flavor, whose saltiness cannot be restored. Today we consider salt to be cheap and plentiful. But in the ancient world, salt is a highly-sought commodity, literally worth its weight in gold, and prized by the Jews, Greeks, and Romans alike. Some peoples use it as currency, and wars are even fought over it. Because it's essential for animal life, the body craves its flavor; saltiness is one of the basic tastes of the human palate. It's also the most ancient of preservatives: The Greeks have a saying that salt can put a new soul into dead things.

❧ Our Lord's implicit comparison of his disciples to salt is thus a high compliment. Just as they can be the light that illumines the darkness of their world, and the yeast that leavens it, they can bring flavor to their world and preserve it from corruption. But Jesus warns that his disciples must not become like worthless salt. This passage is similar to Matthew's reference to salt (Mt 5:13), but Luke's account is unique in its vivid description of the tasteless salt as being "fit neither for the land nor for the dunghill" (14:35).

To prepare for small group discussion, turn ahead now to this session's "Digging Deeper" and "Life Application" sections.

Rome to Home

Thus the Church, at once "a visible association and a spiritual community," goes forward together with humanity and experiences the same earthly lot which the world does. She serves as a leaven and as a kind of soul for human society as it is to be renewed in Christ and transformed into God's family.

Second Vatican Council, Gaudium et Spes, 40

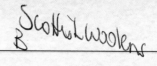

Opening Prayer

Let the words of my mouth and the meditation of my heart be acceptable in your sight, O Lord, my rock and my redeemer!

—Psalm 19:14

Teaching Video

This first video, hosted by Dr. Paul Thigpen, focuses on certain themes and passages from the Gospel of Luke. Here are some key highlights of his presentation, with room to take notes as you view the video to assist you in the group discussion.

The history and meaning of the Sabbath

_____

_____

_____

_____

Difficulties in applying the Sabbath law

_____

_____

_____

_____

The Lord of the Sabbath

_____

_____

_____

_____

The crippled woman in the synagogue

_____

_____

_____

_____

Jesus' response to his critics

_____

_____

_____

_____

Catechism Connections

These readings from the Catechism of the Catholic Church (CCC) will deepen your understanding of this session's presentations and discussions. The numbers identify the relevant paragraphs in the Catechism.

✤ Salvation: CCC 74, 2822

✤ Leaven: CCC 2660, 2832

✤ Christ as the center of Christian life: CCC 1618, 2544–2545

✤ Jesus' ascent to Jerusalem: CCC 557–558

✤ Jesus and the Sabbath: CCC 582, 2173–2176

✤ Humility and prayer: CCC 2559

Small Group Discussion

DIGGING DEEPER

1. How does the story of the fig tree illustrate the mercy of God, a theme that is so prevalent in the Gospel of Luke?

_____

_____

_____

(handwritten: Fruit is the virtues; spiritual works of mercy prayer)

(handwritten top right: Romans 5:2-5   Precepts of the Cat. Church   Tattoos on the Heart Fr Greg Boyle)

The Barren Fig Tree, illustration for 'The Life of Christ', c.1886-94 (w/c & gouache on paperboard), Tissot, James Jacques Joseph (1836-1902) / Brooklyn Museum of Art, New York, USA / Bridgeman Images

2. It appears that neither the woman who is bent over nor the man with the withered hand specifically asks Jesus for healing. He seems to have healed them, not only to make them whole, but also to make a point about the Sabbath. What does this tell us about the importance of understanding the Sabbath? How is the Jewish Sabbath fulfilled in our celebration of the Lord's Day? (See CCC 2173–2176.)

_____

_____

_____

_____

3. In Luke 13:24, Jesus tells us to "strive to enter by the narrow door; for many, I tell you, will seek to enter and will not be able." Does this mean that there are many who will not be saved? Does God desire that all people be saved? (See 1 Tm 2:4; Mt 7:13–14; CCC 74, 2822.)

[handwritten: The Light of Christ (bk)]

4. Jesus makes it clear that all men and women are invited to enter by the narrow gate, but not all will want to enter because the cost of discipleship is high. Why is the cost so high? Does Jesus want us literally to hate everything other than him? (See 14:25–33; CCC 1618, 2544–2545.)

[handwritten: Communion of heaven / Eucharist]

5. In Luke 14:15–24, Jesus tells the story of a man who gives a great banquet. What is this banquet an image of? What role do banquets play throughout salvation history? (See Gn 26:28–31, 31:44–54; Ex 24:9–11; 2 Sm 3:20–21; Is 25:6–9.)

[handwritten: Call to responsibility / Phillipians]

LIFE APPLICATION

1. What does it mean to me that Jesus Christ is the lord of the Sabbath?

2. Do I understand that good religion builds up people and communities? How have I used my faith to help others?

_____

_____

_____

_____

3. Do I look for opportunities to serve and assist other people in their needs?

_____

_____

_____

_____

Voices of the Saints

Great and noble leaders provoke the mighty in arms to deeds of valor, not only by promising them the honors of victory, but by declaring that suffering is in itself glorious. Such we see is the teaching of the Lord Jesus Christ. For he had foretold to his disciples that he must suffer the accusations of his enemies, be killed, and rise again on the third day. But to keep them from thinking that Christ was to suffer persecution for the life of the world, so that they themselves could lead a soft life, he shows them that they too must pass through similar struggles, if they desire to obtain his glory.

—*St. Cyril of Alexandria, Catena Aurea*

Life Application Video

After breaking from your small group discussion, gather to watch the second video, a pastoral reflection from Fr. Jeffrey Kirby, STD.

Christ Healing the Paralytic, c.1619 (oil on canvas), Dyck, Anthony van (1599-1641) / Royal Collection Trust © Her Majesty Queen Elizabeth II, 2016 / Bridgeman Images

How Then Shall We Live?

Silently review the following summary of Fr. Kirby's reflection to prepare for answering the questions in "Living It Out."

The Sabbath: a day of blessing and of rest. It's a reminder that everything we do should lead us to worship. After six days of labor and responsibility, God calls us to set things aside, to relax, and to worship him. The Sabbath is about worship, family, and rejuvenation. In the Old Testament, the Sabbath was protected by an array of ceremonial laws that were binding on all people. The laws were a way for God to teach his people how to observe and enjoy the Sabbath.

The Sabbath was a gift to humanity to renew us by rest and relaxation. Luke recounts that Jesus heals on the Sabbath, but such a healing raises serious legal questions, since the healing seems to break the ceremonial law. By healing on the Sabbath, however, Jesus isn't breaking the law; rather, he's fulfilling it. He is again showing humanity the purpose of the Sabbath: to rest, to worship, but also to be healed. Every Sabbath is an opportunity for each of us to be healed from the battering and bruising of the previous week.

In the hustle and bustle of our lives, do we realize that the Sabbath is a gift? We must rest and enjoy life! The Lord calls us to this consecrated rest. It should not be an optional observance.

The healing on the Sabbath is full of lessons for us. As we look at the powerful work of God in the healing and strengthening of his people, we should be inspired to look for new ways to observe and honor the Sabbath. We should also examine how we can better use our faith to unite and help those around us. This is the lesson the Lord Jesus is giving us and the lesson that Luke is recounting.

| *A Sunday on La Grande Jatte, 1884-86 (oil on canvas) , Seurat, Georges Pierre (1859-91) / The Art Institute of Chicago, IL, USA / Helen Birch Bartlett Memorial Collection / Bridgeman Images*

Living It Out

On your own, spend three to five minutes praying, discerning, and writing down the specific ways that God might be calling you to make changes in your life. Share and discuss afterwards only if you feel comfortable doing so.

Consider this week how God is calling you to …

❧ Give greater attention to the healing power of the Holy Mass: "Lord, I am not worthy to receive you, but only say the word and my soul shall be healed."

❧ Honor the Sabbath (Sunday) more highly by attending Mass (or doing so more reverently), refraining from work, or giving more of your time to loved ones or those in need.

❧ Avoid rash judgment of others and to extend graciously "the benefit of the doubt" to all.

Words to Know

Simile: A figure of speech comparing two unlike things in order to show a particular similarity, usually introduced by "like" or "as"; for example, "his voice is like thunder."

Dropsy: An abnormal swelling of the body.

Hyperbole: A figure of speech that employs extravagant exaggeration; for example, "a mountain of paperwork."

Vinedresser: Literally, someone who prunes and cultivates grapevines; in general, a caretaker of grapevines and fruit trees.

Closing Prayer

Our most holy Father … Your will be done on earth as it is in heaven, so that we may love You with all our heart by always having You in mind; with all our soul by always desiring You; with all our mind by directing all our intentions to You and by seeking Your glory in everything; and with all our strength by spending all our energies and affections of soul and body in the service of Your love and nothing else. Amen.

—St. Francis of Assisi, from *"The Prayer Inspired by the Our Father"*

| *Communion cup and host, encircled with a garland of fruit, Heem, Jan Davidsz. de (1606-84) / Kunsthistorisches Museum, Vienna, Austria / Bridgeman Images*

Return of the Prodigal Son, 1773 (oil on canvas),
Batoni, Pompeo Girolamo (1708-87) /
Kunsthistorisches Museum, Vienna, Austria /
Bridgeman Images

SESSION 12

THE

PRODIGAL SON

"It was fitting to make merry and be glad, for this your brother was dead, and is alive; he was lost, and is found."

LUKE 15:32

SESSION READING

LUKE 15:1–32

Introduction

Luke's fifteenth chapter records three of Our Lord's parables, all with a common theme: The divine mercy is watchful and persistent, seeking out those who are lost to bring them back where they belong. Jesus tells these parables in response to the scribes and Pharisees who are scandalized that he would spend time with notorious sinners.

The parables also share the theme of joy—the celebration that ensues when the lost have been found. This element of rejoicing makes it clear that when Jesus speaks of those who are lost, he doesn't mean they are simply out of place and out of sight. He means they are separated from a God who prizes them dearly.

As usual, the three parables employ imagery that would be familiar to Our Lord's listeners: a stray sheep, a lost coin, a wayward child. The last of the three, the parable of the prodigal son, supplements the themes of lost-and-found and rejoicing with a sharp lesson for the scribes and Pharisees: Those who have never wandered must not resent those who have, but have now returned.

| *Praying the Divine Mercy Devotions, Stock Photo 111, eCatholic.com*

Prayer to Prepare for Study

Lord, my God, bestow upon me an understanding that knows You, diligence in seeking You, wisdom in finding You, a way of life that is pleasing to You, perseverance that waits trustfully for You, and confidence that I shall embrace You at the last. Amen.

—Prayer of St. Thomas Aquinas before study

Study Notes

These notes provide insights to help you understand and reflect upon the biblical text.

* In chapter 15 of Luke's Gospel, three stories are told about repentance and God's search for humanity: the parable of the lost sheep (15:1–7), the parable of the lost coin (15:8–10), and the parable of the prodigal son (15:11–32). They are told in response to an observation by the Pharisees: "This man receives sinners and eats with them" (15:2).

* Each of these stories emphasizes the Lord's desire to reconcile all sinners to himself. They are told not just to show God's compassion, but also to urge the religious leaders of his day

to rejoice over this universal opportunity for mercy and reconciliation. Unfortunately, the illustration of God's mercy falls on hardened hearts among the religious leaders. Nevertheless, as Jesus approaches Jerusalem to begin his passion, his mind and heart turn to the sinner. In each of the three accounts, the Lord is proclaiming mercy.

✤ The parables of Luke 15 also stress an important lesson: God is searching for us. In our time, so many people emphasize their search for God or meaning or purpose. While this search has some validity, we must remember that long before we search for God, he is already searching for us.

✤ Luke begins this trilogy of stories with a pastoral scene. The Lord asks which of his listeners, if he were to own a hundred sheep, would not leave the ninety-nine in order to look for a lost sheep (15:4). The frustration of a lost sheep would have been well known or understood by the Lord's hearers. The question raised is a rhetorical one, since any good shepherd would certainly search for a lost sheep.

✤ Some readers of this passage may wonder about the other ninety-nine sheep: Couldn't they be in danger or wander away themselves if the shepherd leaves them alone while he searches? Our Lord's listeners, however, would know that shepherds typically work as a team. (Consider, for example, the shepherds to whom the angels announced Jesus' birth.) So the assumption would be that the shepherd of the parable leaves the ninety-nine sheep in the care of a coworker; they aren't left alone.

✤ In speaking about the search for a lost sheep, the Lord implicitly addresses the risk of *becoming* a lost sheep. If a sheep is lost, he loses the protection of his shepherd and the comfort of his herd. The lost sheep becomes an easy meal for predators and can fall into traps or holes or off a steep cliff. It's important to realize the imminent danger of being a lost sheep. This parable illustrates the difficulties awaiting those who stray from the Lord.

✤ When the owner finds his lost sheep, he places it on his shoulders (15:5). He cares for his sheep and guides it back to the fold. The image of a shepherd carrying a sheep is one of the most popular images of the Lord in the history of Christian sacred art. Until the legalization of Christianity in A.D. 313, the

Sculpture depicting Christ as a good shepherd in Santa Maria D (photo) / Godong/UIG / Bridgeman Images

image was more popular than any other, even the cross. Only after the legalization of the Faith, and the end of crucifixion as a Roman method of execution, did the cross and crucifix emerge as prominent symbols in Christian art and worship.

❧ When St. Ambrose comments on this parable, he notes that the shepherd is Christ, and he beautifully elaborates on the imagery. "The shoulders of Christ are the arms of the Cross," he writes. "There, I laid down my sins. I rested on the neck of that noble yoke" (*Exposition of the Gospel of Luke*, 7.209). Pope St. Gregory the Great, a sixth-century Church Father, observes: "Christ put the sheep on his shoulders because, in taking on human nature, he burdened himself with our sins" (*In Evangelia homiliae*, 2, 14).

❧ When the owner returns with his lost sheep, he calls on his neighbors to rejoice with him (15:6). The Lord uses this occasion to denounce self-righteousness by teaching that there is more rejoicing over the repentance of one sinner than ninety-nine people who don't need repentance (15:7). The irony, of course, is that there truly are none who need no repentance.

❧ After the parable of the lost sheep, the Lord continues by telling the story of the woman and the lost coin (15:8–10). The coin may be a Greek drachma, a small silver coin. It represents a full day's wage for an agricultural worker in the ancient world, so the woman's search, which is diligent and extensive, isn't motivated by greed or vanity. Her family needs it.

❧ In many respects, the description of the woman lighting a lamp and sweeping the house (15:8) is a description of God's work, not just with individuals, but throughout salvation history. God has worked through the patriarchs, judges, kings, and prophets in his search for humanity. He has lit many lamps and swept the house of Israel many times looking for his wayward children (Heb 1:2), and he ultimately has come as the Light of the world (Heb 1:2; Jn 8:12; Lk 2:32).

❧ The last of the three parables, the story of the prodigal son, is a grand summary of the themes of chapter 15 and the most dramatic of the stories. Much like the parable of the Good Samaritan, the parable of the prodigal son has become one of the most beloved of biblical stories. Yet surprisingly, it's recounted only in Luke's Gospel.

❧ As the Lord has already presented two parables to stress God's mercy, we may need to recall what prompted him to tell these stories in the first place. They are his response to the wrong

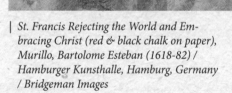

| *St. Francis Rejecting the World and Embracing Christ (red & black chalk on paper), Murillo, Bartolome Esteban (1618-82) / Hamburger Kunsthalle, Hamburg, Germany / Bridgeman Images*

attitude of the religious leaders: "Now the tax collectors and sinners were all drawing near to hear him. And the Pharisees and the scribes murmured, saying, 'This man receives sinners and eats with them' " (15:1–2).

✦ In the story of the prodigal son especially, this context is critical, because these religious leaders are themselves represented by the figure of the older brother. In many respects, then, the story is not just addressed to sinners to call them home, but also to the scribes and Pharisees, the "older brothers." They should rejoice over God's universal invitation to mercy and reconciliation, and the resulting repentance of sinners and Gentiles.

✦ In this parable, the younger son demands his inheritance and squanders it on sinful living (15:11–13). Because the inheritance is typically distributed either when the father dies or when he retires, the son's offense to the father is obvious: He's essentially saying to him, "I've been waiting for you to die or at least go away so I can get what's mine. But I just can't wait any longer." The young man's sinful living is an extension of this offense.

✦ While the Lord is telling a story of two brothers, and it has an application for any family or community that has had a similar experience, he's also using the story to describe the reconciliation of the Gentiles to God. In salvation history, God initially worked with all the nations of the world. But the nations rebelled against him, they "demanded their inheritance" from him, and they lived wayward lives as if God were dead. So God chose the Semitic people, the children of Shem (the firstborn son of Noah after the Great Flood), and worked through their descendants (the Jews) what he desired to do among all the nations.

| *The Repentant Prodigal's Return to his Father (oil on panel), Etty, William (1787-1849) / Ashmolean Museum, University of Oxford, UK / Bridgeman Images.*

* We should note that the price of the disobedience of the Gentiles and the pride of the scribes and Pharisees will be paid by Jesus Christ himself, the God-Man. The spiritual tradition of the Church imagines the prepared comments of the prodigal son in the mouth of Jesus as he prays in the Garden of Gethsemane. As the Lord carries the weight of humanity's sins ("in the likeness of sinful flesh and for sin," Rom 8:3), he will feel the sentiments of the prodigal and pay the price for all of humanity's sins.

* Even so, the scribes and Pharisees will not allow themselves to understand this portion of the Lord's life and teachings. They are adamant that the Law must be obeyed by sinners for salvation, not realizing that it will be obeyed and fulfilled by the eternal Son of God made Man in Jesus Christ.

* The father orders a great celebration upon the return of his younger son (15:22–24). When the elder son returns from working in the fields, he's upset that his father has called for a celebration for his younger brother (15:28). The father goes to the elder brother and consoles him, calling him to rejoice (15:32). Luke records and stresses this exchange because it's the story of the relationship between the Jews and the Gentiles. While we should learn many things from the prodigal son, an important lesson that cannot be forgotten is Jesus' focus on the older brother. The story calls on the Jewish leadership to welcome and rejoice in the admittance of the Gentiles into God's kingdom.

* While the parable of the prodigal son portrays salvation history, it's also a simple story of conversion. The younger brother comes to himself (15:17) while in the pigpen and decides to return to his father's house. God gives this grace of conversion to all people. He calls each of us—in whatever pigpens we find ourselves—to repentance and reconciliation.

* Some may think this teaching is directed only toward more "serious" sinners. But the call to conversion is actually for everyone, for God desires to transform us all more and more by his grace. The graces of conversion must for that reason never be underestimated or taken for granted. They are given at unique moments and may be fleeting. When they come to us, we should respond generously.

* Meanwhile, the figure of the older brother represents any one of us who bears resentment, for whatever reasons, toward converted sinners. In a sense, the prodigal son sins against the older brother as well: He leaves the entire responsibility of working the estate on the shoulders of his more responsible sibling. Then he selfishly wastes his portion of an inheritance that might have eventually been larger for both of them if the younger man had stayed and worked hard to increase the value of the estate. Like the older brother, then, we too are called to forgive those who have wronged us, and to rejoice in their repentance and conversion.

* Note as well that the older brother has worked dutifully but joylessly for his father as if he himself were a hired hand, and he has never asked for a feast to enjoy with his friends. In a sense, he represents as well all those who fail to appreciate and enjoy the spiritual riches they possess as children of God and members of his household, the Church. Cradle Catholics, for example, often comment that the testimonies of Catholic converts have made them

more aware of their spiritual inheritance and helped them to view their faith not as a grim duty, but as a gift to be celebrated. The same can be said of others who have left the Faith and returned, and even those who have simply had an awakening of their faith.

✤ When we consider the parable of the prodigal son, its lessons must be applied to the Sacrament of Reconciliation. People are often hesitant to receive this sacrament because they focus on their sins, or the difficulty of naming them, or the response of the priest. But this parable gives us a different perspective. As we go to Confession, we should understand that our heavenly Father is waiting for us, looking for us, ready to greet us with mercy and great joy. This is the proper focus of such a great and liberating sacrament.

✤ Finally, we should note with the ancient Christian writer Tertullian that the parables in this chapter teach as well the essential virtue of patience: "Our Lord's parables display a breadth of patience. The shepherd's patience makes him seek and find the straying sheep. Impatience would have made him dismiss the loss of a single sheep as unworthy of the effort to find it, but patience takes on the laborious search. … In the case of the prodigal son, it's his father's patience that welcomes, clothes, feeds, and defends the young man from the anger of his brother. … Repentance isn't wasted when it meets up with patience" (*On Patience*, 12).

| *Mary Magdalene with a night light, c.1640-35 (oil on canvas), Tour, Georges de la (1593-1652) / Louvre-Lens, France / Bridgeman Images*

To prepare for small group discussion, turn ahead now to this session's "Digging Deeper" and "Life Application" sections.

Rome to Home

When Jesus speaks in his parables of the shepherd who goes after the lost sheep, of the woman who looks for the lost coin, of the father who goes to meet and embrace his prodigal son, these are no mere words: they constitute an explanation of his very being and activity. His death on the Cross is the culmination of that turning of God against himself in which he gives himself in order to raise man up and save him. This is love in its most radical form.

—*Pope Benedict XVI, Deus Caritas Est, 12*

Opening Prayer

Let the words of my mouth and the meditation of my heart be acceptable in your sight, O Lord, my rock and my redeemer!

—Psalm 19:14

Teaching Video

This first video, hosted by Dr. Paul Thigpen, focuses on certain themes and passages from the Gospel of Luke. Here are some key highlights of his presentation, with room to take notes as you view the video to assist you in the group discussion.

The scribes and Pharisees reject Jesus' mission of mercy

_____

_____

_____

_____

The parable of the lost sheep

_____

_____

_____

_____

| *Farm collection / Sheep sketch © Canicula, Shutterstock*

The parable of the lost coin

_____

_____

_____

_____

_____

_____

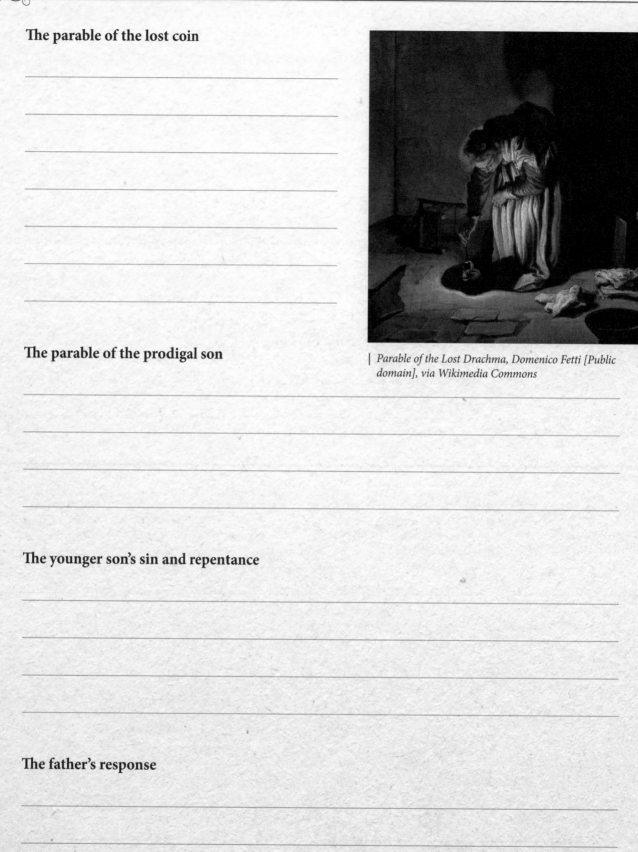

| *Parable of the Lost Drachma, Domenico Fetti [Public domain], via Wikimedia Commons*

The parable of the prodigal son

_____

_____

_____

_____

The younger son's sin and repentance

_____

_____

_____

_____

The father's response

_____

_____

_____

_____

The older brother's response

_____

_____

_____

_____

The father's appeal to the older brother

_____

_____

_____

_____

Catechism Connections

These readings from the Catechism of the Catholic Church (CCC) will deepen your understanding of this session's presentations and discussions. The numbers identify the relevant paragraphs in the Catechism.

✤ Jesus invites sinners to the table of the Kingdom: CCC 545

✤ The priest as shepherd: CCC 1465

✤ God takes the initiative in redemption: CCC 604–605

✤ The prodigal son and the process of conversion: CCC 1439, 1700, 2839

✤ Reconciliation with the Church: CCC 1443

✤ God's patience: CCC 2822

Small Group Discussion

DIGGING DEEPER

1. The parable of the lost sheep tells of the shepherd leaving his flock to go after the one sheep that is lost. What does this parable tell us about the nature of God and his desire to save us? (See CCC 604–605.)

_____

_____

_____

_____

| *The Calling of St Matthew, c.1620 (oil on canvas), Strozzi, Bernardo (1581-1644) / Worcester Art Museum, Massachusetts, USA / Bridgeman Images*

2. Why are the Pharisees so upset that Jesus eats with sinners? What do Jesus' actions show us about the effects of forgiveness? (See CCC 1443.)

_____

_____

_____

_____

3. What does the parable of the prodigal son tell us about the love of God the Father? How does the father in the parable "reintegrate" the son back into the community?

_____

_____

_____

4. What view of his father does the older brother have? Why isn't he able to enter into the joy that the father has at the return of his brother?

_____

_____

_____

5. What do the stories of the lost sheep and the prodigal son reveal about the role of priests in the Church? (See CCC 1439, 1465.)

_____

_____

_____

LIFE APPLICATION

1. Do we have a strong understanding of God as a merciful and loving Father?

_____

_____

_____

2. Do we readily seek the mercy of God and go to Confession regularly?

_____

_____

_____

_____

3. Do we look for ways in which we can spread a culture of mercy, compassion, and gentleness?

_____

_____

_____

_____

Voices of the Saints

Faith is the lost coin that the woman in the Gospel seeks diligently. We read that she lights a lamp and sweeps her house. After finding it, she calls together her friends and neighbors, inviting them to rejoice with her because she has found the coin that she had lost. The damage to the soul is great if one has lost the faith, or the grace that he has gained for himself at the price of faith. So light your lamp. … Search for the coin, the redemption of your soul.

—*St. Ambrose, Letter 20*

Life Application Video

After breaking from your small group discussion, gather to watch the second video, a pastoral reflection from Fr. Jeffrey Kirby, STD.

How Then Shall We Live?

Silently review the following summary of Fr. Kirby's reflection to prepare for answering the questions in "Living It Out."

In the parable of the prodigal son, the younger son squanders everything he receives, and he decides to return to his father's house as a servant. The father is vigilant in waiting for his son, and when he returns, he hosts a party. It's a powerful sequence of events. It's the sequence of events that should be running through our hearts as we prepare to go to Confession.

Now is the time to repent. That's great advice and counsel to us all. If we haven't been to Confession in a while, now is the time. If we have something grave or heavy on our hearts, now is the time to go to Confession. The Lord waits for us, just as that father waited for his younger son.

Living It Out

On your own, spend three to five minutes praying, discerning, and writing down the specific ways that God might be calling you to make changes in your life. Share and discuss afterwards only if you feel comfortable doing so.

Consider this week how God is calling you to …

- ✤ Know the Father who loves you and seeks to embrace you in his loving kindness.
- ✤ Prepare well for and make a good sacramental Confession.
- ✤ Reflect God's loving kindness to those around you (family members, coworkers, neighbors, fellow parishioners, people in authority).

Words to Know

Drachma: A coin of Greek origin. The name is derived from the Greek word for "handful" since the drachma originally consisted of six oboloi, another type of Greek coin representing a smaller denomination. One of these coins is thought to be the equivalent of a day's wage for a laborer in the ancient world.

Prodigal: Marked by wasteful spending, an imprudence or recklessness in expending one's money so as to reduce one to poverty.

Closing Prayer

O Lord, show Your mercy to me and gladden my heart. I am like the man on the way to Jericho who was overtaken by robbers, wounded and left for dead; O Good Samaritan, come to my aid. I am like the sheep that went astray; O Good Shepherd, seek me out and bring me home in accord with Your will. Let me dwell in Your house all the days of my life and praise You for ever and ever with those who are there.

—St. Jerome

Lazarus, Fyodor Andreyevich Bronnikov
[Public domain], via Wikimedia Commons

SESSION 13

LAZARUS
AND THE
RICH MAN

He said to them, "If they do not hear Moses and the prophets, neither will they be convinced if some one should rise from the dead."

LUKE 16:31

SESSION READING
LUKE 16:1–17:37

Introduction

Luke's sixteenth and seventeenth chapters continue to focus on Jesus' teaching rather than on a narrative of events unfolding. But the emphasis now shifts from mercy to the demands of discipleship in this life and the finality of divine judgment in the next life.

The parable of the dishonest steward offers some difficulties in interpretation. But the admonitions of Our Lord that follow it suggest that his primary point is about proper stewardship of the riches God has given us. The Pharisees, who tend to love money, are not surprisingly displeased. So Jesus goes on to tell another story that is guaranteed to upset them: the tale of Lazarus and the rich man.

The Lord also reveals how following him calls for heroic commitment and sacrifice. His disciples must refuse to be greedy; care for those in need; forgive those who offend them, even repeatedly; and embrace marriage as a lifetime commitment. They must maintain grateful hearts and have faith that can uproot a tree and throw it into the sea. In the end, they must be prepared for the day when the Son of Man returns in judgment.

His final summary of discipleship is succinct: Whoever seeks to gain his life will lose it, but whoever loses his life will preserve it.

Betrothal of the Holy Virgin and Saint Joseph (gouache on paperboard), Tissot, James Jacques Joseph (1836-1902) / Brooklyn Museum of Art, New York, USA / Bridgeman Images

Prayer to Prepare for Study

Lord, my God, bestow upon me an understanding that knows You, diligence in seeking You, wisdom in finding You, a way of life that is pleasing to You, perseverance that waits trustfully for You, and confidence that I shall embrace You at the last. Amen.

—Prayer of St. Thomas Aquinas before study

Study Notes

These notes provide insights to help you understand and reflect upon the biblical text.

✤ Only Luke tells Jesus' parable of the dishonest steward (16:1–9). In the story, the steward is squandering a rich man's property and is found out. The rich man tells him he will have to give an account of his stewardship before his dismissal, so the steward reduces the debts of each of the rich man's debtors. The debtors are now grateful to the steward and more likely to help him in the days to come, when he no longer has a job. He may also have gained some leverage with them because he has now involved them in his own crimes. If necessary, he could threaten to blackmail them if they refuse to assist him in the future.

✤ Surprisingly, the master now commends the steward for what he has done (16:8). Is Jesus praising the unrighteous man for his dishonesty? Not at all. The master simply commends the man for his prudence and foresight for the future. The lesson here, as Our Lord goes on to state it, is this: If even the unrighteous are prudent in this way to secure their future in this world, how much more prudent should the righteous be to secure their future in the world to come!

✤ Some have speculated that the steward has been cheating the rich man's debtors by inflating the amounts they owe, and his reduction of their debts returns them to the proper amounts. This would explain why the rich man wants an accounting, and why the steward is able to reduce the debts of the others. In this interpretation of the story, the steward is making things right, so he is also being praised for finally treating the debtors justly.

| *The Unjust Steward (engraving), English School, (19th century) / Private Collection / © Look and Learn / Bridgeman Images*

✤ St. Augustine, St. Ambrose, and others consider this parable an exhortation to almsgiving. All that we own in this life belongs to God; we are only stewards of what we possess. By giving to those in need, we use "unrighteous mammon" (money) to gain "friends" for our future in heaven (16:9). As the rabbis used to say, "The rich help the poor in this world, but the poor help the rich in the world to come."

✦ Our Lord makes additional points related to this parable. First, he declares that how we handle small matters will determine how we handle greater matters (16:10). If we can't properly handle the temporary material goods of this world, how can we be entrusted with the eternal spiritual goods of the next world? The principle has other applications as well. In nearly every important realm of life, we must start out by managing lesser responsibilities before we're ready to manage greater ones. The disciple must grow into a role of leadership.

✦ Jesus concludes his teaching about this parable by again drawing the boundaries of discipleship: "No servant can serve two masters; for either he will hate the one and love the other, or he will be devoted to the one and despise the other. You cannot serve God and mammon" (16:13). The servant here is actually a slave. He's not an employee who can work at two jobs, working for two bosses; he's owned by the master exclusively. Every moment, every effort, belongs to his lord. So serving God can never be one occupation among many. This is especially the case when the other master attempting to claim his loyalty is his true master's enemy. Sooner or later, his allegiance will be compromised.

✦ Remember that Jesus is on his way to Jerusalem for his passion, so he wants to be very clear with his followers about what it means to follow him. There can be no half-hearted disciples, no compromises with the world.

The Tribute Money, illustration from 'The Life of Our Lord Jesus Christ', 1886-94 (w/c over graphite on paper), Tissot, James Jacques Joseph (1836-1902) / Brooklyn Museum of Art, New York, USA / Purchased by Public Subscription / Bridgeman Images

❋ This admonition about money is followed by a rebuke to the Pharisees' self-righteousness (16:14–15). Jesus is challenging a common attitude of the time that material prosperity is an indication of a man's holiness. The Pharisees scoff at Our Lord's teaching (literally, they "make faces at him") because they love money and consider their wealth to be a sign of God's favor.

❋ Next, several of Jesus' teachings are presented that appear to be a small collection of his sayings brought together by Luke and placed in this context. First, Our Lord firmly declares the immutability and stability of God's law (16:16–17). Not a "dot" of it will become void. The Greek word translated here as "dot" apparently refers to the tiny serif that appears on the top of certain Hebrew letters, the language in which the Law has been written. Not even so much as a serif of the Law will be made empty; instead, Christ himself will fulfill the Law perfectly (Mt 5:17–18).

| *The Biblical Tetragrammaton YHWH, the Hebrew Name for God,* © *Architecteur, Shutterstock*

❋ Jesus speaks next of the indissolubility of marriage (16:18). Chastity is highly prized in the Jewish culture of the day; Jews are expected to give up their lives rather than commit idolatry, murder, or adultery. Nevertheless, the marriage bond has become cheapened through easy divorce.

❋ In speaking of divorce, the Law of Moses says: "When a man takes a wife and marries her, if she then finds no favor in his eyes because he has found some indecency in her … he writes her a bill of divorce and puts it in her hand and sends her out of his house" (Dt 24:1). In the time of Jesus, the rabbis have become divided in their interpretation of that word "indecency." One rabbinic school claims that it refers only to adultery. But another school, which has become much more popular, claims that it can mean spoiling a dish of food, talking to a strange man, talking about her in-laws in the presence of her husband, speaking so loudly that she can be heard in the next house, and other such minor offenses. One rabbi even goes so far as to say that a man can divorce his wife if he finds a more beautiful woman. Jesus is once again challenging the assumptions of his culture by declaring that marriage cannot be dissolved in this way.

❋ After these brief teachings, the Lord tells the story of Lazarus and the rich man (16:19–31). The latter is traditionally called *Dives,* from the Latin word for "rich man" in the Vulgate, the ancient Latin translation of the Bible. This parable is well placed after the Lord's teachings about money, and it stands as a reminder to care for the poor. Only Luke records this story from Jesus, and he does so precisely because of its emphasis on serving the forgotten and those in need.

❋ The rich man's wealth is amply illustrated by his personal habits. He dresses in "purple and fine linen" (16:19). Purple dye at this time is made at great cost from a type of shellfish; only the rich can afford clothes dyed with it, so it comes to symbolize both wealth and royalty. Linen is finer and more expensive to produce than other fabrics of the time, so it too denotes luxury.

- The rich man feasts "sumptuously" every day (16:19). The word used here for feasting is typically employed of a connoisseur dining on costly, exotic foods. He eats this way every day in a society where most people manage to eat meat only once a week. If he's able to enjoy such a banquet every day, he probably doesn't have to work.

- The poor man Lazarus waits for the crumbs that fall from the rich man's table (16:20–21). Neither tableware nor napkins are used for dining in this culture; people typically eat with their fingers. In wealthy homes, people clean their hands by wiping them on pieces of bread, which are then thrown out. Apparently, Lazarus must await these pieces of bread for his sustenance—a humiliating way to survive.

- In the story, Dives is not abusive or mean to Lazarus; he doesn't have him chased away. But the rich man is nevertheless negligent; he does absolutely nothing to help Lazarus; he seems to have no pity on him at all. (We know that he's aware of Lazarus' presence, and even of his identity, because he calls the poor man by name; 16:24.)

- The stray dogs of the city compete with Lazarus for the morsels. Such dogs are generally despised by the ancient Jews, so their presence only deepens his humiliation. Even so, as St. Cyril of Alexandria observes, these animals seem to have more compassion for Lazarus than Dives does: They lick his wounds to soothe his suffering (16:21). But the rich man ignores the beggar completely.

- What we have here is an example of sins of omission: things we should do, but fail to do. Recall the words of the *Confiteor* as we pray at the beginning of the Holy Mass: "I confess … that I have sinned … in what I have done and in what I have failed to do." This confession is an acknowledgment, not only of our sins of commission, but also of our sins of omission.

- Because of his sinful avoidance of the poor man, the rich man is sent to the netherworld, where he is tormented. He sees Lazarus in the "bosom of Abraham." The image suggests that Lazarus is now reclining at the banquet of the Old Testament patriarch. In fact, he's the guest of honor who has been positioned immediately next to Abraham, so he can lean his head back on his breast.

- The "bosom of Abraham" is a reference either to heaven or the "limbo of the fathers." The latter is the Church's name for a holding place for the souls of all the righteous men and women of the Old Covenant. They are destined for heaven, but they cannot enter it until Jesus' sacrifice on Calvary is complete. After his coming crucifixion, while his body rests in the tomb, the Lord's human soul will visit this limbo, which the Apostle's Creed calls "hell" (Greek *hades,* "realm of the dead"). Then he will usher the righteous ones into paradise.

- The word "limbo" is often associated with a similar holding place ("limbo of the children"), which some theologians have thought exists for unbaptized babies. But the Church has never officially endorsed this doctrine. These two kinds of "limbo" should not be confused.

- The words of this parable have found their way into the Church's liturgy. "Abraham's bosom," "paradise," and "Lazarus" all appear in various texts used in funeral Masses and burial rites.

| *Lazarus and the Rich Man, c.1400 (oil on panel), German School, (15th century) / The Barnes Foundation, Philadelphia, Pennsylvania, USA / Bridgeman Images*

✤ Dives begs for cooling water, then asks whether a warning can be given to his brothers. Both requests are refused, and the man is left in torment. Note that the once-rich man continues to display a dismissive attitude toward the once-poor man, even in hades: Lazarus is now an honored guest at Father Abraham's table, yet Dives wants the patriarch to dispatch Lazarus with a message to his brothers, as if Lazarus is only a slave to be sent on an errand.

✤ Luke uses this story to emphasize the Christian responsibility to care for and attend to the poor among us. The one who refuses to show compassion and mercy in this life will receive no compassion or mercy in the next life.

✤ We should observe that in this story, the Lord comfortably addresses Abraham as "father" (16:24, 30). This statement helps us understand another of the Lord's teachings, which is misinterpreted by some Christians: "Call no man your father on earth, for you have one Father, who is in heaven" (Mt 23:9). If this statement is intended to be absolute, then we must avoid calling even a biological father by that name. Since Our Lord himself uses the term, however, his point is clearly not that we must avoid using the title. Rather, he instructs us to avoid exalting another human being to the status in our lives that only God the Father should have. At the same time, it's a rebuke to those who seek such status because of their pride and vanity.

❧ No other parable of our Lord recorded in the Gospels assigns a name to a character. In fact, Luke doesn't even call this story a parable, so some Bible scholars have wondered whether it might be a story with some historical basis. Even though Lazarus is named, the rich man is not, so some speculate that the story is a veiled reference to the wealthy Sadducee high priests of the time, who dress in "purple and fine linen" (16:19). In addition, Jesus has the rich man speak of his father's house with five brothers, and there's actually a real family of high priests among Jesus' contemporaries who fit that description: Annas is the father-in-law of Caiaphas, both of whom are high priests; and Annas has five sons, all of them high priests at one time or another.

| *The question of the Sadducees, Copping, Harold (1863-1932) / Private Collection / © Look and Learn / Bridgeman Images*

❧ In the medieval period, Lazarus was widely viewed as an actual historical figure and was considered the patron saint of lepers. Twelfth-century crusaders in the Kingdom of Jerusalem founded the Order of St. Lazarus to care for those with leprosy (Hansen's disease).

❧ The Lord follows this story with various exhortations to discipleship. Jesus somberly warns that his followers must not cause "temptations to sin" (17:1). The Greek word here, *skandala*, means literally "stumbling blocks," from which we get the English word "scandals." It originally referred to the bait-sticks in traps.

❧ The imagery used to describe the consequences of such behavior is terrifying (17:2). A typical millstone of the time is quite heavy, round with a large hole in the center. The picture is of a person's head squeezed through the hole so that the stone cannot be removed and remains around the neck when he is cast into the depths of the sea.

❧ Jesus also exhorts his disciples to mutual correction (17:3), perhaps implying that the failure to rebuke sin is itself a form of stumbling block: It permits the sinner to continue in his wrongdoing. Yet such correction must of course be offered, not proudly or self-righteously, but in the knowledge that when a brother has a speck in his eye, we may well have a log in ours (Mt 7:3–5). Meanwhile, the pain of correction must be soothed by the balm of forgiveness (Lk 17:3–4).

❦ Our Lord's teaching that the disciples are unworthy servants doing only what they owe the master appears only in Luke (17:7–10). It emphasizes how we owe all that we are and have to God's mercy, and our response should be to serve him wholeheartedly, faithfully, and gratefully.

❦ Throughout his Gospel, Luke includes events and lessons that show Jesus dealing with tax collectors, Samaritans, and Gentiles in order to emphasize how abundant is God's mercy and compassion. Luke now tells how Jesus heals ten lepers, but only one returns to give thanks (17:11–19). The one who returns is one of the Samaritans so despised by the Jews of Jesus' day. Jesus rebukes the other lepers (presumably fellow Jews) and praises the faith of the Samaritan (17:17–19). Luke records this event to illustrate once more that God's love and mercy are for everyone.

❦ The healing of the ten lepers is a powerful lesson about gratitude as well. The Lord calls us to be grateful to God for his mercy and compassion. St. Augustine observes, "No duty is more urgent than that of returning thanks."

| *Christ and the Lepers, Gebhard Fugel [Public domain], via Wikimedia Commons*

✤ After the healing of the ten lepers, Jesus responds to a question about the coming of the kingdom of God. He wants them to understand that with his coming to earth, the Kingdom is already present (17:20–21). But he goes on to warn of difficult times still to come (including his own passion and death), and he wants them to be prepared (17:20–37).

✤ A parallel to this passage in Matthew's Gospel (Mt 24) provides more details of Jesus' teaching on this matter. In that account, the disciples ask two questions: When will the Temple be destroyed (as Jesus has prophesied), and what will be the signs of his second coming at "the close of the age" (Mt 24:3)?

✤ The disciples seem to assume that these events are simultaneous. But we know now that they are not: The Temple (and all Jerusalem) was destroyed in A.D. 70, yet the end of the world has yet to come. In his reply as recorded in both Gospels, Jesus answers both questions, but we must sort out which events he foretells have to do with A.D. 70, and which ones have to do with the end of the world.

| *Destruction of Temple of Jerusalem/ De Agostini Picture Library / A. Dagli Orti / Italy, Lombard, Bridgeman Images*

✤ Failure to make this and other distinctions lies behind much of the misinterpretation of these texts, which has led some Christians to certain popular but misguided apocalyptic notions. While the Church acknowledges that there will be tribulations and difficulties before the Lord returns in glory, she does not subscribe to ideas such as a secret "rapture."

✤ "Rapture" believers teach that before Christ's visible and glorious second coming at the end of the world, he will return secretly and invisibly to snatch away true believers to heaven, leaving unbelievers behind. That way, Christians can be spared the terrifying events that will come at the very end of human history.

✤ They cite this passage in Luke to support this teaching because Jesus says, "There will be two men in one bed; one will be taken and the other left. There will be two women grinding together; one will be taken and the other left" (17:34–35). These interpreters conclude that those who are taken are the "raptured" true believers, while those who are left behind are the ungodly who will be punished by the world's great tribulations.

✤ Since ancient times, however, most Christian traditions have viewed this passage as an account of the final judgment day when Christ appears in glory. If we read the entire passage, we find Jesus saying that these events will take place "as it was in the days of Noah" and "in the days of Lot" (17:26, 28). Now in the days of Noah and of Lot, who was taken *away*, and who was left behind? The *wicked* were swept away in the judgment of Noah's flood and Sodom's fire and brimstone; the *righteous* were the ones left behind. So this passage is speaking of Our Lord's final judgment, not a secret rapture.

✢ The disciples want more details about Jesus' second coming. He replies to their query, enigmatically, "Where the body is, there the eagles will be gathered" (17:37). Perhaps he intends such an obscure response to discourage them from seeking more details. Perhaps it's a common proverb of the time meaning simply that when the necessary conditions are in place, it will happen. The word translated "eagles" can also mean "vultures"; either way, the speedy manner in which these birds swoop down on their prey may suggest the sudden, unexpected nature of Our Lord's return.

✢ At every Holy Mass the faithful pray for the Lord's return when the priest, after the Lord's Prayer, prays on behalf of the community: "Deliver us, Lord, we pray, from every evil, graciously grant peace in our days, that, by the help of your mercy, we may be always free from sin and safe from all distress, as we await the blessed hope and the coming of our Savior, Jesus Christ."

To prepare for small group discussion, turn ahead now to this session's "Digging Deeper" and "Life Application" sections.

Rome to Home

The parable of the rich man and Lazarus must always be present in our memory; it must form our conscience. ... All of humanity must think of the parable of the rich man and the beggar. ... We cannot stand idly by when thousands of human beings are dying of hunger. Nor can we remain indifferent when the rights of the human spirit are trampled upon, when violence is done to the human conscience in matters of truth, religion, and cultural creativity.

We cannot stand idly by, enjoying our own riches and freedom, if, in any place, the Lazarus of the twentieth century stands at our doors. In the light of the parable of Christ, riches and freedom mean a special responsibility. Riches and freedom create a special obligation. And so, in the name of the solidarity that binds us all together in a common humanity, I again proclaim the dignity of every human person: the rich man and Lazarus are both human beings, both of them equally created in the image and likeness of God, both of them equally redeemed by Christ, at a great price, the price of "the precious blood of Christ" (1 Pt 1:19).

—*St. John Paul II, Homily in Yankee Stadium, October 2, 1979, 7*

Opening Prayer

Let the words of my mouth and the meditation of my heart be acceptable in your sight, O Lord, my rock and my redeemer!

—Psalm 19:14

Teaching Video

This first video, hosted by Dr. Paul Thigpen, focuses on certain themes and passages from the Gospel of Luke. Here are some key highlights of his presentation, with room to take notes as you view the video to assist you in the group discussion.

Difficult or puzzling sayings of Jesus

_____

_____

_____

_____

Words of justice

_____

_____

_____

_____

The rich man's luxury and Lazarus' misery

_____

_____

_____

_____

Lazarus' reward and the rich man's torment and fate

_____

_____

_____

_____

Parable, historical account, or historical fiction?

_____

_____

_____

_____

Debates about what the story teaches about the afterlife

_____

_____

_____

_____

Three moral lessons

_____

_____

_____

_____

| *Three Pharisees with Caesar's Coin, from the Redemption Triptych (oil on canvas),*
Weyden, Rogier van der (1399-1464) / Prado, Madrid, Spain / Bridgeman Images

Catechism Connections

These readings from the Catechism of the Catholic Church (CCC) will deepen your understanding of this session's presentations and discussions. The numbers identify the relevant paragraphs in the Catechism.

⚜ Christ's descent into hell: CCC 632–635

⚜ Christ's second coming: CCC 675–679

⚜ The Last Judgment: CCC 1021–1022, 1038–1041

⚜ "Give us this day our daily bread": CCC 2828–2835

⚜ Marriage and divorce: CCC 2382–2386

⚜ Sins of omission: CCC 1853

⚜ Stewardship of material goods: CCC 952

⚜ God and mammon: CCC 2424

Small Group Discussion

DIGGING DEEPER

1. Why did the Old Covenant allow men to divorce their wives? Why does Jesus abrogate this law? (See CCC 2382–2386; Dt 24:1–4; Lk 16:18; Mk 10:2–12.)

    _____

    _____

    _____

    _____

Wedding rings and rosary,
© Vaclav Mach, Shutterstock

2. In the discussion of the coming of the Kingdom, Jesus refers to the "Son of Man." Who is the "Son of Man"? Where else (other than in the Gospels) can this title be found in the Bible? (See Nm 23:19; Jb 25:6; Ps 8:4; Dn 7:1–28; Lk 5:24; 6:5; 9:22, 26; CCC 1038–1041.)

_____

_____

_____

_____

3. In the story of the rich man and Lazarus, is the rich man maliciously evil? Why does he end in torment? What does this tell us about sins of omission? (See CCC 2828–2835.)

_____

_____

_____

_____

4. In the story of the rich man and Lazarus, the rich man asks Abraham to send someone from the dead to go and warn his five brothers about "this place of torment" (16:28). Abraham says that even if someone rises from the dead to warn them, they will not believe. Who is the person who will rise from the dead that Abraham is talking about?

_____

_____

_____

_____

5. Does Jesus heal the ten lepers immediately? Why is it significant that the one who comes back to thank Jesus is a Samaritan?

_____

_____

_____

_____

LIFE APPLICATION

1. Are we attentive to the needs and concerns of those around us?

    _____

    _____

    _____

    _____

2. Do we stop the activities of our day in order to give time and attention to those in great need?

    _____

    _____

    _____

    _____

3. Are we receptive when others recognize our needs and try to help us?

    _____

    _____

    _____

    _____

Voices of the Saints

I ask you and I beseech you and, falling at your feet, I beg you: As long as we enjoy the brief respite of life, let us repent, let us be converted, let us become better, so that we will not have to lament uselessly like that rich man when we die, and tears can do us no good. For even if you have a father or a son or a friend or anyone else who might have influence with God, no one will be able to set you free, for your own deeds condemn you.

—*St. John Chyrsostom, Homily on 1 Corinthians*

Life Application Video

After breaking from your small group discussion, gather to watch the second video, a pastoral reflection from Fr. Jeffrey Kirby, STD.

How Then Shall We Live?

Silently review the following summary of Fr. Kirby's reflection to prepare for answering the questions in "Living It Out."

Luke tells us the story of Lazarus, the poor man who lies each day at the doorway of the rich man. Every day, the rich man walks over or around Lazarus. He isn't mean or crude to Lazarus; he's simply uninterested and focused on himself.

The rich man spends his life this way, and when he dies, he's not welcomed into paradise. Instead, he finds himself separated from paradise by a great abyss. His requests for relief go unanswered. He has neglected the poor man, and now he suffers an eternal neglect in torment.

The rich man isn't a maliciously evil man. Luke never says that he has mistreated Lazarus in any way. The rich man just doesn't care! He's apathetic to the needs of others.

We are called to see and recognize those around us and to do what we can to help. We're also called to show humility when we are the ones who need help, and others turn to us to offer assistance. This is the life of the Christian believer, and this is the life that we're called to live.

| *A homeless man sitting in the ground with dogs at his feet,* © Jne Valokuvaus, Shutterstock

Living It Out

On your own, spend three to five minutes praying, discerning, and writing down the specific ways that God might be calling you to make changes in your life. Share and discuss afterwards only if you feel comfortable doing so.

Consider this week how God is calling you to …

- ⚜ See more clearly and more deeply the needs of those around you.

- ⚜ Seek to make the lives of others better (even if only by a friendly smile).

- ⚜ Assess how much you truly give to those in need and seek to be more self-giving in time, talent, and treasure to those who need love, help, or attention.

| *Family and friends sitting at a dining table, © monkeybusinessimages, iStock*

Words to Know

Dives: Traditionally, the name given to the rich man in Jesus' story about the poor man named Lazarus (Lk 16:19–31); it comes from the Latin word for "rich."

Hades: A Greek word for the habitation of the souls of the dead, similar to the Hebrew term *Sheol* (see below). Though *hades* has traditionally been translated into English as "hell" (as it is in the Apostles' Creed), it doesn't necessarily refer to the place of torment for the damned, which in the New Testament is usually called *Gehenna* (named after a worm-infested, perpetually burning garbage heap outside the walls of Jerusalem, accursed as a place where child sacrifice was once practiced).

Limbo of the fathers: A place and state of rest where the souls of the righteous under the Old Covenant were detained until he opened heaven to them by his life, death, and resurrection.

Mammon: A term, from Hebrew or Aramaic (the native language of Jesus), which means "riches." In the New Testament, it is associated with the greedy pursuit of wealth. By the medieval period, Mammon came to be commonly depicted as a demon of avarice.

Rapture: An historically recent religious notion, held by some Christian traditions, that before Christ's visible and glorious second coming at the end of the world, he will return secretly and invisibly to snatch away true believers to heaven, leaving unbelievers behind; this supposed event is called "the rapture."

Sheol: A Hebrew word referring to the abode of the souls of the dead, whether righteous or wicked (Ps 49:14; 88:3). Eventually, God revealed to the Jews that the dead would be raised, "some to everlasting life, and some to shame and everlasting contempt" (Dn 12:2).

Vulgate: The ancient Latin translation of the Bible in common use in the Catholic Church until recent times (with revisions); it is largely the work of the fourth-century biblical scholar St. Jerome.

Closing Prayer

It is good to give thanks to you, Lord, to sing praises to your name, O Most High; to declare your merciful love in the morning, and your faithfulness by night. Amen.

—Adapted from Ps 92:1–2

*The Pharisee and the Publican Praying in the Temple,
illustration for 'La Vie de notre Seigneur Jesus-Christ',
published in Tours 1896 (colour litho), Tissot, James
(1836-1902) / Bibliotheque des Arts Decoratifs, Paris,
France / Archives Charmet / Bridgeman Images*

SESSION 14

THE PHARISEE
AND THE
TAX COLLECTOR

*"I tell you, this man went down to his house justified
rather than the other; for every one who exalts himself will be
humbled, but he who humbles himself will be exalted."*

LUKE 18:14

SESSION READING
LUKE 18:1–43

Introduction

Luke's eighteenth chapter begins with a parable that teaches the value of persistence in prayer. That lesson is later illustrated by a blind man who receives his sight because he doggedly seeks out Jesus for healing.

A second parable presents a Pharisee and a tax collector who both go to the Temple to pray. Contrary to the expectations of Jesus' listeners, the tax collector's prayer is acceptable to God, but the Pharisee's prayer is rejected.

Children rarely appear in the Gospel accounts. But when they do, they always have a lesson to teach their elders. Luke tells us how Jesus' disciples try to keep the little ones from bothering him, but he insists that they be allowed to come, and he blesses them. They show us how to enter the kingdom of God.

Christ and the Rich Young Ruler, Heinrich Hofmann [Public domain], via Wikimedia Commons

Our Lord's warnings about attachment to worldly goods continue when a rich ruler approaches him and asks how he can inherit eternal life. The man seems eager to follow God's Law, but when Jesus points out what he must do—give away his wealth to the poor—he shrinks back from the demand.

Yet again Jesus foretells his approaching passion and death. But the disciples understand nothing of what he says; its meaning remains hidden from them.

Prayer to Prepare for Study

Lord, my God, bestow upon me an understanding that knows You, diligence in seeking You, wisdom in finding You, a way of life that is pleasing to You, perseverance that waits trustfully for You, and confidence that I shall embrace You at the last. Amen.

—Prayer of St. Thomas Aquinas before study

Study Notes

These notes provide insights to help you understand and reflect upon the biblical text.

❧ Only Luke recounts the Lord's parable of the persistent widow (18:1–8). In the story, a widow continually presses an unrighteous judge until he gives a just verdict in her favor. The judge eventually gives in, not because of justice, but because he wants the widow to leave him alone (18:5).

❧ Unjust judges are a familiar reality to Jesus' listeners. Many public officials of the time regularly accept bribes or charge fees for a favored verdict or service. This tendency to corruption is found as well among the infamous tax collectors, who overtax their own people and serve the Roman occupying power.

❧ Everyday disputes among the Jews of the day are taken before the elders, not the public courts. If a case goes to arbitration, three judges always serve: one selected by the plaintiff, one by the defendant, and one appointed independently. So this particular judge must be one of the paid magistrates appointed by Herod or by the Romans. Such judges are notorious for their corruption; only money or influence sways them. Among the people, they have the well-earned nickname "robber judges."

❧ To make matters worse, the widows and orphans of Jesus' day are an extremely vulnerable class. In the patriarchal society of the ancient world, widows and orphans have no immediate family protection or network of assistance. Often they must rely on charity or even begging for survival. The widow in the Lord's story has no defense against the judge, and yet she is persistent in her pleas.

❧ Commenting on the parable, Jesus calls on his followers to stay the course in prayer and to trust in God's goodness. If even an unjust human judge will respond to persistent petition, how much more will a loving Father in heaven do so? This teaching of the Lord is consistent with Luke's focus on prayer as essential to the disciple.

| *The Unjust Judge (engraving), English School, (19th century) / Private Collection / © Look and Learn / Bridgeman Images*

The Christian Martyr's Last Prayer, 1863-83 (oil on canvas), Gerome, Jean Leon (1824-1904) / © Walters Art Museum, Baltimore, USA / Bridgeman Images

✣ At the same time, Jesus draws out an apocalyptic dimension of the parable. The time will come when his followers are violently persecuted, and they will cry out for heaven's intervention. "Will not God vindicate his elect, who cry to him day and night? Will he delay long over them? I tell you, he will vindicate them speedily" (18:7–8). This image of persecuted believers crying out for justice—a justice that will come fully only when Christ returns to judge the world—echoes the cry of the martyrs in the Book of Revelation: "They cried out with a loud voice, 'O Sovereign Lord, holy and true, how long before thou wilt judge and avenge our blood on those who dwell upon the earth?'" (Rv 6:10).

✣ The implicit apocalyptic theme becomes explicit when Jesus says of this divine vindication, "Nevertheless, when the Son of man comes, will he find faith on the earth?" (18:8). Citing this passage in Luke's Gospel, the Catechism notes: "Before Christ's second coming the Church must pass through a final trial that will shake the faith of many believers" (CCC 675). As we move through history toward its inevitable end, we should find Our Lord's question both sobering and motivating.

✣ Next comes the endearing parable of the Pharisee and the tax collector in the Temple, which only Luke records (18:9–14). Already in his Gospel we have seen the self-righteousness of the Pharisees and the sinfulness of the tax collectors. The parallel between the two groups presents a striking contrast of character, as does their different approaches to God and his mercy.

* In the story, the Pharisee praises himself before God; in fact, he is so self-absorbed that Jesus says he prays "with himself," not to God (18:11). Not only does he indulge in smug self-righteousness, listing his religious practices in a pretense of piety (18:12); he speaks with contempt of "other men," and he singles out the nearby tax collector for his scorn (18:11).

* The Pharisee thinks he sees himself and others clearly. But in truth, he is willfully blind to his own sins, so he doesn't ask for God's mercy, and he fails to receive it. We can apply to him what Jesus says to the Pharisees on another occasion: "If you were blind, you would have no guilt; but now that you say, 'We see,' your guilt remains" (Jn 9:41).

* Meanwhile, the tax collector stands off in the distance, beats his breast, and asks God for mercy. The Lord tells us that the tax collector goes home justified, not the Pharisee. Jesus explains that those who exalt themselves will be humbled, but those who humble themselves will be exalted (18:14). The Pharisee exalts himself in his arrogant boasting, but the tax collector humbles himself by acknowledging his need for mercy.

* St. Augustine says of the Pharisee, "His fault was not that he gave God thanks, but that he asked for nothing further. Those who need nothing have no need to say, 'Forgive us our trespasses.'" Luke includes this parable in his Gospel because it highlights his emphasis on humility, mercy, and the universal invitation of salvation to all people, including the tax collector.

* Following the Lord's exhortation to humility, parents are bringing "even infants to him that he might touch them" (18:15). The word "even" suggests that people are bringing him not only the sick and demon-possessed, as we have seen before, but also even the babies who are well.

* Why do they want Jesus to touch the little ones? Matthew's Gospel adds the detail that the parents come hoping "that he might lay his hands on them and pray" (Mt 19:13). The parents are asking Jesus to pray a blessing on their children; in fact, it's a custom of the day to have rabbis bless children on their first birthday. The parents do well to seek that favor from Jesus: If only a touch from him can heal the woman with the flow of blood (Lk 8:43–48), how much benefit might the babies receive (continuing good health and more) from having him lay hands on them to impart his blessing!

* Though the disciples seek to turn the children away, we can't necessarily blame them for it; they are probably seeking to protect their Master from too many demands at a time when he is weary and deeply burdened by the prospect of his fast-approaching passion and death (18:15). When Jesus instructs the disciples to let the children come, he doesn't rebuke them for arrogance, selfishness, or hardness of heart; he simply reminds them that "to such belongs the kingdom of God" (18:16).

* St. Cyril of Alexandria confirms this insight: "The blessed disciples rebuke the parents for doing this, not because they envied the babies; rather, they were paying Jesus due respect as their teacher, and preventing him from getting unnecessarily tired" (*Commentary on Luke*, Homily 121).

✤ So Jesus receives the children and praises them as a model of humility, docility, and innocence (18:16–17). To enter the Kingdom, he declares, we must in certain respects be childlike. St. Ambrose explains, "So why does Jesus say that children are fit for the kingdom of heaven? Perhaps because they are usually without malice. They aren't deceitful; they don't dare to get revenge; they have no experience of lust; they don't covet; they aren't ambitious. Even so, the virtue of all these qualities doesn't lie in ignorance of evil, but rather in its rejection; it doesn't consist in being unable to sin, but rather in not consenting to sin. So the Lord isn't referring to childhood as such, but to the innocence that children have in their simplicity" (*Expositio Evangelii sec. Lucam*).

✤ At another level, it's critical to note in our world today the Lord's command: "Let the children come to me" (18:16). As abortion and contraception lead humanity into viewing children as a burden or a commodity, the Lord calls for the believer to break from such a fallen mindset and instead generously to accept and welcome children.

✤ Next, a rich ruler approaches Jesus with the question, "Good Teacher, what shall I do to inherit eternal life?" (18:18). It is quite rare for a rabbi of the day to be addressed as "Good Teacher." Jesus offers a slight rebuke, saying, "Why do you call me good? No one is good but God alone" (18:19).

✤ Our Lord's reply seems to be probing the inquirer's motivation in approaching him. On the one hand, the ruler may be trying to flatter him, and if so, Jesus' question undermines that attempt. But if he is sincere, does he see something in Jesus that he doesn't see in other rabbis? And if, as Jesus says, God alone is good, is the ruler getting a glimpse of God himself when he sees such goodness in Jesus?

✤ In this response, then, Jesus is revealing his divinity. The man has spoken truly: Jesus is good, and Jesus is God. None of the Lord's initial hearers are ready to understand such a reality; they simply cannot fathom yet that God has become a Man. But today we can truly understand that Jesus is the God-Man, fully human and fully divine. This understanding of his divine nature should lead us into a sincere praise of his goodness.

✤ The ruler's question must not be overlooked. What more powerful question could someone ask God: "What shall I do to inherit eternal life?" (18:18). This question represents both an initial inquiry of faith and a source of constant conversion and renewal within the believer. It's a question we should regularly ask of God.

✤ In response to the ruler's question, Jesus lists five of the great commandments that have to do with love for neighbor: You shall not commit adultery, or steal, or kill, or bear false witness. Honor your father and mother (18:20). The Lord's answer to the ruler indicates the permanence of the moral law.

✤ The ceremonial laws of the Old Testament are fulfilled in Jesus Christ (sacrifices, dietary restrictions, and the like); such laws are no longer binding on God's people. But the moral law—including the five commandments that Jesus notes—still remains, since it corresponds to our unchanging human nature and is given for our well-being. The moral law is still in effect for the Christian disciple, and it can now be lived in greater depth through the grace given to us in Jesus Christ.

✤ Luke's mentor, the Apostle Paul, tells us that the moral law is a demanding tutor (or "custodian") that teaches us how to love God, ourselves, our neighbor, and the world around us (Gal 3:24). As we cooperate with the moral law, grace gives us freedom, and virtue can flourish within us. In this process, we grow in holiness. The help of the moral law is necessary for us to begin living the life of grace and following the path to holiness. This is the insight that Jesus offers the rich ruler.

✤ "All these [commandments] I have observed from my youth," the ruler replies (18:21). He sounds confident of his own righteousness; he believes that he knows himself well. And if he is speaking truly, he is a rare man indeed; who has never, for example, borne false witness—who has never lied?

✤ In any case, Jesus now calls the ruler to a more perfect life of virtue. Our Lord has already discerned the man's heart. So he doesn't ask him about the last two commandments, which have to do with coveting—and by extension, with greed, materialism, attachment to possessions. Instead, Our Lord gives the ruler a directive that will immediately reveal the state of his soul in that regard: "One thing you still lack. Sell all that you have and distribute to the poor, and you will have treasure in heaven; and come, follow me" (18:22).

✤ The Lord knows that this wealthy man is too attached to his possessions; he has failed to follow the commandment against coveting. So Jesus has offered a remedy, though it will be a bitter medicine to swallow (18:22). The ruler grieves to hear Jesus' words; his wealth is considerable (18:23).

| *Saint Paul the Apostle (oil on canvas), Pino, Marco (c. 1520-79) / Galleria Borghese, Rome, Italy / Bridgeman Images*

✤ In truth, the Lord is summoning him to let go of whatever has a hold on him, so he can focus his attention on God. Jesus is calling him to freedom, true virtue, and holiness. But apparently the man's money has too firm a grip on his heart. In recounting this incident, Matthew's Gospel adds the detail that "when the young man heard this he went away sorrowful" (Mt 19:22). His sad response presses us to ask ourselves: In our own life of discipleship, is there something that keeps us away from the call to follow the Lord more perfectly?

✤ Those in the Church who aspire to the consecrated life (monks, nuns, friars, sisters, consecrated men and women, hermits) see in this passage a biblical basis for their unique call to live in poverty. Poverty is one of the three "evangelical counsels" (along with obedience and chastity) that mark the vocation of consecrated persons.

✣ While only some within the Church are called to live this summons radically, all of us are called to evaluate our discipleship, remove whatever gets in the way of following the Lord, and seek to live the evangelical counsels spiritually, according to our state in life (as married couples, single people, diocesan priests, and so on).

✣ In light of the ruler's dismay, Jesus laments the difficulty of entering the Kingdom for those who have riches (18:24–25). Here appears the famous declaration about a camel going through the eye of a needle, whose meaning has been long debated.

✣ St. Cyril of Alexandria insists that among mariners, thicker cables on ships were called "camels." Jesus is speaking, he says, of trying to thread a needle with a thick cable.

✣ One ancient text (wrongly attributed to St. John Chrysostom) features a gloss offering an interpretation that has today become popular: "At Jerusalem there was a certain gate, called 'the needle's eye,' through which a camel could pass only on its bended knees, after its burden had been taken off. Similarly, the rich man cannot pass along the narrow way that leads to life, until he has put off the burden of sin, and of riches—that is, by ceasing to love them" (*Pseudo-Chrysostom*).

View of Damascus Gate with Camel Drivers, Jerusalem, c.1844 (oil on board), Caffi, Ippolito (1809-66) / Museo d'Arte Moderna di Ca' Pesaro, Venice, Italy / © Mondadori Electa / Bridgeman Images

✤ Even the obvious meaning makes sense if we consider this statement another example of hyperbole in Our Lord's teaching. The rabbis often speak in a similar way about getting an elephant through the eye of a needle as something impossible. Jesus' listeners certainly interpret his words to mean that such an outcome is an impossibility, so he must reassure them, "What is impossible with men is possible with God" (18:27). Even the rich may find eternal life.

✤ When the Apostle Peter points out poignantly that he and the others have left everything to follow the Lord, Jesus reassures him that they will be repaid for their sacrifice many times over, both in this life and the next (18:30). The disciples will soon need such consolation as they witness the coming events in Jerusalem. Once again, Luke's Gospel focuses on the demands of discipleship.

✤ Yet once more, the Lord now foretells plainly his passion, death, and resurrection. He reminds his Apostles that he is on his way to Jerusalem. The ministry of Jesus at this time must all be read within the immediate scope of this journey to Jerusalem. The Lord tells the Apostles that everything the prophets wrote about the Son of Man will be accomplished (18:31).

✤ The reference to the prophets is highly significant. The prophets frequently spoke about the coming of the promised Savior and the suffering of the just man—for example, see the prophet Isaiah's famous "Songs of the Suffering Servant" (Is 42:1–9; 49:1–13; 50:4–11; 52:13—53:12). Later, Jesus explains these teachings of the prophets to the two disciples on the way to Emmaus (24:25–27).

✤ At various times in his public ministry, Jesus refers to himself as the "Son of man" (18:31). The title is taken from the apocalyptic literature of the Old Testament, especially from the Books of Daniel (Dn 7:13–14; 8:17) and Ezekiel (where the title is used more than ninety times in multiple ways). Sometimes the phrase means simply "human being," but at other times, it describes a heavenly figure who has a human appearance, even though the figure seems to be much more than a mere mortal.

✤ Apocalyptic literature references the end times by merging it with the author's contemporary situation. This genre of literature is difficult to understand and requires explanation. Because the title "Son of Man" comes from this source, it's a mysterious one, and its full meaning is highly debated among biblical scholars. It appears that the Lord uses "Son of Man" both to refer to his own humanity and to identity himself with the images described in Daniel and Ezekiel. Most of these images deal with heavenly realities and can be seen as portrayals of the Lord's divinity.

✤ As before, the Apostles don't understand what the Lord is saying. This is not a reflection of obstinacy or a weak intelligence, but of the completely unexpected work of redemption. No one could have imagined that the long-awaited Savior would be God himself, that he would suffer a torturous passion and death, and that he would destroy sin and death by rising on the third day. Only after the events of the paschal mystery and the sending of the Holy Spirit will the Apostles begin to understand what Jesus has done and is seeking to do in the life of the Church (Jn 14:26; Lk 24:31–32).

✦ After the Lord's third foretelling of his passion, death, and resurrection, he passes Jericho (18:35), the ancient city whose walls were destroyed by God through the supplications and songs of the early Israelites (Jo 6:1–21). As Jesus passes Jericho, a blind man calls to him for healing, addressing him with the messianic title "Son of David" (18:38–39). The Lord asks him what he wants and then heals the man (18:41–43). As the ancient city had its walls, so the blind man had "walls" blocking his sight, and the Lord removes them just as the ancient walls were removed.

Jesus Opens the Eyes of a Man Born Blind, 1311 (tempera on panel), Duccio di Buoninsegna, (c.1278-1318) / National Gallery, London, UK / Bridgeman Images

✦ Several lessons can be gleaned from this incident. First, the blind man's determination in asking for the Lord's help, even when others try to silence him, illustrates the need for persistence in prayer that Jesus taught about in the earlier parable of the widow and the unrighteous judge (18:1–8).

✦ Second, the blind man takes immediate advantage of an opportunity to receive God's grace when it presents itself. As soon as the others in the crowd tell him that "Jesus of Nazareth is passing by," he begins shouting to get the Lord's attention (18:37–38). We too must not fail to let such grace-filled moments pass us by.

✦ Finally, each one of us has blind spots in our spiritual lives. Like the man in Jericho, we must seek healing and the removal of the "walls" before our eyes and in our hearts so that we can draw closer to the Lord.

To prepare for small group discussion, turn ahead now to this session's "Digging Deeper" and "Life Application" sections.

Rome to Home

The question which the rich young man puts to Jesus of Nazareth is one which rises from the depths of his heart. It is an essential and unavoidable question for the life of every man, for it is about the moral good which must be done, and about eternal life. . . . People today need to turn to Christ once again in order to receive from him the answer to their questions about what is good and what is evil. . . . If we therefore wish to go to the heart of the Gospel's moral teaching and grasp its profound and unchanging content, we must carefully inquire into the meaning of the question asked by the rich young man in the Gospel and, even more, the meaning of Jesus' reply, allowing ourselves to be guided by him. Jesus, as a patient and sensitive teacher, answers the young man by taking him, as it were, by the hand, and leading him step by step to the full truth.

—*St. John Paul II, Veritatis Splendor, 8*

Opening Prayer

Let the words of my mouth and the meditation of my heart be acceptable in your sight, O LORD, my rock and my redeemer!

—Psalm 19:14

Teaching Video

This first video, hosted by Dr. Paul Thigpen, focuses on certain themes and passages from the Gospel of Luke. Here are some key highlights of his presentation, with room to take notes as you view the video to assist you in the group discussion.

Self-knowledge is essential for knowing God

_____

_____

_____

_____

The problem of inflated self-confidence

_____

_____

_____

_____

The Pharisee

_____

_____

_____

_____

The tax collector

The Pharisee's "prayer"

The tax collector's prayer

| *The Pharisee and the Publican, Dore, Gustave (1832-83) / Private Collection / Photo © Liszt Collection / Bridgeman Images*

The crowd's response

Catechism Connections

These readings from the Catechism of the Catholic Church (CCC) will deepen your understanding of this session's presentations and discussions. The numbers identify the relevant paragraphs in the Catechism.

* The three parables about prayer: CCC 2613

* Praying with humility: CCC 2559

* Evangelical counsels: CCC 915–916, 1973–1974

* The rich ruler: CCC 2052–2055

* Prayer: CCC 2613, 2616, 2631

* "And forgive us our trespasses": CCC 2839

Small Group Discussion

DIGGING DEEPER

1. By the end of chapter 18, Luke has given us three important parables on prayer: the importunate friend knocking on his neighbor's door (11:5–13), the persistent widow (18:1–8), and the Pharisee and the tax collector (18:9–14). What important principles of prayer are illustrated by each of these stories? (See CCC 2613.)

_____

_____

_____

View of the cloister courtyard of famous Cistercian Abbey of Fontenay, Burgundy, France, © canadastock, Shutterstock

2. How does the blind man sitting by the side of the road outside Jericho put into practice the principles of prayer discussed in the answer to Question 1?

_____

_____

_____

_____

3. Why is the prayer of the tax collector heard by God, while the prayer of the Pharisee is not? How do Jesus' words about becoming like children support the point made in this parable about humility?

_____

_____

_____

_____

4. The blind man at Jericho calls out to Jesus, calling him "Son of David." What is the significance of this title? (See 2 Sm 7:12–16.) What does he realize about Jesus' identity?

_____

_____

_____

_____

5. In the story of the rich ruler, Luke is once again highlighting the need to give up everything to follow Jesus. Why is the rich ruler unable to leave everything behind to follow Jesus? How does this story highlight the importance of the evangelical counsels (poverty, chastity, and obedience) for all followers of Jesus?

_____

_____

_____

_____

LIFE APPLICATION

1. Have we ever found ourselves judging others or seeking to alienate people we don't like or who need extra compassion and love?

_____

_____

_____

_____

2. Have we ever found ourselves in situations when we were self-righteous and thought we were better than others?

_____

_____

_____

_____

3. What have been the spiritual fruits of our lives by living a life of repentance and humility?

_____

_____

_____

_____

Voices of the Saints

Our Lord adds this to show, that when faith fails, prayer dies. In order to pray then, we must have faith, and so that our faith doesn't fail, we must pray. Faith pours forth prayer, and the pouring forth of the heart in prayer gives steadfastness to faith.

—*St. Augustine, Catena Aurea*

Life Application Video

After breaking from your small group discussion, gather to watch the second video, a pastoral reflection from Fr. Jeffrey Kirby, STD.

How Then Shall We Live?

Silently review the following summary of Fr. Kirby's reflection to prepare for answering the questions in "Living It Out."

Let's look at the Lord's parable about the Pharisee and the tax collector. The Pharisee thinks he's got everything under control. He thinks he's so amazing. In fact, if you want to know how amazing he is, well, just ask him!

But what about the guy in the back? Yes, that guy, the one beating his chest and not looking up. What about him? The tax collector, the public sinner. He knows he's a sinner. He knows he needs God. And just look at that humility and sincere repentance. There's something very attractive and encouraging about this tax collector.

Portrait of the Artist's Sister in the Garb of a Nun, detail of her prayer book (oil on canvas) (detail of 79749), Anguissola, Sofonisba (c.1532-1625) / Southampton City Art Gallery, Hampshire, UK / Bridgeman Images

So we have these two figures to consider: the Pharisee and the tax collector. Let's be honest with ourselves here: Which of these two figures are we most like right now? Are we with the Pharisee up front? Or are we in the back with the tax collector?

We can examine how we approach the sin in our own lives as a help in discerning an answer to this question. We can also consider how we approach the sins of those around us as a help in deciphering an answer. Do we show humility and compassion? Do we realize that we need the Lord Jesus and his abundant mercy?

I said "need"—that's important. Do we know that we need, really need, the Lord Jesus—need him as our bodies need air and water? We have to realize that we need Jesus. The tax collector understands this need.

We cannot remove our sins and we cannot live an abundant life by our own powers. We have to ask for help! Will we? The tax collector does, and he goes home justified. We're invited to do the same. Will we go home justified?

Living It Out

On your own, spend three to five minutes praying, discerning, and writing down the specific ways that God might be calling you to make changes in your life. Share and discuss afterwards only if you feel comfortable doing so.

Consider this week how God is calling you to …

* Acknowledge how much you need the Lord Jesus.

* Examine your conscience for any self-righteousness or Pharisaic attitudes in your heart.

* Repent of your sins and seek the mercy of those around you (family members, coworkers, neighbors, clergy, fellow parishioners).

Words to Know

Apocalyptic: From the word "Apocalypse" (literally, the "uncovering"), the Greek name of the last book of the Bible (also called in English "Revelation"). Because this book is traditionally interpreted as revealing events to unfold at the end of the world, things related to that subject have come to be called "apocalyptic."

Elect: "The elect" or "God's elect" refers to those whom God has "elected" or chosen.

Evangelical counsels: Voluntary poverty, chastity, and obedience. Their observance in a vowed form is not necessary for salvation; they are a rule of perfection, instruments for seeking it, to be voluntarily taken up by those who are called to do so.

Gloss: A brief explanation written in the margin or between the lines of a text, usually referring to a difficult or obscure word or passage.

Son of Man: A title found in the Old Testament Books of Daniel and Ezekiel whose full meaning is highly debated among biblical scholars. Sometimes the phrase means simply "human being," but at other times, it describes a heavenly figure who has a human appearance, even though the figure is obviously much more than a mere mortal. Jesus appears to use "Son of Man" both to refer to his own humanity and to identify himself with the Old Testament images, which can be seen as portrayals of his divinity.

Closing Prayer

Lord Jesus Christ, Son of God, have mercy on me, a sinner.

—Traditional Eastern prayer known as the "Jesus Prayer"

*Entry of Christ into Jerusalem, by Charles Le Brun (1619-1690), oil on canvas /
De Agostini Picture Library / G. Dagli Orti / Bridgeman Images*

SESSION 15

ZACCHAEUS

"For the Son of man came to seek and to save the lost."

LUKE 19:10

SESSION READING

LUKE 19:1—20:47

Introduction

Jesus is fast approaching the Holy City, where the Cross awaits him. Luke tells us that his last stop is Jericho, about eighteen miles from Jerusalem. In this wealthy city, he dines with the chief tax collector, making more enemies—yet saving one more soul.

Our Lord's mission of mercy is coming to its culmination. Soon, he will enter Jerusalem on a humble donkey, acclaimed by the jubilant crowds as the Messiah-King. He will preach his last public sermons and teach his last parables. He will work his last miracles of healing and share his heart more deeply than ever with his closest friends, the Apostles.

At the same time, Jesus' conflict with the scribes, Pharisees, and Sadducees will also find its culmination. He will forcefully, fiercely chide and challenge them, even denounce them publicly as hypocrites who deserve God's condemnation. He will engage the spies sent by the high priests to trap him in his words. He will even overturn the tables of the moneychangers in the Temple.

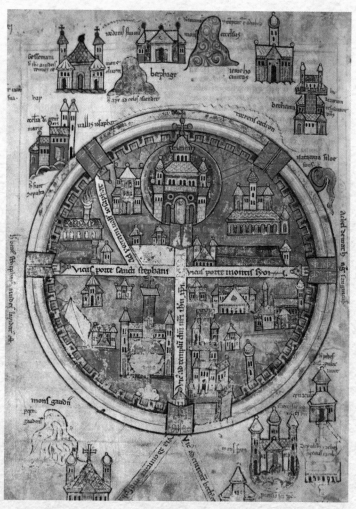

Map of Jerusalem, with the cities of Gethsemane, Jericho, Bethany, and Hebron, miniature from Robert the Monk's History of the first Crusade (Historia Hierosolymitana), by Robert le Moine, manuscript C 691, folio 39, verso, France, 13th century / De Agostini Picture Library / Bridgeman Images

Yet in these pages we see much more than just the Lord's righteous anger. In a deeply touching scene, Luke tells us how Jesus weeps openly over Jerusalem as he prophesies its coming destruction.

Prayer to Prepare for Study

Lord, my God, bestow upon me an understanding that knows You, diligence in seeking You, wisdom in finding You, a way of life that is pleasing to You, perseverance that waits trustfully for You, and confidence that I shall embrace You at the last. Amen.

—Prayer of St. Thomas Aquinas before study

Study Notes

These notes provide insights to help you understand and reflect upon the biblical text.

✤ Luke's emphasis on the universality of salvation led him to include the story of Zacchaeus in his Gospel, which no other Gospel reports (19:1–10). It stresses the openness of Jesus Christ to all.

✤ Jesus encounters Zacchaeus in Jericho, his last stop before Jerusalem (19:1). Again, the destruction of the ancient walls of this city serves as a symbol of removing barriers to our encounter with God. In addition, we should note that Jericho is a wealthy city and a center of Roman taxation. It's no surprise, then, that Jesus encounters here yet another tax collector.

✤ In fact, Zacchaeus is not only a tax collector; he's a *chief* tax collector (19:2). He evidently has made a long and profitable career out of exploiting his neighbors, so his sins are even more despicable than those of other tax collectors. This depth of depravity seems implied by the mention that he was "rich" (19:2).

✤ Zacchaeus has heard of Jesus and desires to see him. He's a short man, so he has trouble seeing over the heads of the crowd, and the crowd may even be hostile to him (19:3). But Zacchaeus is determined to see Jesus. So he lays aside his pride and does something that seems undignified for such a man: He runs ahead of the crowd and climbs up a sycamore fig tree, as a boy might do (19:4).

✤ Jesus sees Zacchaeus and asks him to come down from the tree so he can dine in his home (19:5). The crowd grumbles, since tax collectors are viewed as sell-outs to their people and public sinners (19:7). But Jesus goes to Zacchaeus' house anyway, and this act of mercy and kindness leads the chief tax collector to convert and make amends to those he has cheated (19:8). Zacchaeus makes the promise to give half of his possessions to the poor, and those he has defrauded will receive back from him four times as much as he took from them.

✤ Beyond this liberal act of almsgiving to the poor, Zacchaeus is in fact making a generous restitution that goes far beyond what is required by the Law of Moses. According to

Jesus summoning Zacchaeus the publican to entertain him at his house, Hole, William Brassey (1846-1917) / Private Collection / © Look and Learn / Bridgeman Images

that Law, if a voluntary confession of theft is made, and a voluntary restitution is offered, only the value of the original stolen goods is to be repaid, plus one fifth more (Lv 6:1–5; Nu 5:5–7). So the tax collector's gracious offer demonstrates that his repentance is sincere.

✤ Jesus praises the man's repentance and declares, "Today salvation has come to this house, since he also is a son of Abraham" (19:9). Our Lord is saying to those who have despised and ostracized Zacchaeus, "You have rejected him as a traitor. But in truth, he is still an heir, along with you, of God's promises to Abraham. You must receive him back into your hearts as your brother." The story is consistent with Luke's stress on repentance, conversion, and reconciliation, especially for the most wayward or forgotten.

✤ Jesus concludes by reminding the crowd, "For the Son of man came to seek and to save the lost" (19:10). His actions are vividly illustrating the parable of the lost sheep (15:4–7).

✤ Neither Luke's Gospel nor his Book of Acts has any more to say about Zacchaeus. But the second-century Christian writer Clement of Alexandria claims that the Apostles later surnamed him Matthias, and he was the same Matthias who was chosen by lot to take the place of Judas as an Apostle. A fourth-century text called the *Apostolic Constitutions* suggests that he went on to become the first bishop of the city of Caesaria.

✤ After this encounter with Zacchaeus, the Lord tells the crowd the parable of the ten pounds (19:11–27) because he is "near to Jerusalem," and his disciples continue to assume "that the kingdom of God [will] appear immediately" (19:11). These words give us a clue that the parable is warning them that their messianic expectations are about to be dashed. In Luke's account, the parable is the last reported of the Lord's public teachings before he enters Jerusalem and begins the immediate preparation for his passion and death.

| *The Lost Sheep, 1864 (oil on canvas), Webbe or Webb, William J. (1831-1904) / Astley Cheetham Art Gallery, Stalybridge, Greater Manchester / Bridgeman Images*

✤ In the parable, a nobleman leaves for a faraway country to receive kingly power. He entrusts one pound to each of ten servants (19:12). The word translated here as "pound" is *mina,* the name of a silver coin worth about three months' wages for an agricultural laborer.

✤ When the nobleman returns, he demands an accounting. One servant has turned the one pound he received into ten more by astute trading; another has turned it into five; while a third has only hidden it away out of fear (19:15–21). The king rewards the first two, but punishes the third (19:22–24). The story is a reminder to use well all that we have received because an accounting will be expected. This parable is told as the Lord prepares to enter Jerusalem, where he himself will give an accounting to the Father.

| *The Parable of the Talents (engraving), English School, (19th century) / Private Collection / © Look and Learn / Bridgeman Images*

✤ Some elements of this particular story that seem inessential to the parable may actually have been included by Jesus because they allude to historical events that would be familiar to his listeners. In fact, Matthew recounts another version of this parable without these details (Mt 25:14–30). The story still makes perfect sense without any reference to a nobleman who travels to a far country to receive kingly power, whose citizens send a delegation rejecting his kingship, who is made a ruler anyway, and who slays his opponents (19:12, 14, 15, 27).

✤ These details, however, correspond to an historical episode that Jesus' audience would know about. Herod the Great died in 4 B.C., leaving his kingdom to three sons, who were to divide it among themselves. This arrangement had to be approved by the Romans. So one of the sons, Archelaus, traveled to Rome to persuade the Emperor Augustus to permit him to receive his inheritance. But the Jews sent a delegation of fifty men to Rome to tell the Emperor that they didn't want Archelaus to rule over them. As it turned out, Augustus approved his rule (though without the actual title of king). We should also note that Archelaus reportedly massacred three thousand people who had gathered at the Temple to oppose him. All these parallels between history and parable are striking. Perhaps Jesus uses them to make the story more memorable for his listeners.

✤ At last Jesus is now "going up to Jerusalem" (19:28). For the Jewish people, a journey to Jerusalem is always a journey *up* (Mt 20:18; Jn 5:1; 7:8). This may be in part because the city is perched on Mount Zion at about 2,500 feet above sea level. But in addition, the Temple is the religious center of the nation, so "going up to Jerusalem" also means ascending to the holy place where worship and sacrifices to God are offered. In fact, Psalms 120 through 134 have been known since ancient times as "Psalms of Ascent," probably because they were sung by pilgrims as they climbed their way up to Jerusalem and the Temple. Luke presents Our Lord's entire public ministry as a continuous ascent to Jerusalem. There, his life reaches its pinnacle as he is lifted high on the Cross to die for the world's salvation.

⚜ When the words of the prophets of ancient Israel fell on deaf ears, God's messengers often resorted to presenting a dramatic gesture that would grab the attention of the people. At various times, for example, divine judgment on Jerusalem had been portrayed at God's command in varying scenes of prophecy that were acted out.

⚜ Jeremiah used a rotten waistcloth to show the people the rottenness of their national life, then thongs and a yoke to show that the people would be taken captive (Jer 13:1–11; 27:1–11). Ezekiel acted out a siege with a model of Jerusalem made of a brick to warn the people of impending judgment. Then he shaved his head and beard and used the hair to act out a second drama of judgment (Ez 4:1–3; 5:1–4). Isaiah even walked through the city barefoot and naked (Is 20:1–6) to portray the coming humiliation of his people by their enemies!

⚜ Our Lord's triumphant entrance into the Holy City of Jerusalem to begin his passion and death (19:28–40) can be seen as a similar prophetic gesture. His actions that day speak loudly of his true identity and mission as the promised Messiah-King.

| *The Entry of Christ into Jerusalem* (oil on canvas), Leullier, Louis Felix (1811-82) / Musee des Beaux-Arts, Arras, France / Bridgeman Images

❧ The arrival in Jerusalem initiates a shift in the Lord's ministry (and in Luke's Gospel). This dramatic scene is commemorated and celebrated by the Church every year in the liturgies for Passion (Palm) Sunday.

❧ For his entrance into the city, the Lord secures a colt of a donkey, riding it in humility (19:33–35). Matthew's Gospel provides the additional detail that he comes with both an adult donkey and a colt, and that in doing so, Jesus fulfills ancient prophecies of Isaiah and Zechariah (Is 62:11; Zech 9:9; Mt 21:1–5). Majestic kings and military commanders enter a city on horses or in horse-drawn chariots in order to show their power. But the Lord enters on a colt without such a display of earthly force. The image of a future king riding on a colt might also stir up the memory of many to recall Solomon, who rode a colt to his anointing as king (1 Kgs 1:33).

❧ As the Lord rides the colt, the disciples throw down their garments. The act is an acknowledgment of royal authority and obedience to it (19:36). Earlier in salvation history, a similar act of submission was given to Jehu when he was named king (2 Kgs 9:13). King Jehu was a great religious reformer (although he was later denounced by the prophet Hosea because of the massive bloodshed of his reforms).

❧ While Luke mentions garments being thrown down, he doesn't mention palm branches. Matthew and Mark note branches without specifying which kind (Mt 21:8; Mk 11:8). John is the only Evangelist to note that these branches are from palm trees (Jn 12:13). This is only one tiny example of how the four Gospels complement one another and provide together a more complete picture than any one of the four offers us by itself.

❧ Palm fronds are an ancient symbol of victory; Jesus is being welcomed as a triumphant king. In time, palms come to be associated with Christian martyrs, who have "fought the good fight" and won it by their sacrifice (2 Tm 4:7; Rv 7:9). Palms are considered "goodly trees," whose fronds are to be used in the celebration of the Feast of Tabernacles (Lv 23:40). They also figure as a prominent decorative motif in the Temple (1 Kgs 6:29; 7:36; 2 Chr 3:5; Ez 40:16; 41:18).

| *Palm leaves © zhu difeng, Shutterstock*

❧ Luke is the only Gospel writer to include the word "king" in the praise offered by the crowd (19:38): "Blessed is *the King* who comes in the name of the Lord!" The others say, "Blessed is *he* …" (Mt 21:9; Mk 11:9; Jn 12:13). No doubt the boisterous crowds aren't speaking in unison; they are shouting out several variations on this phrase. These shouts echo a passage in Psalm 118:26: "Blessed be he who enters in the name of the LORD!" The words "peace in heaven and glory in the highest!" recall the jubilant declaration of the angels when Jesus was born (2:14).

✤ Luke's Gospel is the only one to record that the Pharisees admonish Jesus to rebuke his disciples during the procession (19:39). However, Matthew does report that later, after Jesus throws the moneychangers out of the Temple (see below), the chief priests and scribes are indignant that the children in the Temple are crying out, "Hosanna to the Son of David!" and they challenge him about it (Mt 21:10–16).

✤ In both situations, the Pharisees are offended on religious grounds and fearful on political grounds. A declaration of Jesus' kingship not only challenges their religious authority; it sounds treasonous to the occupying Romans. Throughout his public ministry, Jesus has admonished his followers to remain quiet about his identity. But now he permits a clear declaration of his status. He tells the Pharisees, "I tell you, if these were silent, the very stones would cry out" (19:40).

✤ Note that for Our Lord, this first Passion Sunday procession is an act of heroic courage. He knows the authorities are out to kill him. We might have expected him to slip into the city quietly at night to avoid detection. But instead he comes dramatically, publicly, royally, making one last, great, glorious statement to the world of his true identity: The Messiah, the King, the Savior has arrived!

The Destruction of Jerusalem in 70 AD, engraved by Louis Haghe (1806-85) (litho), Roberts, David (1796-1864) (after) / Private Collection / The Stapleton Collection / Bridgeman Images

✤ As he nears the city, Jesus weeps and cries out his famous lament over Jerusalem, which is contained only in Luke's Gospel (19:41–44), though it echoes an earlier cry of grief over the city that Luke also records (13:34–35). Jesus knows the fate of the Holy City. He weeps as he prophesies its destruction.

❧ This tragedy took place in A.D. 70 when a Roman army under the general Titus (later the emperor) responded to a Jewish uprising by razing the city and destroying the Temple. The devastation was reportedly so thorough that a plow could be drawn across the city. The massive stone Arch of Titus in Rome, which commemorates that victory, depicts the spoils taken from the Temple.

❧ Though Jesus is warning of judgment, he weeps at the prospect of the people's failure to repent and be converted (19:41). This merciful heart is displayed again in his exhortation to his disciples to watch at all times and pray for the strength to escape the judgment and stand before the Judge (found only in 21:34–36).

❧ Upon entering the Holy City, Jesus goes to the Temple and drives out those who are making a profit there (19:45). Two kinds of merchants are the subject of his ire: those who exchange currencies and those who sell animals for sacrifice.

Christ Driving the Money-Changers from the Temple (panel), Garofalo, Benvenuto Tisi da (1481-1559) / © Scottish National Gallery, Edinburgh / Bridgeman Images

❧ In Jesus' day, each adult Jewish male must pay an annual Temple tax. Many other types of coins are in circulation, but the people are not permitted to pay the Temple tax with pagan Roman and Greek coins. So moneychangers are needed to provide acceptable local coins in place of Greek, Roman, Egyptian, or Syrian currency, but they do this for an excessively high price.

❧ Those who are selling sacrificial animals in the Temple often sell them at inflated prices, especially during the Passover season, when demand is high. Animals can be bought elsewhere, but the Temple has inspectors to make sure that the sacrifice is without blemish. So the safer strategy is to buy the animals at the booths set up in the Temple. In Jesus' time these are known as the Booths of Annas and are the property of the high priest's family, who receive a commission from their income.

❧ Citing as justification the words of the prophets Isaiah (Is 56:7) and Jeremiah (Jer 7:11), Jesus manifests a just anger toward those who offend God's glory and turn the Temple into "a den of robbers" (19:46). His concern is both to reestablish the reverence due to his Father's house and to stop the profiteers from exploiting the people, many of whom are poor. This expression of righteous anger by the Lord should not surprise us. Jesus has often spoken of divine anger, just as the Old Testament prophets did many times before him.

⚜ The Temple in Jerusalem is the center of Jewish national life and worship. In Jesus' day it's the second temple to stand on that sight, built after the return from the Babylonian exile and renovated by King Herod the Great. It's considered a special dwelling place of God and is protected by ceremonial law and local custom. For Jesus to enter the Temple and cleanse it of corruption is thus a bold move. It demonstrates that as the Son of God, he has the authority to enter his Father's house (2:49) and take care of his business. The act also has severe repercussions, since many of the priests and leaders of the people benefit financially from the commerce in the Temple.

⚜ There are times in life, especially when sacred things are being profaned, that the use of a just and tempered anger is appropriate and even virtuous. But we must not confuse this kind of anger with unrighteous anger—the kind that is wrongly expressed, undeserved, uncontrolled, or out of proportion to the offense.

⚜ In Luke chapter 20, we find Jesus teaching in the Temple after his triumphal entrance into the city (20:1). This chapter could rightly be called "the great trial," since the passage is filled with challenges to Jesus' authority. Some have called it "the day of questions," since the challenges are presented through questions.

⚜ First, Our Lord's authority is challenged directly by his adversaries: "Tell us by what authority you do these things, or who is it that gave you this authority" (20:1–2). This challenge gets to the heart of the matter: Does Jesus have God's own authority to interpret the Law, forgive sins, heal on the Sabbath, cleanse the Temple? If not, he's a fraud, and worse yet, a blasphemer. If so, his adversaries are in deep trouble; they are opposing God.

⚜ Note that the challengers are "the chief priests and the scribes with the elders" (20:1). These represent the religious aristocracy associated with the Temple. The chief priests are all the men who have served as high priest and certain members of the families from which the high priests are selected. The scribes (or lawyers) we have met before. Along with the elders, these three groups form the Sanhedrin, the highest council and governing body of the Jewish people at the time. The question they present may well have been formulated by the Sanhedrin in order to manufacture a charge against the Lord.

⚜ Jesus replies to them with a brilliant tactic. He will answer their question if they answer one of his (20:3–4): "Was the baptism of John from heaven or from men?" They recognize, as he does, that this question presents them with a dilemma: If they say from heaven, they show themselves disobedient to God, for they have rejected John's ministry. But if they say from men (that is, that John had no mission from God; he was speaking on his own), then the people will stone them as blasphemers, because the people have accepted John's ministry as valid.

But No Man Laid Hands on Him, illustration for 'The Life of Christ', c.1884-96 (w/c & gouache on paperboard), Tissot, James (1836-1902) / Brooklyn Museum of Art, New York, USA / Purchased by Public Subscription / Bridgeman Images

✤ This question also has implications for Jesus' authority and identity. In a sense, their answer to Jesus' question will answer their own question. We know from the Gospel of John that John the Baptist has publically identified Jesus as the Son of God (Jn 1:34). If Our Lord's adversaries say that the Baptist was sent by God, then they are admitting that he was right about Jesus.

✤ Jesus' question quiets his enemies. They dare not respond, so he declines to respond to their challenge. If he admits plainly that he is the divine Son of God, they will immediately drag him to the religious authorities on blasphemy charges. But this is not yet the hour for his arrest. In any case, he has actually declared many times already the divine Source of his authority; he need not repeat himself at this point.

✤ Next comes the parable of the wicked tenants (20:9–18), yet another declaration of Our Lord's approaching death. The vineyard is the nation of Israel; its owner is God. Such imagery comes from numerous Old Testament passages (Is 5:1–7; Jer 10:21; Hos 10:1; Ez 19:10–14; Ps 80:8–19). The tenants are the religious rulers of the Jewish people. The servants sent by the owner to look for fruit are the prophets of the Old Covenant who were rejected. The owner's "beloved son" is Jesus himself—the title echoes the words from heaven at his baptism (3:22). He is murdered by the tenants, who want the vineyard all for themselves. They refuse to recognize God's ownership of his Chosen People. So God will destroy them and give the place they have occupied to someone else: the Gentiles. Those who reject the Son are courting disaster.

✦ "God forbid!" Jesus' listeners exclaim (20:16). But he quotes Psalm 118:22–23, a prophecy that the stone (himself) rejected by the builders (his adversaries) will become the cornerstone—that is, the foundational stone on which everything else is built. Luke tells us in the Book of Acts that the Apostle Peter will use this vivid image when speaking to the high priests and Sadducees after Jesus' resurrection (Acts 4:11). Peter's first epistle cites it again, along with a prophecy of Isaiah, calling Jesus the "living stone" on which the Church is built (1 Pt 2:4–7; Is 28:16). But as a stone, Christ is more than a sure foundation; he is also a stumbling block, a crushing weight, to those who reject him (Lk 20:18; Is 8:14–15; 1 Pt 2:8).

✦ When the religious authorities realize that the parable is about them, they want to arrest Jesus, but don't yet have the proper pretext. So they send spies who pretend to be sincere, trying to trick Jesus into saying something they can use to hand him over to the Roman governor (20:20). Their tactic: Put Jesus in a bind by asking him whether it's lawful to pay taxes to Caesar (that is, to the despised pagan Romans who occupy the land). They refer specifically to the hated annual poll tax that every adult must pay, a tax that has in the past led to Jewish rebellions. So if Jesus says yes, the people will be furious and turn on him as a traitor; if he says no, the spies can report him to the Roman governor for sedition.

✦ Our Lord's response is profound yet utterly simple. He asks for a *denarius*, a silver Roman coin that is used to pay the poll tax. It represents a day's wage for a common laborer of the time.

✦ "Whose likeness and inscription has it?" he asks (20:24). They reply, "Caesar's." The likeness on this particular coin is probably that of Tiberius; the inscription (translated from the Latin), "Caesar Augustus Tiberius, son of the Divine Augustus." (Ironically, Tiberius is claiming to be "the son of [a] god.")

✦ The very suggestion that the emperor is divine would be blasphemous to the Jews, and the image might well seem idolatrous. Yet they use this coin casually, daily. So Jesus' conclusion shows up their pretensions to piety, even as he declares a spiritual principle that will fortify Christians martyred by the State for ages to come: "Render to Caesar the things that are Caesar's, and to God the things that are God's" (20:25). We owe our ultimate allegiance to our Father in heaven.

✦ At the same time, Jesus tells us that as citizens, we must fulfill our obligations that

| Altarpiece of the Guild of Minters, 1602 (oil on panel), Vos, Maarten de (1532-1603) / Koninklijk Museum voor Schone Kunsten, Antwerp, Belgium / © Lukas-Art in Flanders VZW / Photo: Hugo Maertens / Bridgeman Images

don't contradict God's will. As the Apostle Paul, Luke's mentor, will later put it, "Pay all of them their dues, taxes to whom taxes are due, revenue to whom revenue is due" (Rom 13:7).

✤ Next, the Sadducees (who deny the resurrection of the dead) pose a question they hope will make Jesus stumble and demonstrate the truth of their teaching (20:27–40). The Law of Moses (Dt 25:5–6) required that if a man dies without a male heir, the widow is to be married by one of his brothers, so that she can bear a son who becomes the dead man's heir. This particular provision is probably not followed widely in Jesus' time, but it gives the Sadducees a pretext: What if this happens seven times to the same woman? If there is truly a resurrection of the dead, which of the brothers will be her husband then?

✤ Jesus' answer has two parts. First, their question is moot, because there is no marriage in heaven (20:34–36). Second, he shows how even a scriptural text they accept as authoritative—the story of Moses at the burning bush—demonstrates that the Sadducees are wrong on this point (20:37–38). Despite their previous hostility, some of the scribes, who probably side with the Pharisees against the Sadducees on this point, are pleased with his answer (20:39).

✤ Our Lord poses a question that, if answered correctly, will point to his divinity (20:41–44). In one of David's psalms, the ancient king speaks of his son (descendant), the Messiah, as his Lord (Ps 10:1). How could David call his descendant "my Lord"? The answer, which Jesus doesn't provide at this time, is that the Messiah (Jesus himself) is actually God in the flesh, and thus David's Lord.

✤ While they are left pondering the puzzle he proposes, Jesus concludes with a denunciation of the vanity and greed of the scribes (20:45–47).

To prepare for small group discussion, turn ahead now to this session's "Digging Deeper" and "Life Application" sections.

Rome to Home

This appeal to the moral value of spiritual worship should not be interpreted in a merely moralistic way. It is before all else the joy-filled discovery of love at work in the hearts of those who accept the Lord's gift, abandon themselves to him, and thus find true freedom. The moral transformation implicit in the new worship instituted by Christ is a heartfelt yearning to respond to the Lord's love with one's whole being, while remaining ever conscious of one's own weakness. This is clearly reflected in the Gospel story of Zacchaeus (Lk 19:1–10). After welcoming Jesus to his home, the tax collector is completely changed: He decides to give half of his possessions to the poor and to repay fourfold those whom he had defrauded. The moral urgency born of welcoming Jesus into our lives is the fruit of gratitude for having experienced the Lord's unmerited closeness.

—*Pope Benedict XVI, Sacramentum Caritatis, 82*

Opening Prayer

Let the words of my mouth and the meditation of my heart be acceptable in your sight, O Lord, my rock and my redeemer!

—Psalm 19:14

Teaching Video

This first video, hosted by Dr. Paul Thigpen, focuses on certain themes and passages from the Gospel of Luke. Here are some key highlights of his presentation, with room to take notes as you view the video to assist you in the group discussion.

The culmination of Jesus' ministry

_____

_____

_____

_____

_____

_____

Zacchaeus' background, motives, and strategy for seeing Jesus

_____

_____

_____

_____

_____

_____

_____

| *Conversion of Zaccheus (oil on canvas), Strozzi, Bernardo (1581-1644) / Musee des Beaux-Arts, Nantes, France / Bridgeman Images*

Jesus' invitation and the crowd's response

_____

_____

_____

_____

Zacchaeus' conversion and restitution

_____

_____

_____

_____

Jesus' instruction to the people of Jericho and their response

_____

_____

_____

_____

Traditions about Zacchaeus' later life

_____

_____

_____

_____

Catechism Connections

These readings from the Catechism of the Catholic Church (CCC) will deepen your understanding of this session's presentations and discussions. The numbers identify the relevant paragraphs in the Catechism.

⚜ Jesus and the Temple: CCC 583–586

⚜ Passions and the moral life: CCC 1767–1770

⚜ Jesus as a stumbling block: CCC 587–589

⚜ Jesus' entry into Jerusalem: CCC 557—560

⚜ Reparation for injustice: CCC 2412

⚜ Jesus reconciles sinners to the community: CCC 1443

Small Group Discussion

DIGGING DEEPER

1. How does Zacchaeus differ from the rich ruler in Luke 18:18–30? What do their different responses show us about the appropriate relationship to money?

   _____

   _____

   _____

   _____

2. On Palm Sunday, Jesus rides triumphantly into Jerusalem on a colt of a donkey. Why is it important that the donkey has never been ridden before? What prophecy does Jesus fulfill by his entry into Jerusalem? Where in the celebration of the Mass do we use words similar to the ones the Jews use to acclaim Jesus? (See Nm 19:2; 1 Sm 6:7; Zec 9:9–10; Ps 118:26; CCC 559–560.)

   _____

   _____

   _____

   _____

3. After his triumphant entry into Jerusalem, Jesus goes to the Temple, where he cleanses it of those engaging in commerce. Why is it appropriate for Jesus to be angry and to drive out the sellers? Is he showing dishonor to the Temple by his actions? (See Jer 7:11, Is 56:7, CCC 583–584, 1767.)

_____

_____

_____

_____

4. In Luke 20:17, Jesus refers to himself as the stone rejected by the builders that has become the cornerstone. Where else in the Scriptures is the idea of the Messiah as the cornerstone presented? What does it mean to say that "every one who falls on that stone will be broken to pieces" (Lk 20:18)? (See Ps 118:22; Is 8:14–15; Dn 2:44–45; Rom 9:33; 1 Pt 2:6–8; CCC 587–588.)

_____

_____

_____

_____

5. How is the parable of the wicked tenants a retelling of Old Testament history? (See Is 5:1–7; Jer 12:10; Ps 80:7–18.)

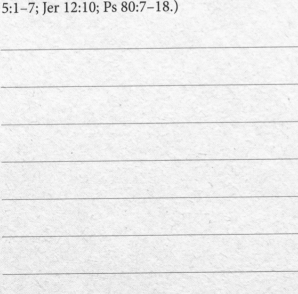

_____

_____

_____

_____

_____

| *Initial capital letter with the parable of the tenants, by Liberale of Verona, from a choral conserved in the Piccolomini Library in the cathedral of Siena, Tuscany, Italy 15th-16th Century. / De Agostini Picture Library / G. Nimatallah / Bridgeman Images*

| *Sinite Parvulos (Let the Little Ones), 1851 (fresco) / Mondadori Portfolio/Electa/Paolo Manusardi / Bridgeman Images*

LIFE APPLICATION

1. How far are we willing to go to see Jesus and have him in our lives?

_____

_____

_____

_____

2. Do we realize that Jesus invites us to his table at every Holy Mass? Are we receptive to this unmerited invitation?

_____

_____

_____

_____

3. Do we realize that to follow Jesus means that we have to change? What does the Lord desire to change in our lives?

_____

_____

_____

_____

Voices of the Saints

Once, indeed, the aged Simeon met the Savior, and received in his arms, as an infant, the Creator of the world, and proclaimed him to be Lord and God. But now, in the place of foolish elders, children meet the Savior, even as Simeon did, and instead of their arms, they strew under him the branches of trees, and they bless the Lord God seated upon a colt, as if upon the cherubim: "Hosanna to the son of David! Blessed is he who comes in the name of the Lord!" Together with these let us also exclaim, "Blessed is he who comes, God, the King of Glory, who for our sakes became poor. ... Blessed is he who once came in humility, and who will one day come again in glory!"

—*St. Methodius of Olympus, Oration on the Palms, V*

Life Application Video

After breaking from your small group discussion, gather to watch the second video, a pastoral reflection from Fr. Jeffrey Kirby, STD.

How Then Shall We Live?

Silently review the following summary of Fr. Kirby's reflection to prepare for answering the questions in "Living It Out."

Look at what moves us in life. People receive something in love, and they want to give something back in gratitude. Doesn't that summarize the story of Zacchaeus in St. Luke's Gospel?

In fact, it also summarizes the life of St. Francis of Assisi. Francis received in love, and it moved him profoundly. So he sought to give in gratitude. It's the story of Francis; it's the story of Zacchaeus. Is it our story? This should be the life of the Christian believer.

Look at Zacchaeus, a chief tax collector, who climbs a tree to see Jesus. He must look ridiculous. The man has nothing to gain in terms of this world; in fact, he has everything to lose: his reputation, social status, and human respect.

But Zacchaeus doesn't care. He climbs the tree, and when the Lord sees him and says that he will eat at his house, Zacchaeus is profoundly changed. The supper converts the tax collector.

While others see only a sinner, the Lord Jesus sees a man who needs and wants conversion. When Zacchaeus is converted, he promises monumental reimbursements to anyone he has cheated. This is the story of St. Francis, the story of our beloved Zacchaeus. And this could be our story. We must decide!

Living It Out

On your own, spend three to five minutes praying, discerning, and writing down the specific ways that God might be calling you to make changes in your life. Share and discuss afterwards only if you feel comfortable doing so.

Consider this week how God is calling you to …

- ✣ "Climb a tree"—to go beyond whatever barrier there might be in your life so you can see Jesus better.

- ✣ Evaluate how you treat your neighbors. Do you rob them of their reputations, honor, or dignity?

- ✣ Follow a new path of repentance that includes making reparation to those whom we have harmed by our words or actions (or lack of words and actions).

Entry of Christ into Jerusalem, detail of tile from Episodes from Christ's Passion and Resurrection, reverse surface of Maesta' of Duccio Altarpiece in the Cathedral of Siena, 1308-1311, by Duccio di Buoninsegna (ca 1255 – pre-1319), tempera on wood / De Agostini Picture Library / G. Nimatallah / Bridgeman Images

Words to Know

Chief priests: In New Testament times, the chief priests are all the men who have served as high priest, along with certain members of the families from which the high priests are selected.

Denarius: A small, silver Roman coin in common use in New Testament times; it is used to pay the annual Roman poll tax.

Mina: A silver coin used in New Testament times, worth about three months' wages for an agricultural laborer; translated in some English Bibles as "pound."

Sanhedrin: The highest religious council and governing body of the Jewish people in New Testament times.

Closing Prayer

O Jesus, King most wonderful! O Conqueror renowned!
O Sweetness inexpressible in whom all joys are found!

May every heart confess Your name, forever You adore,
and seeking You, be kindled new to seek You more and more.

—From *"Iesu, Dulcis Memoria,"* St. Bernard of Clairvaux

| *Appian Way / Rome, Italy, Photographer Craig Mace*

SESSION 16

THE
NEW
COVENANT

"This cup which is poured out for you is the new covenant in my blood."

LUKE 22:20

Introduction

The hour that Jesus has long anticipated is rapidly approaching. With his disciples gathered around him, he commends the great generosity and faith of a widow in the Temple who gives to God her last few coins. When the disciples comment on the beauty of the Temple, he prophesies again, with great sadness, that the Temple will be torn down, stone by stone.

His listeners ask for more details about the future, and he warns them of false messiahs, persecutions, natural calamities, and the destruction of all Jerusalem. The Son of Man will return, Jesus adds to reassure them. But they must watch for him diligently.

A few days later, at the Feast of the Passover, Jesus leads the Apostles in the ancient ceremony celebrating the rescue of their ancestors from Egypt. But he transforms his last Passover into the first Eucharist. The New Covenant is being established in his Body and Blood.

After the meal, the Lord offers agonized prayer in the Garden of Gethsemane. Then he is arrested by the Temple officials, having been betrayed by Judas. Peter denies him; the others abandon him. Brought before the high priest and then the Sanhedrin, he is mocked and mistreated. His passion has begun.

Prayer to Prepare for Study

Lord, my God, bestow upon me an understanding that knows You, diligence in seeking You, wisdom in finding You, a way of life that is pleasing to You, perseverance that waits trustfully for You, and confidence that I shall embrace You at the last. Amen.

—Prayer of St. Thomas Aquinas before study

Study Notes

These notes provide insights to help you understand and reflect upon the biblical text.

✤ After warning his disciples about the greed of the scribes, the Lord is in the Temple when he sees a poor widow who makes an offering to God (21:1–4). She is standing in the Temple in the section known as the Courtyard of the Women, where there are thirteen boxes to collect donations. These boxes are called the Trumpets, because they are shaped liked that instrument, with the narrower part at the top and the wider part at the foot. Each box is designated for a particular aspect of the Temple's upkeep, such as wood to burn the sacrifices, incense used on the altar, and maintenance of the golden vessels.

✤ The widow is poor, a common situation for widows of this time. She might well look around at the lavish furnishings of the Temple and say, "They don't need my little contribution." Nevertheless, she contributes all she has: two of the coins called in Greek the *lepton*. (Older Bible translations use the English word "mite," from which we get the expression "the widow's mite.")

❧ The *lepton* is the smallest of coins in use in the Holy Land at this time; its name means "small" or "thin." Made of copper rather than silver, it's the least valuable of coins in circulation. But in God's eyes, these two coins are worth more than all the others the people around her are giving that day.

❧ The widow's generosity to God is in sharp contrast to that of the religious leaders. Jesus praises the offering of the poor widow because she has given out of her poverty, from her limited resources that she needed to live.

❧ This incident, and Our Lord's commentary on it, should shake us a little. If we want to know what we love, we need only look at how we spend our money.

| *The Widow's Mite, by Gustave Doré, 1832 - 1883, French. Engraving for the Bible. 1870, Art, Artist, Holy Book, Religion, Religious, Christianity, Christian, Romanticism, Colour, Color Engraving, Dore, Gustave (1832-83) / Private Collection / Photo © Liszt Collection / Bridgeman Images*

Our discipleship calls us to love the Lord, and to give a tithe (ten percent) of our earnings to God. Our offering should be given in a spirit of surrender and gratitude. It shouldn't come just from our abundance, but even from resources that might be limited.

❧ After the incident with the widow, the disciples marvel at the beauty of the Temple (21:5). It is a massive and splendid edifice. The pillars of its porticoes are forty feet high, each one carved from a single block of white marble. One of its ornaments, above the Temple gate, is a grape vine made of solid gold; each cluster of its grapes is as tall as a man. The outward face of the Temple is covered in many places with heavy plates of gold, gleaming brilliantly in the sun, with the rest built of dazzling white marble.

❧ According to the ancient Jewish historian Josephus, "the Temple appeared to strangers, when they were at a distance, like a mountain covered with snow, for those parts that weren't covered with gold were exceedingly white" (*Antiquities of the Jews*, XV, 11).

❧ In response to the disciples' praise of the Temple, Jesus prophesies, with a heavy heart, the destruction of the Temple and the fall of Jerusalem (21:5–9; 21:20–24). He has prophesied these events before (13:34–35; 19:41–44), but these thoughts are pressing on his sacred heart because he is now in Jerusalem, standing within the Temple, and about to begin his passion. He knows what will happen to the beauty of the Temple and the grandeur of the Holy City.

✦ Such statements are considered blasphemy by the Jewish people for several reasons. First, the Temple is the center of worship and Jewish identity, especially during the current Roman occupation.

✦ Second, the Temple of which Jesus speaks is actually the Second Temple. The First Temple was built by King Solomon many generations earlier and was destroyed by the Babylonians. That disaster was one of the most horrific events in Jewish history. After destroying the Temple, the Babylonians took the Jewish people into exile. Only after the Babylonians were conquered by the Persians were the Israelites able to return home and eventually rebuild the Temple.

✦ Finally, at the time of Jesus, the Second Temple is actually being renovated. The renovation takes eighty-three years, from 20 B.C. until A.D. 63/64. At the time Jesus is speaking, the process has been going on about fifty years. For all these reasons, the Lord's hearers are shocked and offended to hear him speak of the Temple's destruction.

✦ Even so, Jerusalem on the whole rejects the Lord and his invitation to conversion, and the Second Temple is later destroyed, in A.D. 70. A Jewish revolt against the Romans, followed by a two-year siege, is crushed by the Roman army when Jerusalem falls.

✦ With the fall of the Holy City, the Roman general Titus tears down the Temple, stone by stone, and brings its treasures to Rome. To this day, the destruction of the Temple is depicted on the Arch of Titus in the Roman Forum. Incidentally, Jewish slaves are also brought to Rome and forced to build the new Coliseum, whose ruins can still be seen near the Roman Forum.

✦ In this series of teachings, the Lord's pronouncements follow a common pattern of apocalyptic literature: He weaves together statements about the present, the immediate future (the

The Taking of Jerusalem by Titus (oil on panel), Flemish School, (15th century) / Museum voor Schone Kunsten, Ghent, Belgium / Bridgeman Images

destruction of Jerusalem and the Temple), and the end of the world (events leading up to his return in glory to judge the earth). This juxtaposition suggests that the catastrophe of Jerusalem's destruction is a foreshadowing of the terrors God's people will endure at the end of the world. Such a parallel is strengthened by the ancient Christian tradition, expressed most clearly in Revelation 21:2, that Jerusalem is a symbol (type) of the Church and of God's eternal city in heaven.

✤ Next Jesus talks about signs of the end times (21:10–19). He describes persecutions, wars, natural disasters, and heavenly activity (21:10–11), as well as the betrayal of friends and family (21:16). The leaders of the synagogues will oppose his followers, just as they have opposed him, and will have them thrown into prison (21:12).

✤ Jesus promises his persecuted followers, "Not a hair of your head will perish" (21:18). Since he has just declared that some of them will be "put to death" (21:16), he obviously doesn't mean here that they will escape bodily injury. Rather, they will not "perish" in the sense of dying eternally (Jn 3:16), suffering "the second death" (Rv 20:14–15)—that is, they will be saved from eternal damnation. Our Lord simultaneously warns and encourages his disciples when he tells them, "By your endurance you will gain your lives" (21:19).

✤ After providing a glimpse of the end of the world, the Lord returns to the destruction of Jerusalem (21:20–24). In his prophecy he notes the Holy City "surrounded by armies" (21:20), the violence of the "sword," and the captivity of the inhabitants of Jerusalem (21:24). These details correspond to the events in A.D. 70 that fulfilled his prophecy.

✤ We should note, however, that Jesus warns his followers here to "flee to the mountains" when they see Jerusalem surrounded by siege forces (21:21). Some ancient writers report that the Christians living in Jerusalem at that time were able to escape the terrible fulfillment of this prophecy by obeying their Master's command to escape from the city. According to one tradition, an angel gave them specific instructions to flee across the Jordan to the city of Pella in the Decapolis region. The ancient Church historian Eusebius reports, "The people of the Church in Jerusalem were commanded by an oracle given by revelation before the war to those in the city who were worthy of it to escape and move to one of the cities of Perea, which they called Pella. Those who believed in Christ traveled there from Jerusalem" (*Ecclesiastical History*, 3, 5, 3).

✤ Having described the destruction of Jerusalem, Jesus again returns to the end of the world (21:25–28). He warns his disciples against fear, telling them, "Now when these things begin to take place, look up and raise your heads, because your redemption is drawing near" (21:28). The Christian believer should never be afraid in distress or calamity, or even when the end of the world approaches, since the Lord is with us and will lead us through the darkness and into his own light.

✤ After the Lord's somber apocalyptic teaching, he offers a simple parable about a fig tree. The fig is a popular fruit in Jesus' time and a regular part of the people's diet. The Lord tells them that just as they know it's summer when the fig tree blossoms, so the signs of the times must be watched and discerned to tell them when the end is near (21:29–31).

✤ The Lord concludes this portion of his teaching by saying, "Truly, I say to you, this generation will not pass away till all has taken place" (21:32). This comment has led to considerable confusion, since the events leading up to the end of the world did not happen within the lifetime of the Lord's original hearers, and they have yet to happen in our day.

✤ Several interpretations of this statement have been offered by biblical scholars. One opinion is that "this generation" refers, not to the generation of those listening to the Lord, but the

| *The barren fig tree, vintage engraved illustration, © Morphart Creation, Shutterstock*

generation that witnesses these signs. Those who see the signs will see the end as well; it will all happen that quickly.

✤ Finally, the Lord admonishes his disciples to watch and remain attentive (21:34–36). Watchfulness is necessary because someone might be caught off guard, and his salvation be in question (21:36). In contrast to the views of some that a person is "once saved, always saved," the Lord's repeated exhortation to watch and be ready reminds us that salvation can be lost by "dissipation and drunkenness" (21:34) and other sins.

✤ The religious leaders are still plotting to do Jesus harm (22:2). Luke tells us that Satan enters into Judas Iscariot (22:3), who for payment conspires with them to find Jesus when he is away from the multitudes. Judas is one of the Apostles and dear to the Lord. He is a trusted friend; this is the highest form of betrayal. St. Cyril of Alexandria comments tersely here: "Judas lost heaven for a little silver" (*Commentary on Luke*, Homily 140).

✤ Luke has reported that after Jesus' temptation in the wilderness, the Devil "departed from him until an opportune time" (4:13). His reference to Satan's involvement in Judas's betrayal now suggests that such an opportune time has come.

| *Conspiracy of the Jews, illustration from 'The Life of Our Lord Jesus Christ', 1886-94 (w/c over graphite on paper), Tissot, James (1836-1902) / Brooklyn Museum of Art, New York, USA / Purchased by Public Subscription / Bridgeman Images*

✤ Some Catholics claim they have left the Church because of weak bishops, bad priests, or mean religious sisters or brothers. While evil can never be justified, the sinfulness of the Church's leadership—and of her lay members as well, for that matter—does not negate her sacred teachings or the call to discipleship. Beginning with Judas, the Church has always struggled with bad leadership within her ranks. The Holy Spirit, however, continues to accomplish the great work of the gospel in and through us. Bad leadership, whenever it exists, calls for greater fidelity and perseverance on the part of the faithful.

✤ Having completed his teachings, Jesus now begins to prepare for the Passover, when he will at last suffer his passion and death (22:7–13). The Lord tells his Apostles, "I have earnestly desired to eat this passover with you before I suffer" (22:15).

✤ St. Cyril of Alexandria suggests that the unusual instructions Jesus gives to Peter and John for locating and preparing the room (22:8–13) is his way of keeping the location hidden from Judas. This way, he makes sure that they can celebrate the Passover before his adversaries come to arrest him.

✤ The Last Supper is the seventh meal described by Luke. (There will be two other meals described later in his Gospel.) Luke recognizes the meal context as an ancient sign of the friendship offered by the Lord (Is 25:6).

| *The Last Supper, called 'The Little Last Supper' (oil on canvas), Champaigne, Philippe de (1602-74) / Louvre, Paris, France / Bridgeman Images*

✤ Of course, the Last Supper is no ordinary meal. This meal celebrates the Passover, an ancient observance marking the liberation of God's people from their slavery in Egypt many centuries before (Ex 12:1–29). On the night of their deliverance, the Lord instructed each Hebrew family (the Hebrews were the ancient ancestors of the Jews) to sacrifice an unblemished lamb. The blood of the lamb was to be sprinkled on the doorframes of their homes. Then the flesh of the lamb was to be consumed, together by each family, that very evening.

✤ Later that night, the angel of the Lord passed through Egypt, striking dead the firstborn children and livestock of all the Egyptians, but passing over every Hebrew home that was covered by the blood of the lamb. As a result, Pharaoh, the king, commanded that the Hebrews be set free and allowed to leave the country. The Passover commemorating these events became one of the most important feast days of the Jewish people.

✤ To understand the Passover more fully, we must understand the Jewish concept of remembering. It is not simply a recalling of historical events or information, but a true re-presentation of sacred events, a type of spiritual reliving of the events in the present day. This type of remembering is now largely unknown because of the modern concept of knowledge, which is based on facts, calculations, statistics, and other measurable and materialistic means.

✤ Such a development has been accentuated by the information age in which we find ourselves. Our minds are perceived, not as a source of transcendence and spiritual activity, but rather as biological computers collecting and dispersing facts. With the prevalence of this misperception, the celebration of Passover becomes difficult (and the Holy Mass as well, because it also makes present an event of the past).

✤ The Lord begins his passion with the Passover, fulfilling the ancient ritual and giving us the first Eucharist. The Passover is thus revealed to be the foreshadowing of what God will do in Jesus Christ. The Lord himself becomes the Lamb of sacrifice. He will shed the definitive blood of redemption, saving God's people from the slavery of sin and death. What begins in the Passover celebration is played out and accomplished throughout the Lord's passion, his death on the Cross, and his resurrection from the dead.

✤ The Church's teaching about the Holy Mass parallels the ancient Jewish understanding of Passover: "Do this in remembrance of me" (22:19). In every Mass, in every place and at every time, the one historical sacrifice of Jesus Christ is sacramentally made present under the appearances of bread and wine. By the power of the Holy Spirit, the faithful remember what was done and participate in the Sacrifice by offering their own lives with Jesus Christ to God the Father. They are at table with Jesus Christ himself, enjoying his eternal life, abiding in him.

✤ In receiving Holy Communion, the Christian receives the true Body and Blood of Jesus Christ, truly offered for us, and truly risen. This Communion will be evident in one of the last meals recorded in Luke's Gospel, as two disciples in the town of Emmaus recognize the Lord's presence in "the breaking of the bread" (an early way of referring to the Holy Mass; 24:30–31, 35).

✤ Toward the end of the meal, Jesus declares that one of the men present will betray him, and they question one another to try to determine who it is (22:21–23). The statement that the betrayal will take place "as it has been determined" has led some interpreters to claim that Judas's betrayal is not an act of free will; God

| *Detail of the Crucifixtion from Isenheim altarpiece (detail of a lamb), c.1512-16, (oil on panel), Grunewald, Matthias (Mathis Nithart Gothart) (c.1480-1528) / Musee d'Unterlinden, Colmar, France / Bridgeman Images*

has destined him to be the traitor. But we might say instead that Judas freely makes the choice, and God, in his foreknowledge of the traitor's crime, has included his choice in the eternal plan.

✤ The Apostles next argue over which one is greater (22:24–30). This isn't the first time they have disputed this way (9:46–48). How it must have grieved Our Lord's heart to hear them debating this matter again, rather than focusing on the eternally significant matters he has revealed that evening! He offers his own humble example of service as their model (22:27) and reassures them that they will sit at his eternal banquet table in the kingdom of God.

✤ The ancient united kingdom of Israel was composed of twelve tribes. Jesus has chosen a corresponding twelve Apostles to have authority in his kingdom as judges (22:30).

✤ Jesus tells Peter that Satan has demanded to "sift" the Apostle's heart, a situation that recalls Satan's demand to test the Old Testament figure Job (Jb 1:12; 2:6). Notice, St. John Chrysostom comments, Jesus doesn't say he has prayed that Peter won't deny him; rather, he has prayed that his faith won't fail (*Homily on Matthew*, 3).

✤ The other Gospels tell us that Jesus has previously revealed Peter's special mission and office among the Apostles and for the whole Church (Mt 16:18–19; Jn 1:40–42). That special mission is once again revealed here: "And when you have turned again, strengthen your brethren" (22:32). These words parallel Jesus' instructions to Peter after his resurrection as recorded by John: "Feed my sheep" (Jn 21:17).

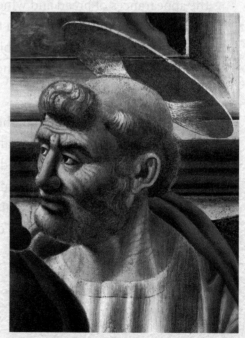

| *Peter's face, detail from The Last Supper, by Andrea del Castagno, 1450, fresco / De Agostini Picture Library / G. Dagli Orti / Bridgeman Images*

✤ Instead of asking for strength to endure this testing, Peter protests that he is willing to die with Jesus. But Jesus prophesies that Peter will deny him three times before the cock crows at sunrise, implicitly extending mercy to him before it happens (22:33–34).

✤ Next, Luke records an exchange between Jesus and all the Apostles that is not found in the other Gospels (22:35–38). In the exchange, Jesus tells them to rely on Divine Providence. He declares that he will fulfill yet another messianic prophecy (Is 53:12). And he exhorts them to sell what they have and buy a sword. The disciples indicate that there are two swords present, and the group leaves for the Garden of Gethsemane.

✤ Why would Jesus have the Apostles bring two swords, only to tell one disciple to put it away when he later draws it in Our Lord's defense (22:49–51)? St. Ambrose suggests that Jesus wants it to be clear that he could defend himself against his enemies' violence, but instead

Olive Trees in the Garden of Gethsemane, 1858 (w/c on paper), Lear, Edward (1812-88) / Mead Art Museum, Amherst College, MA, USA / Bridgeman Images

chooses not to resist. Ambrose also sees the two swords as symbols of the Old and New Testaments, spiritual weapons against the deceits of the Devil (*Exposition of the Gospel of Luke 10:53–55*). In any case, Jesus is calling the disciples to remain strong and be prepared to suffer.

❖ Now the Lord goes to the Mount of Olives (22:39). Luke doesn't specifically name the Garden of Gethsemane there as do Matthew (Mt 26:36) and Mark (Mk 14:32), but instead calls it simply "the place." It was Jesus' custom to pray there (21:37; 22:39), so he considers no further identification necessary. No doubt Judas is also familiar with the spot and with Our Lord's frequent times of prayer there.

❖ Homes crowded within the city of Jerusalem have little room for gardens. Wealthier residents have private gardens on the Mount of Olivet just outside the city. One of them probably has befriended Jesus and allows him to go to his garden regularly for prayer.

❖ Only Luke includes the detail that Jesus kneels when he prays in the garden (22:41). Except for references to Jesus' lifting up his eyes to heaven to pray (Jn 11:41; 17:1), this is the only reference in the Gospels to Jesus' posture in prayer. Since ancient times, kneeling has been a gesture of reverence and submission in prayer (Ps 95:6; Is 45:23; Acts 20:36; 21:5; Eph 3:14; Rom 14:11; Phil 2:10).

❖ The Lord goes to the mount, separates himself from his disciples, and prays to the Father: "Father, if thou art willing, remove this cup from me; nevertheless not my will, but thine, be done" (22:42). The reference to "this cup" is uncertain. Following the Church Fathers,

Christians have long seen it as a symbol of the sufferings to come with the Passion. Matthew records a similar statement made earlier by Our Lord, in which Jesus speaks of the Apostles' drinking the same "cup" that he will drink (Mt 20:22–23). In this setting, the "cup" may also be a reference to one of the cups used during the Passover.

❧ In general, however, the imagery is clear: The Lord's human nature is in great distress and anxiety even to the point of sweating blood (22:44). This is a rare but documented medical phenomenon that can occur under extreme stress and has been observed among prisoners awaiting execution. St. Thomas More observes, "The fear of death and torments carries no stigma of guilt; rather, it is an affliction of the kind that Christ came to suffer, not to escape" (*De tristitia Christi*).

❧ In making this request, Jesus remains steadfast in following the Father's will (22:42). Disobedience is not an option.

❧ Luke tells of an angel assisting the Lord (22:43). The angel does not come consoling or relieving him, but "strengthening" his human nature for the Passion. Sometimes in difficult moments when we ask to be spared, God will not grant that request but will instead give us the strength to persevere and accomplish his will.

❧ Note that the Apostles are "sleeping for sorrow" (22:45). They have fallen asleep not so much through carelessness as through sheer emotional exhaustion. Jesus' rebuke demonstrates that his primary concern is for their spiritual welfare, not their failure to support him in his agony (22:46).

The Taking of Christ (oil on canvas), Caravaggio, Michelangelo (1571-1610) (follower of) / Private Collection / © Lawrence Steigrad Fine Arts, New York / Bridgeman Images

❧ When Judas leads the soldiers to the Mount of Olives, it's evening, and the soldiers might not be able to recognize Jesus. So Judas identifies Jesus with a disciple's kiss—customarily, given with the disciple's hands upon the rabbi's shoulders (22:47). Jesus responds with one of the most sorrowful questions in the entire Gospel: "Judas, would you betray the Son of Man with a kiss?" (22:48). Such a kiss is normally an act of devotion, but Judas empties its meaning as he betrays Jesus. The expression "the kiss of Judas" has been used throughout the ages of Western civilization to indicate betrayal, treason, disloyalty, and bad faith.

✤ Always merciful, Jesus heals the ear of the high priest's slave wounded by one of the Apostles (22:50–51), whom the Gospel of John identifies as Peter (Jn 18:10). The Lord's question to the mob indicates the unjust nature of his arrest and forthcoming trial (22:52).

✤ "This is your hour, and the power of darkness" (22:53): John's Gospel tells us that previously, Jesus could not be arrested or killed because "his hour had not yet come" (Jn 7:30). But the time has now arrived, so Jesus allows himself to be taken away to his death as orchestrated by "the powers of darkness."

✤ Jesus is taken to the house of the high priest for a private and unofficial interrogation. Peter follows him there. Peter is most likely recognized as a Galilean (22:59) because of the unique spoken accent of that region. Jesus no doubt speaks with the same accent. In the course of the night, Peter denies him three times just before the cock crows, as the Lord has

Christ before the High Priest, 1617 (oil on canvas), Honthorst, Gerrit van (1590-1656) / National Gallery, London, UK / Bridgeman Images

prophesied (22:54–62). Only Luke records that Jesus turns and looks at him (22:61). Peter is unable to bear his shame; he flees and weeps bitterly (22:62).

✤ The high priest's house is also his office and center of administration, so the building has a small cell for prisoners, where Jesus is held. He is beaten and mocked by the guards (22:63–65). They blindfold him and tell him, "Prophesy! Who is it that struck you?" (22:64). Only Luke records this specific form of mockery. After the beating, Jesus is held there overnight.

✤ In the morning (22:66), the Sanhedrin, the governing religious body of the Jewish people, is convened. The high priest presides. Although the council's power is limited by the Roman authorities, it holds tremendous moral authority among the Jewish people. In the Lord's trial, due process is not observed; having been beaten and deprived of sleep, he is interrogated by this body, many of whom are his adversaries.

✤ They ask him whether he is the Christ. He refuses to give them an answer because of their hardness of heart, but he tells them, "From now on the Son of man shall be seated at the right hand of the power of God" (22:69). The elders ask the same question using a different title: "Are you the Son of God, then?" (22:70).

✤ The Lord answers, "You say that I am" (22:70). In ancient Greek, this statement implies that the speaker has spoken truthfully; it's the equivalent of the contemporary expression, "You said it!" So this exchange is enough to condemn Jesus, and the council decides to seek his execution at the hands of the Roman authorities.

To prepare for small group discussion, turn ahead now to this session's "Digging Deeper" and "Life Application" sections.

| *The Torn Cloak - Jesus Condemned to Death by the Jews, illustration from 'The Life of Our Lord Jesus Christ', 1886-94 (w/c over graphite on paper), Tissot, James (1836-1902) / Brooklyn Museum of Art, New York, USA / Purchased by Public Subscription / Bridgeman Images*

Rome to Home

And so we must approach this mystery in particular with humility and reverence, not relying on human reasoning, which ought to hold its peace, but rather adhering firmly to divine Revelation. … Hence the Christian people often follow the lead of St. Thomas and sing the words: "Sight, touch and taste in Thee are each deceived; the ear alone most safely is believed. I believe all the Son of God has spoken; than truth's own word, there is no truer token."

—*Pope Paul VI, Mysterium Fidei, 16, 19*

Opening Prayer

Let the words of my mouth and the meditation of my heart be acceptable in your sight, O LORD, my rock and my redeemer!

Psalm 19:14

Teaching Video

This first video, hosted by Dr. Paul Thigpen, focuses on certain themes and passages from the Gospel of Luke. Here are some key highlights of his presentation, with room to take notes as you view the video to assist you in the group discussion.

Jesus weeps over Jerusalem

_____

_____

_____

_____

God prepares the world for the New Covenant

_____

_____

_____

_____

The history and meaning of Passover

_____

_____

_____

_____

Jesus begins his last Passover

_____

_____

_____

_____

Jesus transforms the Passover to create the first Eucharist

_____

_____

_____

_____

The Old Covenant finds its consummation in the New Covenant

_____

_____

_____

_____

Catechism Connections

These readings from the Catechism of the Catholic Church (CCC) will deepen your understanding of this session's presentations and discussions. The numbers identify the relevant paragraphs in the Catechism.

- The Last Supper: CCC 1323, 1328–1329, 1333–1336

- The institution of the Eucharist: CCC 610–611, 1337–1340

- Our Lord's agony at Gethsemane: CCC 612

- Jesus and the Temple: CCC 585–586

- Peter's denial and return: CCC 552, 641, 1429

Small Group Discussion

DIGGING DEEPER

1. In Luke 21:20–24, Jesus foretells Jerusalem's destruction at the hands of the Romans. Why does God allow Jerusalem to be destroyed? What will happen to the city when it is destroyed? (See Jer 21:7; Ez 39:23; Is 63:18; Dn 8:13; 1 Mc 3:45; Dt 28:49; Zec 14:1–2.)

_____

_____

_____

2. When he foretells Peter's denial, Jesus says, "Satan demanded to have you that he might sift you like wheat" (Lk 22:31). What other person in the Bible did Satan similarly demand to test? Why do you think that Satan demanded to test Peter? Why did Peter have the strength to return to Jesus and not give into despair? (See Jb 1:6–12; CCC 552, 641, 1429.)

_____

_____

_____

_____

3. Why did Jesus choose to institute the Eucharist at the Passover meal? (See CCC 610, 1337, 1340.)

_____

_____

_____

_____

4. Who is with Jesus during the Last Supper? What is the significance of who is in attendance? (See CCC 1337–1340.)

_____

_____

_____

5. Jesus endures several trials before he is condemned to death: before the high priests, before the Sanhedrin, before Pilate, and before Herod. In the trial before the Sanhedrin, he is condemned for blasphemy. What has Jesus said that the elders find blasphemous? Why do they consider it blasphemous? (See Ex 3:14; Ps 110:1; Dn 7:13.)

_____

_____

_____

LIFE APPLICATION

1. Do we understand what a covenant is and how blessed we are that God would make a covenant with us?

_____

_____

_____

2. Are we attentive to attending Mass and participating in the life of the New Covenant?

_____

_____

_____

3. Can other people in our lives see a difference in us and discern that we have a relationship with the God of love and mercy?

_____

_____

_____

_____

Voices of the Saints

For God did not regard the smallness of her offering, but the overflowing of her affection. Almsgiving is not the bestowal of a few things out of many, but rather the action of the widow who empties herself of all she has. But if you cannot offer as much as the widow, at least give all that remains over.

—*St. John Chyrsostom, Catena Aurea*

| *The Last Supper (oil on canvas), Verdier, Francois (1651-1730) / Musee des Beaux-Arts, Caen, France / Bridgeman Images*

Life Application Video

After breaking from your small group discussion, gather to watch the second video, a pastoral reflection from Fr. Jeffrey Kirby, STD.

How Then Shall We Live?

Silently review the following summary of Fr. Kirby's reflection to prepare for answering the questions in "Living It Out."

In our lesson today, St. Luke describes the New Covenant that the Lord Jesus establishes with his people. The Lord describes how he has eagerly awaited the celebration of this New Covenant with his Apostles (and with us), and he fulfills the meaning of the ancient Passover meal in establishing this New Covenant. In fulfilling the Passover, the Lord gives us the Eucharist, the Holy Mass.

| *Elevation of the Eucharist, Communion in a church,* © *Bykofoto, Shutterstock*

At every Mass, we receive the fruits of the Lord's crucifixion and resurrection. As those who have been baptized, we are invited to participate in this Sacrifice. In the Mass, we offer the Lord all our prayers, works, joys, and sufferings. We surrender everything to God. If we attempted to do this without the sacrifice of Jesus Christ, our offering would actually be an offense because of our sins and their consequences. In Jesus Christ, however, our sacrifice to the Father is acceptable and is good for ourselves and for the entire body, for the whole Church.

We consummate our participation in the Lord's sacrifice with the reception of Holy Communion, by receiving what has been sacrificed, by receiving the true Body and Blood of Jesus Christ.

Here in this Eucharistic encounter, we see the depth of the Lord's love and concern for us. He will not leave us in our sin, and he will not leave us orphaned. In his Sacrifice, the Lord offers us salvation from our sins, and in the Eucharist, he remains with us under the appearance of bread and wine. No other action can offer us such a deep, personal relationship with the Lord.

Life is busy, but at Mass we must slow things down. The Lord has greatly desired to celebrate the Mass with us. Let's be attentive and encounter him, receive him, and then go and live the way of life he has shown us!

Living It Out

On your own, spend three to five minutes praying, discerning, and writing down the specific ways that God might be calling you to make changes in your life. Share and discuss afterwards only if you feel comfortable doing so.

Consider this week how God is calling you to …

+ Better understand the mystery and reality of the Holy Mass.

+ Better prepare for the Holy Mass by such actions as reviewing the readings beforehand, arriving early to pray, or being more attentive to your spiritual duties during the Mass.

+ Invite and encourage other people to attend the Holy Mass with you.

Words To Know

Hebrews: The ancient ancestors of the Jewish people, descended from the patriarch Jacob (Israel), grandson of Abraham, through his twelve sons.

Lepton: A small copper coin, the smallest and least valuable of coins in use in the Holy Land in New Testament times.

Passover: The first of the three great feasts of the Jewish religious calendar, commemorating the emancipation of the Hebrew slaves in ancient Egypt through God's miraculous intervention.

Pharaoh: The title used by ancient Egyptian kings, including the one who was compelled by God to free the Hebrew slaves and let them emigrate to the Promised Land.

Closing Prayer

What shall I render to the LORD for all his bounty to me? I will lift up the chalice of salvation and call on the name of the LORD. . . . O LORD, I am your servant. . . . I will offer you the sacrifice of thanksgiving and call on the name of the LORD. Amen.

—Adapted from Ps 116:12–13, 16, 17

SESSION 17

THE

GOOD THIEF

And he said to him, "Truly, I say to you,
today you will be with me in Paradise."

LUKE 23:43

SESSION READING
LUKE 23:1–56

Introduction

After the members of the Sanhedrin, the Jewish religious council, condemn Jesus for blasphemy, they take him to the Roman governor, Pontius Pilate. They want Jesus put to death, but Pilate finds no capital offense in the case. When the governor learns that Jesus is from Galilee, he tries to avoid the case by sending him to Herod, the tetrarch of that district. Herod is interested only in seeing Jesus perform a miracle, and when Jesus refuses, he sends him back to Pilate.

Christ Before Pilate (oil on canvas), Munkacsy, Mihaly (1844-1900) / Hungarian National Gallery, Budapest, Hungary / Bridgeman Images

The religious leaders stir up the crowd to demand Jesus' death, and Pilate gives in to their demands. Jesus is led away to be crucified. Only Luke's Gospel records his powerful prayer for his enemies, spoken from the Cross: "Father, forgive them, for they know not what they do" (23:34). And only Luke reports Our Lord's conversation with the thief, crucified beside him, who comes to repentance and faith before he dies.

At last Jesus commits his spirit to his Father and breaths his last. One of his disciples, Joseph of Arimathea, receives permission from Pilate to repose the body in his own tomb. Several women disciples make preparations to embalm the body properly, but they must wait until after the Sabbath.

Prayer to Prepare for Study

Lord, my God, bestow upon me an understanding that knows You, diligence in seeking You, wisdom in finding You, a way of life that is pleasing to You, perseverance that waits trustfully for You, and confidence that I shall embrace You at the last. Amen.

—Prayer of St. Thomas Aquinas before study

Study Notes

These notes provide insights to help you understand and reflect upon the biblical text.

❖ Jesus' appearances before the high priest and then the Sanhedrin have been an interrogation and trial on religious grounds, resulting in a conviction of blasphemy. The Jewish law calls for blasphemers to be stoned to death, but the Roman occupiers reserve to themselves the authority to carry out the death penalty. So the religious leaders must bring Jesus before Pilate, the Roman governor, to seek his execution. Such a strategy is in keeping with Jesus' previous prophecy that he will be turned over to the Gentiles to be killed (18:32–33).

❖ John's Gospel includes the detail that the trial before Pilate takes place in the *praetorium* (Jn 18:28–33). This is the place where the governor discharges his duties. It is probably in the Antonia fortress, where the Roman soldiers are lodged, near the Temple and linked to it by steps.

❖ More about Pilate is known to us from the historical writings of the ancient Jewish authors Philo and Josephus. They report that he has great disdain for the Jews and a history of conflicts with them. Both writers portray Pilate as a wicked man: murderous, vindictive, bad-tempered, inflexible, abusive, corrupt, cruel, unjust, and inhuman. Luke's portrait of Pilate is somewhat more sympathetic. In this case, at least, the governor seems to be reluctant to execute an innocent man, though in the end he succumbs to the pressure of the mob.

❖ Luke presents a more complete account of the accusations against Jesus before Pilate than those found in the other Gospels (23:2, 5, 14). Note that the claims made by Jesus' accusers have nothing to do with blasphemy—a religious dispute among Jews that would be of little concern to a pagan, who might even consider it a superstition. Instead, these accusations are calculated to raise concerns for a Roman governor whose job is to maintain imperial control: Jesus is "perverting" the nation, forbidding the people to give tribute to Caesar (an outright lie), claiming to be the expected messianic king. All these can be construed as a challenge to Roman authority.

❖ Pilate focuses on the last of the accusations, asking Jesus, "Are you the King of the Jews?" (23:3). Although Our Lord's reply ("You have said so") implies that the statement is true (see the study notes for Session 16), Pilate is unconvinced that Jesus is a threat. Still the chief priests and their allies press the matter, claiming that he stirs up civil unrest (23:4–5).

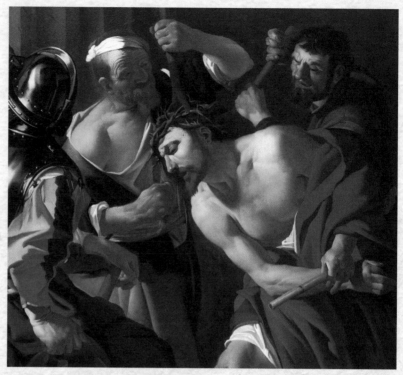

Crowning with Thorns, c.1622 (oil on canvas), Baburen van, Dirck (c.1595-1624) / Private Collection / Bridgeman Images

❧ Only Luke notes that Pilate sends Jesus to Herod Antipas because Jesus is a Galilean (Herod's jurisdiction includes Galilee). The Roman governor hopes to extricate himself from the case (23:6–16). Herod is visiting Jerusalem for the Passover, and he has been wanting to meet Jesus. But he treats him as a spectacle (23:8). When Jesus refuses to perform a miracle at Herod's bidding, Herod and his soldiers mock him, dressing him in "gorgeous apparel" and sending him back to Pilate (23:9, 11). This win's Pilate's favor (23:12).

❧ Pilate and Herod are fulfilling the messianic prophecy in Psalm 2:2, as Peter and John will one day declare: "For truly in this city there were gathered together against thy holy servant Jesus, whom thou didst anoint, both Herod and Pontius Pilate" (Acts 4:24–28).

❧ Once Jesus is returned to Pilate, the governor declares Jesus' innocence multiple times (23:14, 20, 22). He searches desperately for a way to avoid executing Jesus. The detour to Herod's court hasn't worked. So now he offers to "chastise" Jesus instead—that is, to scourge him severely (23:16, 22). The mob refuses the offer.

❧ The other Gospels tell us that the governor customarily releases a prisoner at Passover to placate the people (Mt 27:15–21; Mk 15:6–11; Jn 18:39–40), so Pilate offers them Jesus in a second attempt to release him. Instead, as Luke also notes (23:1–19), they demand the release of the criminal Barabbas, who is actually an insurrectionist (23:18–19, 25). Ironically, this surname means "son of a father," and some ancient manuscripts of the Gospels report that the criminal's first name is actually Jesus (the Greek form of Joshua, a common Jewish name of the time). If that is indeed the case, the people are offered a choice between Jesus, son of a father, and Jesus, Son of the Father.

❧ Luke repeatedly notes Pilate's weakness before the crowd (23:23, 25). The Roman imperial authorities are known to pride themselves on administering impartial justice. So how can the religious leaders and the crowds, whom Pilate so despises, compel him to sentence a man unjustly to death?

| *Ecce Homo (oil on canvas), Ciseri, Antonio (1821-91) / Galleria d'Arte Moderna, Florence, Italy / Bridgeman Images*

❧ A detail in the passion narrative in John's Gospel provides a clue: At one point the crowd shouts at Pilate, "If you release this man, you are not Caesar's friend; every one who makes himself a king sets himself against Caesar" (Jn 19:12). The threat is clear: If Pilate does not agree to their demand, they will report him to the Emperor. Under Roman law, a province has the right to report to Rome a governor's incompetence. We know from secular historians that at this point Pilate already has a history of mishandled dealings with the Jews; he knows (and the crowd knows) that Rome will not take kindly to yet another incident of civil unrest.

❧ So Pilate finally submits to the mob's demands and sentences Jesus to death (23:23–25). He will have Our Lord crucified, as they insist (23:21). Crucifixion—being fixed to a cross and left to die—is a humiliating method of capital punishment first developed by the ancient Persians, but adopted and refined by the Romans to make it excruciatingly painful. (The English word "excruciating," in fact, comes from the Latin word for "crucify.")

❧ Jesus is made to carry his cross to the place of execution, a common custom of the time. Typically, the criminal, accompanied by soldiers, must carry the cross by the longest possible route, thronged by watching crowds. Another soldier goes ahead of him carrying a placard with his name and crime inscribed upon it as a warning to would-be criminals. This practice publicizes the event and intensifies the criminal's pain, humiliation, and exhaustion.

✦ St. Cyril of Alexandria and other Church Fathers teach that in the Old Testament, Abraham's attempted sacrifice of his son Isaac is a foreshadowing of God the Father's offering of his Son, Jesus, as a sacrifice for our sins. For Cyril, when Isaac carries on his back the wood for the fire of the altar of sacrifice (Gn 22:6), he foreshadows Our Lord carrying the wood of the Cross.

✦ As Jesus carries his cross along what is now called the *Via Dolorosa* ("the Way of Sorrows"; also known as "the Way of the Cross") in Jerusalem, he encounters Simon of Cyrene (23:26). Cyrene is in North Africa (near present-day Tripoli), a town with a large Jewish community of the Diaspora (those Jews who have settled down outside of Israel after the people's dispersion among the nations through exile). Simon

Abraham and Isaac carrying the wood for the sacrifice. Engraving. / Private Collection / Photo © Tarker / Bridgeman Images

is most likely a Jew who has come to Jerusalem for the celebration of the Passover; the Cyrenian Jews of the time actually have their own synagogue in the city for use during each year's great feasts. Nevertheless, Simon may be a Gentile, and if so, Luke's reference to him reflects his ever-present concern to show that Gentiles are included in God's plan of salvation.

✦ Simon is compelled by the soldiers to help Jesus carry his cross; no doubt at this point the Lord is sinking under its weight. It's unlikely that they provide him assistance out of some sense of compassion; rather, they fear that he may die before they get to crucify him. According to tradition, Jesus falls three times under the crushing weight of the Cross, but stands up again each time and continues his agonizing journey.

✦ Under Roman law, the soldiers can immediately impress into service any citizen of an occupied land. They need only tap the person on the shoulder with the flat side of a spear blade and make the demand. (This arrangement is also the context for Jesus' famous remark about going the second mile, found in Matthew 5:41.)

✦ Luke doesn't say whether Simon helps willingly or unwillingly, or whether perhaps he begins as an unwilling helper and ends as a willing one. But ancient tradition holds that he went on to become a Christian (Cyrene will become an early center of Christianity), and his sons, Alexander and Rufus (Mk 15:21), will serve as Christian missionaries. In any case, Simon's example reminds us that we too must help Jesus bear the Cross by joining our sufferings to his.

- ❧ On the Way of the Cross, only Luke records Jesus' encounter with the women ("daughters") of Jerusalem (23:28–31). They weep and wail loudly for him to show their extreme distress over his execution. This public expression of grief is especially moving in light of the ancient Jewish tradition forbidding any wailing for someone condemned to death. Jesus warns them of tribulation to come and tells the women not to weep for him, but for themselves and for their children. He no doubt has in mind the coming destruction of Jerusalem.

| *The Procession to Calvary, by Gaspare Landi, 1806 - 1808, 19th Century, oil on canvas, Landi, Gaspare (1756-1830) / Mondadori Portfolio/Electa/Marco Ravenna / Bridgeman Images*

- ❧ In this culture, childlessness is a grave matter, often seen as a sign of God's disfavor. A woman's inability to bear children can be grounds for divorce. So Jesus' declaration that one day people will say, "Blessed are the barren," is startling to his listeners (23:29). The day is coming when what has always been considered a curse will be seen as a blessing, because those children who are alive will suffer a terrifying fate.

- ❧ The statement about green wood and dry wood seems to be a proverb of the time (23:31). Its meaning is debated. St. Ephrem, a fourth-century Church Father, suggests that Jesus means: If they do this to a righteous man who works miracles, what will they do to ordinary righteous people who don't work miracles? (*Commentary on Tatian's Diatessaron*, 20, 21). Others conclude that he means: If they do this to a righteous man, what will they do to guilty sinners?

| *The Crucifixion (oil on canvas), Champaigne, Philippe de (1602-74) / Musee National de Port-Royal des Champs, France / Bridgeman Images*

✤ Jesus is to be crucified along with two criminals (23:32). In this way he fulfills the messianic prophecy of Isaiah: "By oppression and judgement he was taken away. … And they made his grave with the wicked, … although he had done no violence" (53:8, 9).

✤ Luke records that Jesus is crucified at a place called "The Skull" (23:33), which Matthew tells us is the translation of the Aramaic name "Golgotha" (Mt 27:33). Aramaic is closely related to Hebrew and is the common language of the Jewish people living in the Holy Land in Jesus' time. The English name "Calvary" commonly used for this hill is from the Latin *calvaria,* "skull."

✤ St. Ambrose of Milan reports an ancient tradition that Golgotha is situated above the grave of Adam, the first man: "It was fitting that the beginning of death took place where the first fruits of our life were planted" (*Exposition of the Gospel of Luke,* 10.114).

✤ On the Cross, the Lord prays, "Father, forgive them; for they know not what they do" (23:34). Only Luke reports these words. More than any other statement he makes as he is dying, this prayer to the Father on behalf of the world—including his murderers—sums up the mercy that Jesus extends to all people. It is a summons to us to be a people who both receive the Lord's mercy and generously offer it to others, as St. Stephen will later do when he is murdered, echoing his Lord's prayer to forgive his enemies (Acts 7:60).

✤ "They know not what they do" (23:34): Jesus' enemies may know that the man whose death they seek is innocent, but they don't know that he is God. St. Augustine notes that Our Lord's prayer is not in vain; on the day of Pentecost (Acts 2:37–41), thousands in Jerusalem (some of whom no doubt are among the scoffers this day) will come to realize who he is, repent, and receive the forgiveness of their sins through Baptism (Sermon 229G.5).

✤ After Jesus is stripped of his clothing and nailed to the Cross, the soldiers "cast lots to divide his garments" (23:34). Roman soldiers serving as executioners have the legal right to take the criminal's clothing. John's Gospel provides the detail that four soldiers first divide his clothes into four parts, one part for each of them. Then they cast lots for the fifth item, a seamless tunic, because cutting it up would ruin it (Jn 19:23–25). As John also notes, this incident is a fulfillment of Psalm 22:18, which tells of the persecution of a just man.

✤ On the Cross, Jesus is further mocked by the religious leaders and soldiers (23:35–37). The religious offense caused by Jesus in being declared "the Christ" can be seen in the mockery of the rulers: "He saved others; let him save himself, if he is the Christ of God, his Chosen One!" (23:35). The political offense caused by Jesus in being acclaimed as a "king" can be seen in the mockery of the Roman soldiers: "If you are the King of the Jews, save yourself!" (22:37).

| *What Christ Saw from the Cross, illustration for 'The Life of Christ', c.1886-96 (gouache on paperboard), Tissot, James (1836-1902) / Brooklyn Museum of Art, New York, USA / Bridgeman Images*

✤ The "inscription over him" on the Cross (23:38) is the *titulus*, or "title," a technical term in Roman law referring to a statement specifying the grounds on which a criminal is being punished. A summary of the official document stating the charges is inscribed on a wooden placard. As part of the victim's public humiliation, this wooden version of the "title" is displayed by a soldier accompanying the victim as he carries his cross. Then it is nailed to the cross above the head of the condemned prisoner (Mt 27:37).

✤ John's Gospel includes the detail that the title is "written in Hebrew [Aramaic], in Latin, and in Greek" (Jn 19:20). These are the three most commonly spoken languages in Jerusalem; the Romans want everyone to know who this Man is. At the same time, we can view the three languages of the inscription as a sign that Jesus' kingdom is universal.

✤ All four Gospels note that while Jesus is on the Cross, he is offered (sour) wine; that is, wine vinegar (Mt 27:34, 48; Mk 15:23, 36; Lk 23:36; Jn 19:29–30). Laborers and Roman soldiers of the time commonly drink a thin, sour wine each day, so this beverage would be on hand. Matthew and Mark specify that the sour wine is offered twice: The first time, Jesus refuses it (according to Matthew, after first tasting it); the second time, he accepts it. This incident is prophetically described in Psalm 69:21, which reads: "They gave me poison for food, and for my thirst they gave me vinegar to drink."

✤ The first time, Matthew and Mark tell us, a drug is mixed with the drink to relieve pain (Mt 27:34; Mk 15:23). This mixture is probably not intended to comfort Jesus, but rather to mute his cries and groans. Luke's account of the Passion associates the vinegar with the mockery of the rulers and soldiers (23:36), so in this context it seems to be a part of the torture rather than a relief.

✤ In any case, Matthew and Mark tell us that Jesus refuses the drink the first time (Mt 27:34; Mk 15:23). He wants to drink to the dregs the cup that his Father has given him (Lk 22:42). He refuses to deaden the pain he suffers for us, or to lose full consciousness of what he is doing as he willingly offers up his life for the salvation of the world.

✤ All four Gospels note the two thieves who were crucified along with Jesus, one on either side of him (Mt 27:38; Mk 15:27; Lk 23:32; Jn 19:18). But only Luke records the remarkable conversation between Jesus and one of the thieves (23:39–43). He reports the event to show the Lord's generous love and mercy.

✤ One of the thieves is railing at Jesus along with the crowd. But the other one—named "Dismas" according to ancient tradition—defends Jesus against such abuse (23:39–40). The "good thief," as he has come to be called, admits that he and the other are deserving of their punishment. He is offering, essentially, a public confession of his sins (23:41). Then Dismas

Crucifixion (fresco), Luini, Bernardino (c.1480-1532) / Chiesa di Santa Maria degli Angeli, Lugano, Switzerland / Mondadori Portfolio/Archivio Magliani/Mauro Magliani & Barbara Piovan / Bridgeman Images

declares Jesus to be innocent and turns to him with an implicit yet nevertheless startling confession of faith that Jesus is the Messiah: "Jesus, remember me when you come in your kingly power" (23:42).

✤ Jesus responds to the good thief with the promise, "Truly, I say to you, today you will be with me in Paradise" (23:43). The word "Paradise" is used only three times in the entire New Testament: Once here, once by St. Paul speaking of a heavenly vision (2 Cor 12:3), and once by St. John in the Book of Revelation to describe the glorious promise of heaven (2:7).

✤ The term comes from an ancient Persian word that refers to a magnificent garden of the king, full of beauty and pleasure, rest and peace. It was used in the Septuagint (the ancient Greek translation of the Old Testament), to describe the Garden of Eden (Gn 2:8; Ez 28:13; 36:35), also called "the garden of the LORD" (Is 51:3).

✤ No wonder, then, that Jesus chooses this word to speak hope to the good thief. The criminal asks to be remembered when the King comes into his kingdom, and the King replies that the criminal will join him that very day in the royal garden, the garden of the King. St. Ephrem the Syrian observes that, while Adam was cast out of the garden because of his sin, now the thief is welcomed into the garden because of his repentance (*Hymn on Paradise*, 4.5).

| *Christ on the Cross, 1884 (oil on canvas), Munkacsy, Mihaly (1844-1900) / Deri Muzeum. Debrecen, Hungary / Bridgeman Images*

✤ Luke reports darkness (23:44) covering the land from about noon ("the sixth hour") to about 3:00 p.m. ("the ninth hour"). We don't know precisely what type of darkness is meant by the statement "the sun's light failed" (23:45). It cannot be a natural eclipse of the sun; such a phenomenon doesn't take place during the full moon, and the Passover (which is being celebrated) comes at the full moon. In addition, a natural eclipse doesn't last three hours. It may well be a miracle of nature.

✤ This darkness emphasizes the gravity of the Lord's passion and death: Even nature is shocked and grieved by such an assault on the Son of God. As St. Cyril of Alexandria observes, in this moment, "creation itself mourns its Lord" (*Commentary on Luke*, Homily 153).

✤ Luke further reports that "the curtain of the temple" is "torn in two" (23:45). The "curtain" is the veil that divides the Holy of Holies from the rest of the Temple. The Holy of Holies is regarded as the place of God's special presence; no one can enter it except the high priest, once a year, on the great Day of Atonement. The tearing of the veil indicates that the Old Covenant has passed, and a New Covenant has been instituted in the blood of Jesus Christ, the Lamb of God. The presence of God is with his people.

✤ The Gospels of Matthew and Mark include the detail that the Temple curtain is torn in two "from top to bottom" (Mt 27:51; Mk 15:38). Rabbinical tradition reports that this curtain was sixty feet tall, made of fabric as thick as the breadth of a man's hand. It must surely be torn, then, not by human hands, but by the hand of God himself, as a high priest tears his robes in the face of blasphemy, or as a father grieves the death of his son and bares his heart.

✤ Only Luke records this prayer of Jesus from the Cross as he breaths his last: "Father, into thy hands I commit my spirit!" (23:46). The words come from Psalm 31:5; they are in fact the bedtime prayer that Mary, like other Jewish mothers, would have taught Our Lord when he was a small Child. So Jesus falls asleep in the arms of his Father, with his mother close by (Jn 19:26). His last words are a declaration of his ultimate trust in God.

✤ The redemptive power of Jesus' death begins immediately to have its effect. Luke reports that the Roman centurion, a Gentile, praises God and declares Jesus innocent (23:47). The multitudes, many of whom have been either hostile or indifferent, now beat their breasts, the ancient penitential gesture of grieving for sin (23:48).

✤ "The women who … followed him from Galilee" (23:49) include those named by Matthew (27:56) and Mark (15:40–41): Mary Magdalene, Mary the mother of James and Joses, the

| *The Centurion, illustration for 'The Life of Christ', c.1886-94 (w/c & gouache on paperboard), Tissot, James (1836-1902) / Brooklyn Museum of Art, New York, USA / Bridgeman Images*

The Descent of Christ from the Cross (oil on canvas), Weerts, Jean Joseph (1847-1927) / Musee d'Art et d'Industrie, Roubaix, France / Bridgeman Images

mother of James and John, and Salome. Perhaps the soldiers have kept some of them from standing near the Cross with Mary, Jesus' mother (Jn 19:26–27).

✣ Joseph, from the Judean town of Arimathea, is named by all four Gospels. Matthew calls him "a rich man" and a "disciple of Jesus" (Mt 27:57). Mark and Luke call him "a respected member of the council"—that is, the Sanhedrin—"looking for the kingdom of God" (Mk 15:43; Lk 23:50). Luke adds that he is "a good and righteous man" who did not consent to the Sanhedrin's intentions and actions in regard to Jesus (23:51). John notes as well that Joseph is a disciple of Jesus "secretly, for fear of the Jews" (Jn 19:38).

✣ Typically, the Romans leave the bodies of crucified criminals exposed indefinitely on their crosses. Instead of having a dignified burial, the corpses rot and are disposed of by dogs and vultures. Joseph intends to prevent such a desecration of Jesus' body. So he approaches Pilate and asks for it. He may have been a secret disciple before, but now his loyalties are out in the open. Given his religious, social, and financial status, he is taking a terrible risk.

✣ Joseph purchases linen to wrap the body, takes it down from the Cross, wraps it with the linen and spices, and lays it in a rock-hewn tomb. (Nicodemus helps him; Jn 19:39). It's a new tomb in a garden, in which no one has ever been laid, crafted for Joseph himself (Mt 27:58–60; Mk 15:46; Lk 23:53; Jn 19:40–41). According to ancient tradition, this very tomb is inside the Church of the Holy Sepulcher in Jerusalem, where it can be seen today.

✣ The "Holy Women," as they are sometimes called, so often mentioned in Luke's Gospel, make additional preparations for a more complete embalming of the body. But it is Friday, the day of preparation for the Sabbath. Saturday, the holy day of rest, is beginning, so they

| *Burial of Jesus Christ, 1895, by Vidal Gonzalez Arenal. / De Agostini Picture Library / Bridgeman Images*

must wait to finish their task until early Sunday morning (23:56).

⚜ Jesus has truly died. He is not simply in a coma from which he can be revived. The human soul of the Lord has departed his body. According to ancient tradition, while his body rests in the tomb, the Lord's soul descends to the limbo of the fathers (see the study notes for Session 13). There, he preaches the gospel to the souls of the righteous who have died but have had to wait there until his death opens the doors of Paradise. Jesus then brings them with him to heaven (1 Pt 3:18–20; Ps 88:3–6, 10–12).

⚜ This event has come to be known in English as the "harrowing of hell." To "harrow" means to "despoil"; the word hell here refers, not to the realm of the damned, but more generally to the realm of the dead (in Greek, *Hades*), as it does in the traditional English translation of the Apostles' Creed: "He descended into hell." The event is also referenced in the *Exsultet* chant of the Great Easter Vigil on Holy Saturday evening.

To prepare for small group discussion, turn ahead now to this session's "Digging Deeper" and "Life Application" sections.

Rome to Home

The second word spoken by Jesus on the Cross recorded by St. Luke is a word of hope; it is his answer to the prayer of one of the two men crucified with him. The good thief comes to his senses before Jesus and repents; he realizes he is facing the Son of God who makes the very Face of God visible, and begs him; "Jesus, remember me when you come in your kingly power" (Lk 23:42). The Lord's answer to this prayer goes far beyond the request; in fact, he says, "Truly, I say to you, today you will be with me in Paradise" (Lk 23:43). Jesus knows that he is entering into direct communion with the Father and reopening to man the way to God's paradise. Thus, with this response, he gives the firm hope that God's goodness can also touch us, even at the very last moment of life, and that sincere prayer, even after a wrong life, encounters the open arms of the good Father who awaits the return of his son.

—*Pope Benedict XVI, General Audience, February 15, 2012*

Opening Prayer

Let the words of my mouth and the meditation of my heart be acceptable in your sight, O LORD, my rock and my redeemer!

Psalm 19:14

Teaching Video

This first video, hosted by Dr. Paul Thigpen, focuses on certain themes and passages from the Gospel of Luke. Here are some key highlights of his presentation, with room to take notes as you view the video to assist you in the group discussion.

The men surrounding Jesus in his passion and death

Jesus carries the Cross and is crucified

| *Christ's Fall on the way to Calvary, 1772 (oil on canvas), Tiepolo, Giandomenico (Giovanni Domenico) (1727-1804) / Prado, Madrid, Spain / Bridgeman Images*

The conversation between Jesus and the good thief

The meaning of "paradise"

What Jesus sees in the good thief

_____
_____
_____
_____

Jesus gives up his spirit

_____
_____
_____
_____

| *Descent from the Cross, 1617 (oil on canvas), Rubens, Peter Paul (1577-1640) / Musee des Beaux-Arts, Lille, France / Bridgeman Images*

Catechism Connections

These readings from the Catechism of the Catholic Church (CCC) will deepen your understanding of this session's presentations and discussions. The numbers identify the relevant paragraphs in the Catechism.

⚜ The trial of Jesus: CCC 595–598

⚜ Jesus' death on the Cross: CCC 613–618, 2605

⚜ Jesus' burial: 624–628

⚜ "He descended into hell": CCC 631–635

Small Group Discussion

DIGGING DEEPER

1. At the moment of Jesus' death on the Cross, the curtain in the Temple is torn in two. What is this curtain? What is the significance of its being torn in two? (See Ex 26:31–34; Mk 15:38; Heb 9:3, 7; 10:19–22.)

_____

_____

_____

_____

2. In the past, some Christians have engaged in anti-Semitism, justifying their attitudes and actions with the argument that the Jews are responsible for Jesus' death. This belief is against the teaching of the Catholic Church. Why does the Church teach that the Jews are not collectively responsible for Jesus' death? Who is responsible for Jesus' death? (See Lk 23:34; Acts 3:17; CCC 597–598.)

_____

_____

_____

_____

3. While Luke does not record Jesus' quoting Psalm 22 while he is hanging on the cross, Matthew and Mark do (Mt 27:46, Mk 15:34). How do the events that take place during Jesus' crucifixion as described by Luke mirror the words of Psalm 22?

_____

_____

_____

_____

4. After Jesus died, the Apostles' Creed tells us, he "descended into hell." Does this mean that those who died and went to hell had a second chance at salvation? Does Jesus descend to "hell" as we use the word today? (See 1 Pt 3:18–20; CCC 631–635.)

_____

_____

_____

_____

5. On the Cross, the good thief asks Jesus, "Remember me when you come in your kingly power" (Lk 23:42). Why does he ask Jesus to remember him, yet does *not* ask Jesus to save him from death on the cross?

_____

_____

_____

_____

LIFE APPLICATION

1. Do I see Jesus Christ as a loving Savior who is always waiting for me and willing to accept me?

_____

_____

_____

2. Do I approach the Lord for his mercy even in difficult, confusing, or tragic moments in my life?

_____

_____

_____

_____

3. How do I seek to share the radical mercy and compassion of God with others?

_____

_____

_____

_____

Voices of the Saints

If you are a Simon of Cyrene, take up the Cross and follow. If you are crucified with him as a robber, acknowledge God as a penitent robber. If even he was numbered among the transgressors for you and your sin, become law-abiding for his sake. Worship the One who was hanged for you, even if you yourself are hanging; make some profit even from your wickedness; purchase salvation by your death; enter with Jesus into Paradise, so that you may learn from what you have fallen. Contemplate the glories that are there; let the murderer die outside with his blasphemies; and if you are a Joseph of Arimathaea, beg the Body from the one who crucified him; make your own what cleanses the world. If you are a Nicodemus, the worshipper of God by night, bury him with spices. If you are a Mary, or another Mary, or a Salome, or a Joanna, weep in the early morning. Be first to see the stone taken away, and perhaps you will see the angels and Jesus himself. Say something; hear his voice.

—*St. Gregory Nazianzen, Oration, 45, 24*

Life Application Video

After breaking from your small group discussion, gather to watch the second video, a pastoral reflection from Fr. Jeffrey Kirby, STD.

How Then Shall We Live?

Silently review the following summary of Fr. Kirby's reflection to prepare for answering the questions in "Living It Out."

We need to understand that we will receive nothing in this life that we cannot handle with God's grace. Whatever cross the Lord allows, he will give us the grace to carry it well. This is the lesson of the good thief.

The good thief accepted his cross. He knew that he was suffering his lot due to his crimes. The other thief wanted to escape his suffering; he wanted Jesus to remove his sentence and let him go. Yet the good thief asked Jesus only for remembrance in paradise.

If only we all had the faith and trust in God of that good thief! So how are we doing in this regard? Do we accept the sufferings and difficulties of our lives?

These are hard questions to ask ourselves. It's only when we give real

| *Christ Carrying the Cross, 1526 (oil on canvas), Lotto, Lorenzo (c.1480-1556) / Louvre, Paris, France / Bridgeman Images*

answers—such as, "Yes, I think things should be easy and I avoid virtue when it gets hard"—that the Lord Jesus can truly work within us and transform us. Then, like the good thief in Luke's Gospel, we can turn to the Lord, having embraced our crosses, and ask only for remembrance in paradise: "Jesus, remember me when you come in your kingly power!"

This is our call as Christians, and it should be our delight: to carry our crosses well, and to hope for eternal life with the Lord Jesus.

Living It Out

On your own, spend three to five minutes praying, discerning, and writing down the specific ways that God might be calling you to make changes in your life. Share and discuss afterwards only if you feel comfortable doing so.

Consider this week how God is calling you to …

✤ Accept the crosses in your life more faithfully and joyfully.

✤ Affirm interiorly, and give public witness to, God's providence when circumstances are confusing, hard, or stressful for yourself or others.

✤ Understand that the Jesus you need is nailed to the cross you are called to embrace.

| *Jesus Dies on the Cross, 12th Station of the Cross, 1898 (fresco), Feuerstein, Martin (1856-1931) / Saint Anna Church, Munich, Germany / Bridgeman Images*

Words to Know

Aramaic: A language closely related to Hebrew that was the common language of the Jewish people living in the Holy Land in Jesus' time.

Day of Atonement: The highest of Jewish holy days, *Yom Kippur,* which was designated for the atonement of sins (Lv 16:1–34; 23:26–32).

Diaspora: Those Jews who settled down outside of the land of Israel and Judea after the people's dispersion among the nations through forced exile by their conquerors.

Golgotha (Calvary): The name of the hill where Jesus was crucified. "Golgotha" comes from the Aramaic word for "skull;" "Calvary" comes from the Latin word with the same meaning.

Praetorium: The place in Jerusalem where the Roman governor discharged his duties.

Titulus: Latin for "title." A technical term in Roman law referring to a statement specifying the grounds on which a criminal was being punished.

Via Dolorosa (the Way of the Cross): Literally, "Way of Sorrows." The route through Jerusalem taken by Jesus as he carried his cross from the *praetorium* of Pontius Pilate (see above) to Golgotha, the hill where Jesus was crucified.

Closing Prayer

O my God, I thank you and I praise you for accomplishing your holy and all-lovable will without any regard for mine. With my whole heart, in spite of my heart, I receive this cross I feared so much! It is the cross of your choice, the cross of your love. I venerate it; nor for anything in the world would I wish that it had not come, since you willed it. I keep it with gratitude and with joy, as I do everything that comes from your hand; and I shall strive to carry it without letting it drag, with all the respect and all the affection that your works deserve. Amen.

—St. Francis de Sales, *Act of Abandonment*

Christ on the Road to Emmaus (oil on canvas), Stella, Jacques (1596-1657) / Musee des Beaux-Arts, Nantes, France / Bridgeman Images Christ on the Road to Emmaus (oil on canvas), Stella, Jacques (1596-1657) / Musee des Beaux-Arts, Nantes, France / Bridgeman Images

THE ROAD
TO EMMAUS

Then they told what had happened on the road,
and how he was known to them in the breaking of the bread.

LUKE 24:35

Introduction

Luke's concluding chapter begins as the women disciples find Jesus' tomb open and his body missing. Two angels appear and announce that Jesus is risen from the dead. So the women return to tell the Apostles and other disciples what they have witnessed.

The others conclude that the women must somehow be mistaken. But Peter goes to see for himself and finds everything as the women have said. Soon, word of these things ripples out across Jerusalem.

Late that afternoon, two disciples of Our Lord are walking to the village of Emmaus. A stranger joins them on the way. When they tell him about Jesus, he explains how these events fulfill the prophecies of Scripture. At Emmaus they break bread together, when they finally realize that the stranger is Jesus himself. He disappears before their eyes.

| *Holy Women at Christ's Tomb, after Mantegna, 1869, Howard, George, 9th Earl of Carlisle (1843-1911) / Private Collection / Bridgeman Images*

They return to Jerusalem to tell the others, and Jesus appears again to the Apostles and others assembled. He commissions them to preach repentance and forgiveness in his name. They will be his witnesses. But first they must wait in Jerusalem until the Holy Spirit comes upon them.

With these final words, Jesus ascends into heaven, and Luke's Gospel of mercy comes to a close.

Prayer to Prepare for Study

Lord, my God, bestow upon me an understanding that knows You, diligence in seeking You, wisdom in finding You, a way of life that is pleasing to You, perseverance that waits trustfully for You, and confidence that I shall embrace You at the last. Amen.

—Prayer of St. Thomas Aquinas before study

Study Notes

These notes provide insights to help you understand and reflect upon the biblical text.

✤ The resurrection of Jesus Christ (24:1–12) is at the heart of the gospel. The truth of the Christian faith—and the possibility of living the Christian life—hinge upon its reality. As Luke's mentor, St. Paul, observes, "If Christ has not been raised, your faith is futile and you are still in your sins. Then those also who have fallen asleep in Christ have perished. If for this life only we have hoped in Christ, we are of all men most to be pitied" (1 Cor 15:17–19).

✤ Our Lord's resurrection crowns and completes his work of salvation. St. Thomas Aquinas teaches: "By dying he endured all evil in order to deliver us from evil. In the same way, he was glorified in rising again to advance us toward good things, just as Romans [4:25] says: 'He was put to death for our trespasses and raised for our justification.'"

✤ Some interpreters have tried to claim that Jesus' resurrection was "spiritual" rather than "physical," citing the words of the Apostle Paul: "It is sown a physical body, it is raised a spiritual body" (1 Cor 15:44). But we must insist with the Church that Our Lord's body was in fact raised from the dead and reunited to his spirit; his body was not left behind in the tomb or anywhere else. The Resurrection, of course, is a supernatural mystery that we cannot fully grasp. It was certainly *more* than physical. But it wasn't *less* than physical. It was subject to verification in physical ways by human witnesses.

✤ Luke specifies that the Resurrection occurs on "the first day of the week," that is, on Sunday (24:1). Since the Resurrection took place on a Sunday, the early Church observed the Sabbath on that day instead of Saturday to honor the glorious event that makes her very existence possible (Acts 20:7; 1 Cor 16:1–2). Truly, then, every Sunday is meant to be a "little Easter."

| *The Resurrection, 1619-20 (oil on canvas), Caravaggio, Cecco de (1588/90-after 1620) / The Art Institute of Chicago, IL, USA / Charles H. and Mary F. S. Worcester Collection / Bridgeman Images*

❧ Because it is "the first day of the week," the day of Our Lord's resurrection recalls the first creation (Gn 1:5). But it is also "the eighth day," following the seventh day of the Sabbath, so it serves as a symbol of "the new creation" (2 Cor 5:17) that has come into being through Jesus' resurrection. For a similar reason, traditional baptismal fonts have eight sides, recalling the "new creation" of the believer through Baptism.

❧ By the time the Book of Revelation is written, Sunday will be known among Christians as "the Lord's Day" (Rv 1:10). The second-century bishop and martyr St. Ignatius of Antioch writes: "Those who lived according to the old order of things have come to a new hope, no longer keeping the old Sabbath, but now the Lord's Day, in which our life is blessed by him and by his death" (*Epistle to the Magnesians*, 9:1).

❧ Having a tomb carved out of living rock to form a cave-like receptacle is common in Jesus' time. Inside is a large shelf carved from the rock where the body is reposed, covered in a long strip of linen with spices and ointments. The Gospel of John adds the detail that myrrh and aloes (19:39) are among the burial ointments. For this reason, some see the myrrh brought by the Wise Men to Jesus when he was a Child (Mt 2:11) as a foreshadowing of his death and burial.

❧ The entrance to the tomb is covered by a large wheel-like stone that is rolled into place along a groove cut into the stone at the base. The Gospel of Mark notes that the stone is so heavy, the women who are bringing spices and ointments for the body ask themselves as they approach the tomb, "Who will roll away the stone for us from the door of the tomb?" (Mk 16:3). Matthew reports that an angel is sent from heaven to roll it away (Mt 28:2).

❧ Note that the angelic announcement of the Resurrection is given to the Holy Women (24:10). St. Mary Magdalene, one of these women, has been called "the apostle to the Apostles," since she was sent to announce the Lord's resurrection to Peter and the others.

❧ Luke reports that "two men" appear suddenly at the tomb (24:4). Later, however, the disciples walking to Emmaus

Why Seek Ye the Living Among the Dead?, 1905 (oil on canvas), Pyle, Howard (1853-1911) / © American Illustrators Gallery, NYC / www.asapworldwide.com / Bridgeman Images

report that the women have had "a vision of angels" (24:23). We find in Scripture that angelic visitors often take the form of human beings when they appear (Jo 5:13–15; Acts 1:10), so we should interpret "two men" here to mean "two figures who look like men," in "dazzling apparel" (24:4, 23).

❖ The Apostles struggle to accept the resurrection of their Master and think the women's words sound like "an idle tale" (24:11). This English translation makes it sound as if the Apostles are dismissing the women as gossips. But the Greek word chosen here by Luke the physician was actually employed by ancient medical writers to describe the babbling of a patient with a high fever. Luke's intended meaning, then, is more charitable: The men conclude that the women's minds have been overwhelmed, and their senses deceived, by the intense grief that burns in their souls.

❖ In some respects, this doubt about the Resurrection is much like the familiar questioning of the Apostle Thomas (which is fully recounted only in Jn 20:24–29). Even though the Lord has told them that he would rise from the dead, the Apostles aren't yet capable of grasping what he said. At this point the Resurrection is to them completely unthinkable, a radically new reality in human history.

| *Christ and Doubting Thomas, by Paolo Cavazzola (1486-1522) / De Agostini Picture Library / A. Dagli Orti / Bridgeman Images*

| *The Disciples Peter and John Running to the Sepulchre on the Morning of the Resurrection, c.1898 (oil on canvas), Burnand, Eugene (1850-1921) / Musee d'Orsay, Paris, France / Bridgeman Images*

✦ Pope St. Leo the Great, a fifth-century Church Father, concludes that God allows the Apostles to doubt so that their faith ultimately will be strengthened by additional testimony—and in hearing about their experience, our faith will be strengthened as well. "Their seeing instructed us," he observes, "their hearing informed us, their touching strengthened us. Let us give thanks for the divine plan and the necessary 'slowness' of the holy fathers. They doubted so that we need not doubt" (Sermon 73.1.2.444).

✦ Even with his questions, Peter takes the initiative to check out the women's story; he runs to the tomb. There, he finds the Lord's grave clothes "by themselves" (24:12). Commentators have noted the significance of this detail.

✦ When Jesus rises, he doesn't take his grave clothes with him, and he will never appear in them (as a ghost might do) when his followers see him after the Resurrection. He has left death behind. When Lazarus came out of the grave at Christ's command, he was still bound in his grave clothes, because he would need them again one day when he died a second time. But Jesus doesn't need grave clothes anymore. He cannot be bound again that way, because he will never die again. Our Lord will now be robed in heavenly glory; he needs no earthly clothes. Just as the first Adam had to take on clothes when he left Paradise (Gn 3:21–24), Jesus, the last Adam (1 Cor 15:45), must take them off to reenter Paradise.

❧ Thinking about the meaning of everything he has seen (and not seen), Peter goes "home wondering at what had happened" (24:12). It's unclear what Luke means by "home." It may be the home attached to the upper room where the Last Supper was celebrated, or the home of another believer in that neighborhood.

❧ After the events at the tomb, Luke tells about two disciples on their way to Emmaus, seven miles outside of Jerusalem. The whole of the Emmaus event (24:13–35) is described only in Luke's Gospel.

❧ One of the disciples is called Cleopas; the other is unidentified. Some of the Church Fathers speculate that these two may be among the seventy disciples Jesus previously sent out (10:1). The fourth-century Church historian Eusebius quotes a second-century chronicler who claims to have interviewed two grandsons of the Apostle Jude; they told him that Cleopas was a brother of St. Joseph, the husband of Mary (*Ecclesiastical History,* III, 11).

| *The walk to Emmaus, Copping, Harold (1863-1932) / Private Collection / © Look and Learn / Bridgeman Images*

❧ The two disciples, filled with grief about Our Lord's passion and death, encounter a stranger on the road and begin a conversation with him. They tell him about Jesus. Notice that they describe him, not as the Son of God, but as "a prophet mighty in deed and word before God and all the people" (24:19). They once "hoped that he was the one to redeem Israel" (24:21)—that is, the Messiah—but he has been put to death, so their hopes have been dashed.

❧ Jesus "had foretold it all," St. Augustine remarks, "but his death had erased it from their memories. They were so shattered when they saw him hanging on the Cross that they forgot about his teaching. They did not expect him to rise, nor did they hold on to his promise" (Sermon 235.2).

✤ Clearly, though they are devoted followers of Our Lord, the two men haven't yet begun to understand his true identity and mission. To help them develop such an understanding, the stranger opens the Scriptures to them to show how the Christ, the Messiah, had to suffer in order to "enter into his glory" (24:25–27). He teaches them how "Moses" (the Law) and the Prophets point to himself through the kinds of foreshadowings and prophecies we have noted in previous sessions.

✤ This Christ-centered approach to Scripture is summed up by St. Augustine this way: "In the Old Testament the New Testament is concealed; in the New Testament the Old Testament is revealed." We ourselves must approach all of Scripture in the hope that Jesus will be revealed to us in some way. "Everything in those Scriptures speaks of Christ," St. Augustine teaches, "but only to the one who has ears" (Second Homily on 1 John, 1).

✤ Note that the disciples speak of the women's report that Jesus has been raised from the dead on "the third day" (24:21). The day of his death is the first day; the day in which he lies in the tomb, the second; and the day of his resurrection, the third. This timing was prophesied by Jesus (9:22; 13:32; 18:33) and echoed by the angels at the empty tomb (24:7).

✤ The stranger is actually Jesus, but the two disciples don't realize who he is; he conceals his identity at first. St. Augustine notes that "their eyes were kept from recognizing him because their hearts needed more thorough instruction. So recognition is deferred" (Sermon 232.3).

✤ The Lord seems to conceal his identity with Mary Magdalene as well, at the tomb (Jn 20:14) and also with the Apostles beside the sea (Jn 21:4). In each case, however, he eventually reveals himself.

✤ As they reach Emmaus, the disciples ask the Lord to lodge with them rather than walking on, because it is almost evening (24:29). Though he is a guest, at the table Jesus assumes the role of head of the household by blessing and distributing the food. In the breaking of the bread (a reference to the Eucharist), he is made known to them (24:31, 35).

✤ Suddenly, the Lord disappears, and the disciples return to the Church in Jerusalem to tell what has happened. They obviously consider this an urgent matter: The road is dark, and they must walk seven miles, yet they leave the table and get on their way "that same hour" (24:33). The two disciples allow the excitement of the Good News to inspire and motivate them.

✤ The Emmaus account is in some ways the grand climax of Luke's Gospel. Its message is clear: The Lord is still with the Church. He can be encountered in the living Word (the Scripture) and in the breaking of the Bread (the Eucharist). Meet him today.

✤ When the two disciples arrive in Jerusalem, the new Christian community announces to them, "The Lord has risen indeed, and has appeared to Simon!" (24:34). Luke doesn't record this appearance to Simon Peter. The last time we hear specifically of Peter in Luke's Gospel, he is walking home after seeing the empty tomb. So apparently the Lord appears to Peter in some form, but we don't know the details of this encounter.

Christ Appears to Apostles Behind Closed Doors, detail from Episodes from Christ's Passion and Resurrection, part of Maesta' of Duccio Altarpiece in Cathedral of Siena, 1308-1311, by Duccio di Buoninsegna (ca 1255 - pre-1319), tempera on wood / De Agostini Picture Library / G. Nimatallah / Bridgeman Images

- After the exchange between "the eleven" (the Twelve minus Judas) and the two Emmaus disciples (24:33), Luke alone records a post-Resurrection appearance of Jesus to the disciples (24:36–49). It is similar to other post-Resurrection appearances, but not exactly the same.

- The disciples are "startled and frightened" (24:37) because they are seeing what they believe to be the disembodied spirit of a dead man. Since they think he's a spirit, just as they did when he walked on the sea (Mt 14:26), he invites them to touch his body. That way they can be reassured that he is real (24:40). The Gospel of John tells us Jesus did the same for Thomas specifically (Jn 20:27–28).

- Jesus also eats fish with them (24:41–43), as he does again beside the sea (Jn 21:9–14). Recall that when Our Lord raised a young girl from the dead, he instructed those present to give her something to eat (8:55). In all these cases, he seems to be using food to demonstrate that the person raised is truly alive and in the flesh.

- These details are important because they establish the fact that Jesus is neither a mere ghost nor a hallucination. He has truly been raised from the dead and glorified.

✦ After witnessing the Resurrection, the Apostles need to "re-learn" the gospel (24:44–47). He explains to all assembled, as he explained to the two on the road to Emmaus, that "Moses and the prophets and the psalms" foreshadowed him and prophesied about him (24:44). Note that this time he includes the Psalms as well; a number of them have messianic meaning. Once again, he speaks of rising "on the third day" (24:46).

✦ In light of the Resurrection, the disciples can now see the greater meaning and context of what Jesus has done and seeks to do in the world. They are ready to be witnesses (24:48), but they still need the Holy Spirit—the "power from on high"—to help and enlighten them (24:49). So the Holy Spirit will come upon them in this way a little later, at Pentecost. They must await him in Jerusalem (24:49).

✦ Jesus refers to the Holy Spirit as "the promise of my Father" (24:49). Through the prophet Joel in the Old Testament, God promised to "pour out" his Spirit upon all flesh (Jl 2:28–32). When the Spirit descends at Pentecost, the Apostle Peter will declare that event to be the fulfillment of God's promise through Joel (Acts 2:16–18). Speaking through the prophet John the Baptist, God has also promised that the Messiah will baptize his followers in the Holy Spirit (Lk 3:16), another prediction of what will occur at Pentecost. Even Jesus himself has promised that God will give the Holy Spirit to those who ask (11:13), and that the Spirit will teach his followers what to say under trial (12:12).

✦ We can see here once again the importance of the Holy Spirit in Luke's account. He first appears in this Gospel's infancy narrative (1:15), and now he appears at the end as the One who is to come (24:49). All told, Luke refers to the Spirit in this Gospel eighteen times, and in the Book of Acts, a full fifty-eight times.

✦ Luke's theme of mercy is evident here as well. The message that the Apostles are to preach is one of "repentance and forgiveness of sins" in Jesus' name (24:47).

| *Ascension of Christ (oil on panel), Benvenuto Tisi da Garofalo (c.1510–1520), National Gallery of Ancient Art, Rome, Italy / Restored Traditions*

✤ Finally, Luke's emphasis on the universal offer of the Gospel is also manifest in this passage. Though the preaching will begin in Jerusalem, where it will be heard and even embraced by many who had a hand in Jesus' death (Acts 2:22–24), it will eventually spread "to all nations," to the Gentiles as well as the Jews (Lk 24:47).

✤ Only Luke provides certain details of Jesus' ascension into heaven (24:50–53). He notes that the disciples return to the Temple in Jerusalem to pray and worship, but he doesn't go on, as Mark does in his Gospel, to say that they went preaching the gospel and working miracles (Mk 16:20). Why the difference? Luke does in fact go on to chronicle in great detail these events in the early Church, but they appear in the second part of the text, which is now the separate book known as the Acts of the Apostles. In that book, Luke tells about the day of Pentecost, the preaching, the miracles, the early persecutions, the martyrdom of St. Stephen, the missions of St. Paul, and much more.

✤ In the first chapter of that "sequel" to his Gospel, Luke tells us that when Jesus ascends into heaven, he is taken "out of their sight" (Acts 1:9). But Luke's account of the journey to Emmaus should always remind us that even though Jesus is out of our sight, he is still with us: Every time we gather at the sacred Table in remembrance of him, we receive the Bread of Life himself.

To prepare for small group discussion, turn ahead now to this session's "Digging Deeper" and "Life Application" sections.

Rome to Home

He dwelt among us, full of grace and truth. He proclaimed and established the Kingdom of God and made us know in Himself the Father. He gave us His new commandment to love one another as He loved us. He taught us the way of the beatitudes of the Gospel: poverty in spirit, meekness, suffering borne with patience, thirst after justice, mercy, purity of heart, will for peace, persecution suffered for justice sake. Under Pontius Pilate He suffered—the Lamb of God bearing on Himself the sins of the world, and He died for us on the cross, saving us by His redeeming blood. He was buried and, of His own power, rose on the third day, raising us by His resurrection to that sharing in the divine life which is the life of grace. He ascended to heaven, and He will come again, this time in glory, to judge the living and the dead: each according to his merits—those who have responded to the love and piety of God going to eternal life, those who have refused them to the end going to the fire that is not extinguished. And His Kingdom will have no end.

—*Pope Paul VI, Credo of the People of God, 12*

Opening Prayer

Let the words of my mouth and the meditation of my heart be acceptable in your sight, O LORD, my rock and my redeemer!

—Psalm 19:14

Teaching Video

This first video, hosted by Dr. Paul Thigpen, focuses on certain themes and passages from the Gospel of Luke. Here are some key highlights of his presentation, with room to take notes as you view the video to assist you in the group discussion.

From Friday night to dawn on Sunday

_____

_____

_____

_____

The women, then Peter, at the empty tomb

_____

_____

_____

_____

A stranger on the road to Emmaus

_____

_____

_____

_____

| *Supper at Emmaus (oil on panel), Carpaccio, Vittore (c.1450-1522/5) (attr.to) / Ca' Rezzonico, Museo del Sette-cento, Venice, Italy / Cameraphoto Arte Venezia / Bridgeman Images*

The meal in Emmaus

_____
_____
_____
_____

Jesus appears behind closed doors in Jerusalem

_____
_____
_____
_____

Jesus commissions the Apostles and ascends into heaven

_____
_____
_____
_____

SESSION 18 | GROUP STUDY

Catechism Connections

These readings from the Catechism of the Catholic Church (CCC) will deepen your understanding of this session's presentations and discussions. The numbers identify the relevant paragraphs in the Catechism.

- Jesus in the tomb: CCC 625–628
- The resurrection of Jesus: CCC 638–655
- The ascension of Jesus into heaven: CCC 659–664
- The general resurrection of the body: CCC 988–991
- The liturgical structure of the Eucharist: CCC 1346–1347

Small Group Discussion

DIGGING DEEPER

1. Luke's Gospel has more stories about women in it than any of the other Gospels. What important roles do women play in the events surrounding Jesus' death and resurrection?

_____

_____

_____

_____

_____

_____

_____

_____

The Holy Women at the Tomb of Christ, 1890 (oil on canvas), Bouguereau, William-Adolphe (1825-1905) / Koninklijk Museum voor Schone Kunsten, Antwerp, Belgium / © Lukas - Art in Flanders VZW / Photo: Hugo Maertens / Bridgeman Images

2. Jesus is in the tomb for two days and rises from the dead on the third day. Where in the Old Testament do we find this theme of three days repeated? (See Gn 22:4, 13; Jon 1:17; Hos 6:2; Ex 10:21–23; 19:10–11.)

_____

_____

_____

_____

3. When he appears to the Apostles after his resurrection, Our Lord goes to great lengths to show them that he is not a ghost, or spirit, and that he truly is present in his body. Why is it important that they understand that he is present bodily? How is his body different after the resurrection? What hope can we have because of Jesus' bodily resurrection? (See CCC 645–646, 988–991.)

_____

_____

_____

_____

4. How does the unfolding of the episode with Jesus and the disciples on the road to Emmaus parallel the structure of the liturgy? (See CCC 1346–1347.)

_____

_____

_____

5. What does Jesus' ascension into heaven show us about his identity? What does Jesus do now that he has ascended to the Father? (See CCC 659–664; Heb 1:3; 7:23–25; 9:24; 1 Jn 2:1; Eph 1:20–23; Rv 3:21; 11:15; 20:4.)

_____

_____

_____

_____

LIFE APPLICATION

1. In our lives, are we aware that the Lord is with us, walking with us, and accompanying us through life's joys and sorrows?

   _____

   _____

   _____

   _____

2. How do we approach the Sacred Scriptures? Do we read from them regularly and see them as "a lamp" to our "feet" (Ps 119:105)?

   _____

   _____

   _____

   _____

3. Do we see Jesus in the breaking of the Bread and celebrate his presence with the community of faith?

   _____

   _____

   _____

   _____

Life Application Video

After breaking from your small group discussion, gather to watch the second video, a pastoral reflection from Fr. Jeffrey Kirby, STD.

Voices of the Saints

Every passage in the history of our Lord and Savior is of unfathomable depth, and affords inexhaustible matter for contemplation. Everything concerning him is infinite, and what we discern at first is only the surface of what begins and ends in eternity.

—*Adapted from Blessed John Henry Newman, "Mental Sufferings of Our Lord in His Passion"*

| *The Supper at Emmaus (oil on canvas), Bigot, Trophime (c.1595-p.1650) / Musee Conde, Chantilly, France / Bridgeman Images*

How Then Shall We Live?

Silently review the following summary of Fr. Kirby's reflection to prepare for answering the questions in "Living It Out."

Our lesson today takes us to the road from Jerusalem to Emmaus, a journey of about seven miles. Two disciples are walking to Emmaus and are struggling with the events of the Lord's passion and death. They don't understand it.

Suddenly, another figure begins to walk with them. He asks them what they are talking about. The disciples are shocked that their new companion doesn't know what has been happening the past few days in Jerusalem, so they describe the events and express their confusion about such developments. They don't know what will happen next. They conclude that they have been mistaken in thinking Jesus was the Messiah.

The disciples' new companion begins to open up the Scriptures to show them how the Law and the prophets testify that the Messiah had to suffer. The hearts of the disciples burn within them, and they ask their guest to stay with them as they stop. The three begin their meal, and when their guest breaks bread, they finally recognize him as Jesus. But he disappears before their eyes.

This is a great story and one that should encourage each of us. The Lord came to the disciples in their hardship and confusion. Do we realize that the Lord comes to us? Do we know that he is with us even in difficult and confusing times?

The Emmaus story is in some ways the climax of Luke's Gospel. Having recounted the life and ministry of Jesus Christ, Luke concludes his Gospel by describing the very real means of encountering the risen Lord and being with him.

The Emmaus story is the story of discipleship. It contains all the essential elements of what it means to be with Jesus and to follow him. Will we let the Emmaus story inspire us to follow Jesus more faithfully?

Living It Out

On your own, spend three to five minutes praying, discerning, and writing down the specific ways that God might be calling you to make changes in your life. Share and discuss afterwards only if you feel comfortable doing so.

Consider this week how God is calling you to …

| *Celebration of Catholic Mass (photo) / Godong/UIG / Bridgeman Images*

- ✠ Realize more fully that the Lord is with you and desires to hear you express the sentiments of your heart.

- ✠ Understand the great importance of the Bible so that you seek to read and study it regularly.

- ✠ Appreciate and approach with great reverence the Lord's presence in "the breaking of the Bread" by attending the Holy Mass more devoutly and seeking out a time for adoration of the Blessed Sacrament (when it is available in your area).

Words to Know

Easter: The principal feast of the liturgical year, celebrating Christ's resurrection. The English word, derived from the name for a Teutonic goddess associated with sunrise, is a translation of the Latin word "pascha," referring to the Jewish Feast of Passover. The early Christians appropriated this term when referring to the Resurrection, *pashca resurrectionis,* since Christ is the true Paschal Lamb whose death and resurrection is a fulfillment of the Old Testament Passover.

Pentecost: The feast celebrating the descent of the Holy Spirit upon the Apostles. In Greek, the name means "the fiftieth," referring to the fact that the event took place fifty days after Easter on the Jewish Feast of Weeks (Ex 34:22; Dt 16:10), which is also known as Pentecost since it takes place fifty days after Passover.

Closing Prayer

I believe in God, the Father Almighty, Creator of heaven and earth; and in Jesus Christ, His only Son, our Lord; who was conceived by the Holy Spirit; born of the Virgin Mary; suffered under Pontius Pilate; was crucified, died and was buried. He descended into hell. The third day He rose again from the dead. He ascended into heaven and is seated at the right hand of God, the Father Almighty; from there He shall come to judge the living and the dead. I believe in the Holy Spirit, the holy Catholic Church, the communion of saints, the forgiveness of sins, the resurrection of the body, and life everlasting. Amen.

—The Apostles' Creed

| *Descent of the Holy Spirit, by Anton Raphael Mengs, 1751, oil on canvas, 1728-1779, 46x255 cm / State Hermitage Museum, St. Petersburg, Russia / De Agostini Picture Library / A. Dagli Orti / Bridgeman Images*

MY PERSONAL CHECKLIST

After the Study

Your word is a lamp for my feet, a light for my path (Ps 119:105 NAB).

You will know the truth, and the truth will make you free (Jn 8:32).

At the beginning of your study of *Luke: The Gospel of Mercy*, you reviewed a list of some personal benefits that we hoped you would receive through this experience. Now that the study has concluded, it's time to review the list and check all those areas where you may have experienced spiritual growth. In this way, you can reflect on the areas in which you've grown. *This checklist is for you only; it will not be shared with anyone else unless you choose to do so.*

- ❑ I have come to know God more personally and intimately through studying his Word.
- ❑ I have become more familiar with the Bible and learned how to study it.
- ❑ I have found in the Bible new truths about God, myself, and others.
- ❑ I now understand better the people who encounter Jesus in the Gospel, and I have learned from their experience.
- ❑ I now understand more about God's mercy, and I am better able to experience it more fully and extend it to others.
- ❑ I have received more hope and healing for the personal wounds I carry.
- ❑ I have forgiven myself for something in my past, even though it was difficult.
- ❑ I have forgiven someone else for something in my past, even though it was difficult.
- ❑ I am now less attached to material possessions.
- ❑ I am now more attentive and generous to those who are around me and to those who are most in need.
- ❑ I am now more grateful for the mercy and other graces I've received from God.
- ❑ I am now more willing to ask forgiveness from the people whom I've wronged.
- ❑ I am now a more active member of my parish to help build the kingdom of God.
- ❑ I am now more likely to avoid rashly judging others.
- ❑ I now honor the Lord's Day (Sunday) more fully and consistently.
- ❑ I now prepare better for making good sacramental confessions.
- ❑ I now reflect more often God's loving kindness to those around me.
- ❑ I now appreciate more fully the meaning, the reality, and the power of the Eucharist.
- ❑ I now accept more faithfully and joyfully the "crosses" I must bear in my life.

If you've checked some of the boxes above, it shows your spiritual growth in your relationship with God and others. Congratulations for the time, effort, and love that you have invested in your spiritual life. Over time, you will see more and more rewards from this effort. Continue to engage with God's Word on your own, and continue your journey with Christ and your parish with the next CSS program.

Explore the History and Beauty of the Heart of Rome

8 FASCINATING DVD LECTURES
WITH HUNDREDS OF SUPPLEMENTAL IMAGES AND SPECIAL EFFECTS

A Tour of St. Peter's Square and Basilica

FR. JEFFREY KIRBY, STL,
HOST OF *DOORS OF MERCY*

A COMPREHENSIVE TOUR

In this course, Father Kirby takes a look at the history and artwork of St. Peter's square and basilica through the light of faith. This comprehensive tour explains why St. Peter's basilica was significant to the early Christians, and why it is still significant today.

"ECCO ROMA"

Just as the ancient pilgrims exclaimed, "Ecco Roma" (Latin for "Behold Rome"), so too does this course begin with wonder at beholding the Eternal City. Aside from visiting Italy in person, this tour will take you as close as possible to experiencing the splendor of Rome, Vatican City, and St. Peter's Square.

BEGINNING WITH THE FIRST POPE

Rather than starting this tour with the Basilica's construction, Fr. Kirby begins with the Basilica's namesake—St. Peter himself, as well as the origins of Christianity. With this great historical context of the first Pope, one can come to more fully appreciate the treasures contained within Rome and within St. Peter's Square.

A TOUR FOR OUR TIMES

Given in light of the New Evangelization, this tour is not just a tour of Rome's essential history and its artistic masterpieces, but rather one that begs a certain spiritual awareness. St. Peter's is a sacred place, and its basilica is like a living catechism, inspiring us to ask ourselves profound questions and deepen our faith.

TO TAKE THIS WHIRLWIND TOUR OF ST. PETER'S, VISIT US AT TANBOOKS.COM/CATHOLICCOURSES, OR CALL (800) 437-5876

FULL OF *Grace*

BEHOLD, YOUR MOTHER

Hail Mary, full of grace. It is a phrase repeated more often than perhaps any other, recited daily in millions of homes, schools and churches around the world. Its first speaker, the angel Gabriel, uttered these history-altering words over 2000 years ago in the little town of Nazareth. He spoke to a young girl, unknown to the world at the time.

How that has changed.

Today she is the patron of thousands of churches, great and small…the inspirer of countless pieces of art. She has given her name to more communities, places, and persons than any other. She is history's most famous woman.

Never before has the story of Our Lady been told like this, as an eternal biography. Her life did not end when she was assumed into heaven; just as Christ lives on through His Church, she lives on as the Mother of the Church . . .

This spring, with Full of Grace, take a journey into the distant reaches of time and through the winding path of humanity's history, to discover the woman who, from the very beginning, was destined to be our Mother . . . the one, who was full of grace.

Full of Grace is the upcoming parish program from Saint Benedict Press. Stay tuned for more details!

AVAILABLE
SPRING
2017

Image credit: The Annunciation (tempera on panel), Sarto, Andrea del (1486-1530) / Palazzo Pitti, Florence, Italy / Bridgeman Images

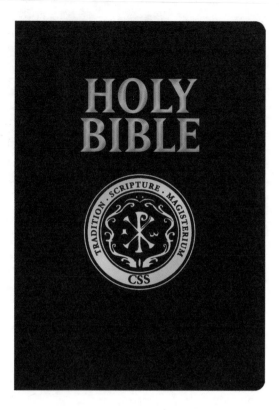
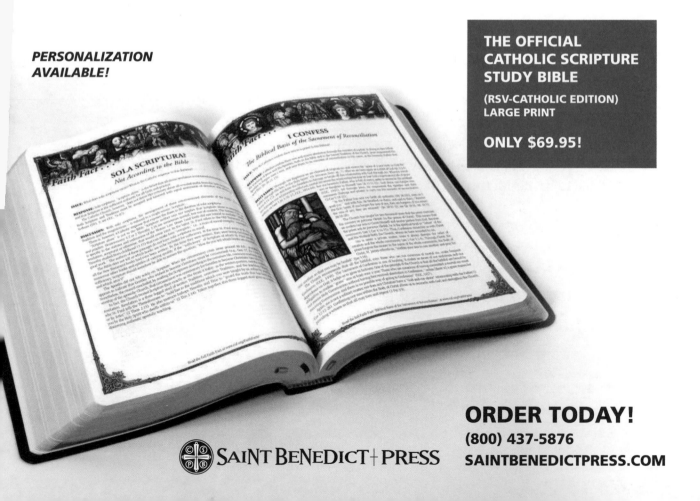